MznLnx

Missing Links Exam Preps

Exam Prep for

Fundamentals of Investments

Alexander & Sharpe & Bailey, 3rd Edition

The MznLnx Exam Prep is your link from the texbook and lecture to your exams.
The MznLnx Exam Preps are unauthorized and comprehensive reviews of your textbooks.

All material provided by MznLnx and Rico Publications (c) 2010
Textbook publishers and textbook authors do not particpate in or contribute to these reviews.

MznLnx

Rico
Publications

Exam Prep for Fundamentals of Investments
3rd Edition
Alexander & Sharpe & Bailey

Publisher: Raymond Houge
Assistant Editor: Michael Rouger
Text and Cover Designer: Lisa Buckner
Marketing Manager: Sara Swagger
Project Manager, Editorial Production: Jerry Emerson
Art Director: Vernon Lowerui

Product Manager: Dave Mason
Editorial Assitant: Rachel Guzmanji
Pedagogy: Debra Long
Cover Image: Jim Reed/Getty Images
Text and Cover Printer: City Printing, Inc.
Compositor: Media Mix, Inc.

(c) 2010 Rico Publications
ALL RIGHTS RESERVED. No part of this work covered by the copyright may be reproduced or used in any form or by an means--graphic, electronic, or mechanical, including photocopying, recording, taping, Web distribution, information storage, and retrieval systems, or in any other manner--without the written permission of the publisher.

Printed in the United States
ISBN:

For more information about our products, contact us at:
Dave.Mason@RicoPublications.com

For permission to use material from this text or product, submit a request online to:
Dave.Mason@RicoPublications.com

Contents

CHAPTER 1
Introduction — 1

CHAPTER 2
Buying and Selling Securities — 7

CHAPTER 3
Security Markets — 14

CHAPTER 4
Efficient Markets, Investment Value, and Market Price — 26

CHAPTER 5
Taxes — 31

CHAPTER 6
Inflation — 35

CHAPTER 7
The Portfolio Selection Problem — 40

CHAPTER 8
Portfolio Analysis — 44

CHAPTER 9
Riskfree Lending and Borrowing — 46

CHAPTER 10
The Capital Asset Pricing Model — 48

CHAPTER 11
Factor Models — 54

CHAPTER 12
Arbitrage Pricing Theory — 57

CHAPTER 13
Characteristics of Common Stocks — 60

CHAPTER 14
Financial Analysis of Common Stocks — 70

CHAPTER 15
Dividend Discount Models — 84

CHAPTER 16
Dividends and Earnings — 89

CHAPTER 17
Investment Management — 95

CHAPTER 18
Portfolio Performance Evaluation — 101

CHAPTER 19
Types of Fixed-Income Securities — 108

CHAPTER 20
Fundamentals of Bond Valuation — 121

Contents (Cont.)

CHAPTER 21
Bond Analysis — 129

CHAPTER 22
Bond Portfolio Management — 136

CHAPTER 23
Investment Companies — 144

CHAPTER 24
Options — 152

CHAPTER 25
Futures — 161

CHAPTER 26
International Investing — 170

ANSWER KEY — 174

TO THE STUDENT

COMPREHENSIVE

The *MznLnx* Exam Prep series is designed to help you pass your exams. Editors at MznLnx review your textbooks and then prepare these practice exams to help you master the textbook material. Unlike study guides, workbooks, and practice tests provided by the texbook publisher and textbook authors, *MznLnx* gives you **all** of the material in each chapter in exam form, not just samples, so you can be sure to nail your exam.

MECHANICAL

The MznLnx Exam Prep series creates exams that will help you learn the subject matter as well as test you on your understanding. Each question is designed to help you master the concept. Just working through the exams, you gain an understanding of the subject--its a simple mechanical process that produces success.

INTEGRATED STUDY GUIDE AND REVIEW

MznLnx is not just a set of exams designed to test you, its also a comprehensive review of the subject content. Each exam question is also a review of the concept, making sure that you will get the answer correct without having to go to other sources of material. You learn as you go! Its the easiest way to pass an exam.

HUMOR

Studying can be tedious and dry. MznLnx's instructional design includes moderate humor within the exam questions on occassion, to break the tedium and revitalize the brain

Chapter 1. Introduction

1. An _____ is a company whose main business is holding securities of other companies purely for investment purposes. The _____ invests money on behalf of its shareholders who in turn share in the profits and losses.
   a. Investment company
   b. AAB
   c. Unit investment trust
   d. A Random Walk Down Wall Street

2. The _____ is that part of the capital markets that deals with the issuance of new securities. Companies, governments or public sector institutions can obtain funding through the sale of a new stock or bond issue. This is typically done through a syndicate of securities dealers.
   a. Primary market
   b. Peer group analysis
   c. Sector rotation
   d. Volatility clustering

3. The _____ is the financial market where previously issued securities and financial instruments such as stock, bonds, options, and futures are bought and sold. The term '_____' is also used refer to the market for any used goods or assets, or an alternative use for an existing product or asset where the customer base is the second market

   With primary issuances of securities or financial instruments, or the primary market, investors purchase these securities directly from issuers such as corporations issuing shares in an IPO or private placement, or directly from the federal government in the case of treasuries.

   a. Delta neutral
   b. Performance attribution
   c. Financial market
   d. Secondary market

4. A _____ is a fungible, negotiable instrument representing financial value. They are broadly categorized into debt securities (such as banknotes, bonds and debentures), and equity securities; e.g., common stocks. The company or other entity issuing the _____ is called the issuer.
   a. Book entry
   b. Securities lending
   c. Tracking stock
   d. Security

5. In finance, a _____ is a debt security, in which the authorized issuer owes the holders a debt and, depending on the terms of the _____, is obliged to pay interest (the coupon) and/or to repay the principal at a later date, termed maturity.

   Thus a _____ is a loan: the issuer is the borrower, the _____ holder is the lender, and the coupon is the interest. _____s provide the borrower with external funds to finance long-term investments, or, in the case of government _____s, to finance current expenditure.

   a. Bond
   b. Convertible bond
   c. Puttable bond
   d. Catastrophe bonds

6. In lending agreements, _____ is a borrower's pledge of specific property to a lender, to secure repayment of a loan. The _____ serves as protection for a lender against a borrower's risk of default - that is, a borrower failing to pay the principal and interest under the terms of a loan obligation. If a borrower does default on a loan (due to insolvency or other event), that borrower forfeits (gives up) the property pledged as _____ ollateral - and the lender then becomes the owner of the _____.
   a. Refinancing risk
   b. Collateral
   c. Future-oriented
   d. Nominal value

Chapter 1. Introduction

7. _____ is a form of corporation equity ownership represented in the securities. It is dangerous in comparison to preferred shares and some other investment options, in that in the event of bankruptcy, _____ investors receive their funds after preferred stockholders, bondholders, creditors, etc. On the other hand, common shares on average perform better than preferred shares or bonds over time.

   a. Stock split
   b. Stock market bubble
   c. Stop-limit order
   d. Common stock

8. A _____ is a bond issued by a corporation. The term is usually applied to longer-term debt instruments, generally with a maturity date falling at least a year after their issue date. (The term 'commercial paper' is sometimes used for instruments with a shorter maturity.)

   a. Government bond
   b. Brady bonds
   c. Serial bond
   d. Corporate bond

9. The coupon or _____ of a bond is the amount of interest paid per year expressed as a percentage of the face value of the bond.

For example if you hold $10,000 nominal of a bond described as a 4.5% loan stock, you will receive $450 in interest each year (probably in two installments of $225 each.)

Not all bonds have coupons.

   a. Revenue bonds
   b. Coupon rate
   c. Zero-coupon bond
   d. Puttable bond

10. _____ refers to any type of investment that yields a regular (or fixed) return.

For example, if you lend money to a borrower and the borrower has to pay interest once a month, you have been issued a fixed-income security. When a company does this, it is often called a bond or corporate bank debt (although preferred stock is also sometimes considered to be _____).

   a. 529 plan
   b. 4-4-5 Calendar
   c. Bond market
   d. Fixed income

11. In economic models, the _____ time frame assumes no fixed factors of production. Firms can enter or leave the marketplace, and the cost (and availability) of land, labor, raw materials, and capital goods can be assumed to vary. In contrast, in the short-run time frame, certain factors are assumed to be fixed, because there is not sufficient time for them to change.

   a. 529 plan
   b. Long-run
   c. 4-4-5 Calendar
   d. Short-run

12. _____ is a life of security. It may also refer to the final payment date of a loan or other financial instrument, at which point all remaining interest and principal is due to be paid.

1, 3, 6 months _____ band can be calculated by using 30-day per month periods.

Chapter 1. Introduction

a. Maturity
b. False billing
c. Primary market
d. Replacement cost

13. _____ mature in one year or less. Like zero-coupon bonds, they do not pay interest prior to maturity; instead they are sold at a discount of the par value to create a positive yield to maturity. Many regard _____ as the least risky investment available to U.S. investors.

a. Treasury securities
b. Treasury bills
c. 4-4-5 Calendar
d. Treasury Inflation Protected Securities

14. _____ are government bonds issued by the United States Department of the Treasury through the Bureau of the Public Debt. They are the debt financing instruments of the U.S. Federal government, and they are often referred to simply as Treasuries or Treasurys. There are four types of marketable _____: Treasury bills, Treasury notes, Treasury bonds, and Treasury Inflation Protected Securities (TIPS.)

a. Treasury Inflation-Protected Securities
b. 4-4-5 Calendar
c. Treasury securities
d. Treasury Inflation Protected Securities

15. A _____ is a measure of the average price of consumer goods and services purchased by households. The _____ can be used to index (i.e., adjust for the effects of inflation) wages, salaries, pensions, or regulated or contracted prices. The _____ is, along with the population census and the National Income and Product Accounts, one of the most closely watched national economic statistics.

a. 4-4-5 Calendar
b. Consumer Price Index
c. Divisia index
d. 529 plan

16. In economics, _____ is a rise in the general level of prices of goods and services in an economy over a period of time. The term '_____' once referred to increases in the money supply (monetary _____); however, economic debates about the relationship between money supply and price levels have led to its primary use today in describing price _____. _____ can also be described as a decline in the real value of money--a loss of purchasing power in the medium of exchange which is also the monetary unit of account.

a. ABN Amro
b. A Random Walk Down Wall Street
c. AAB
d. Inflation

17. A _____ is a normalized average (typically a weighted average) of prices for a given class of goods or services in a given region, during a given interval of time. It is a statistic designed to help to compare how these prices, taken as a whole, differ between time periods or geographical locations.

a. Price discrimination
b. Discounts and allowances
c. Transfer pricing
d. Price Index

18. The institution most often referenced by the word '_____' is a public or publicly traded _____, the shares of which are traded on a public stock exchange (e.g., the New York Stock Exchange or Nasdaq in the United States) where shares of stock of _____s are bought and sold by and to the general public. Most of the largest businesses in the world are publicly traded _____s. However, the majority of _____s are said to be closely held, privately held or close _____s, meaning that no ready market exists for the trading of shares.

a. Protect
b. Federal Home Loan Mortgage Corporation
c. Depository Trust Company
d. Corporation

Chapter 1. Introduction

19. A _____ is a payment made by a corporation to its shareholder members. When a corporation earns a profit or surplus, that money can be put to two uses: it can either be re-invested in the business (called retained earnings), or it can be paid to the shareholders as a _____. Many corporations retain a portion of their earnings and pay the remainder as a _____.

   a. Dividend puzzle
   b. Special dividend
   c. Dividend yield
   d. Dividend

20. _____ in finance is a risk management technique, related to hedging, that mixes a wide variety of investments within a portfolio. Because the fluctuations of a single security have less impact on a diverse portfolio, _____ minimizes the risk from any one investment.

A simple example of _____ is the following: On a particular island the entire economy consists of two companies: one that sells umbrellas and another that sells sunscreen.

   a. 7-Eleven
   b. Diversification
   c. 4-4-5 Calendar
   d. 529 plan

21. _____, is when a company issues common stock or shares to the public for the first time. They are often issued by smaller, younger companies seeking capital to expand, but can also be done by large privately-owned companies looking to become publicly traded.

In an _____ the issuer may obtain the assistance of an underwriting firm, which helps it determine what type of security to issue (common or preferred), best offering price and time to bring it to market.

   a. Interest
   b. Asian Financial Crisis
   c. Insolvency
   d. Initial public offering

22. The _____ is the market for securities, where companies and governments can raise longterm funds. The _____ includes the stock market and the bond market. Financial regulators, such as the U.S. Securities and Exchange Commission, oversee the _____s in their designated countries to ensure that investors are protected against fraud.

   a. Delta neutral
   b. Spot rate
   c. Forward market
   d. Capital market

23.

A _____ is a type of financial intermediary and a type of bank. Commercial banking is also known as business banking. It is a bank that provides checking accounts, savings accounts, and money market accounts and that accepts time deposits.

   a. 529 plan
   b. 7-Eleven
   c. 4-4-5 Calendar
   d. Commercial bank

24. In finance, the _____ is the global financial market for short-term borrowing and lending. It provides short-term liquidity funding for the global financial system. The _____ is where short-term obligations such as Treasury bills, commercial paper and bankers' acceptances are bought and sold.

Chapter 1. Introduction

a. Debt-for-equity swap
b. Consumer debt
c. Cramdown
d. Money market

25. A _____ is an institution, firm or individual who mediates between two or more parties in a financial context. Typically the first party is a provider of a product or service and the second party is a consumer or customer.

In the U.S., a _____ is typically an institution that facilitates the channelling of funds between lenders and borrowers indirectly.

a. Net asset value
b. Savings and loan association
c. Financial intermediary
d. Mutual fund

26. _____ is a type of private equity capital typically provided to early-stage, high-potential, growth companies in the interest of generating a return through an eventual realization event such as an IPO or trade sale of the company. _____ investments are generally made as cash in exchange for shares in the invested company. It is typical for _____ investors to identify and back companies in high technology industries such as biotechnology and ICT.

a. Tail risk
b. Treasury Inflation-Protected Securities
c. Venture capital
d. Probability distribution

27. The term _____ is used to describe a nation's social, or business activity in the process of rapid industrialization. _____ are generally less-wealthy than the developed world, and are wealthier (or the wealthiest of) the developing world. According to The Economist many people find the term dated, but a new term has yet to gain much traction.

a. AAB
b. Emerging markets
c. A Random Walk Down Wall Street
d. ABN Amro

28. In finance, a _____ (non-investment grade bond, speculative grade bond or junk bond) is a bond that is rated below investment grade at the time of purchase. These bonds have a higher risk of default or other adverse credit events, but typically pay higher yields than better quality bonds in order to make them attractive to investors.

a. Sharpe ratio
b. Private equity
c. High yield bond
d. Volatility

29. A _____ occurs when a financial sponsor acquires a controlling interest in a company's equity and where a significant percentage of the purchase price is financed through leverage (borrowing.) The assets of the acquired company are used as collateral for the borrowed capital, sometimes with assets of the acquiring company. The bonds or other paper issued for _____ s are commonly considered not to be investment grade because of the significant risks involved.

a. Limited partnership
b. Pension fund
c. Leverage
d. Leveraged buyout

30. _____, authored by professors Benjamin Graham and David Dodd of Columbia Business School, laid the intellectual foundation for what would later be called value investing. The work was first published in 1934, following unprecedented losses on Wall Street. In summing up lessons learned, Graham and Dodd chided Wall Street for its myopic focus on a company's reported earnings per share, and were particularly harsh on the favored 'earnings trends.' They encouraged investors to take an entirely different approach by gauging the rough value of the operating business that lay behind the security.

a. 4-4-5 Calendar
b. Stock valuation
c. Growth stocks
d. Security analysis

31. An _____ is any government regulation or law that encourages or discourages foreign investment in the local economy, e.g. currency exchange limits.

As globalization integrates the economies of neighboring and of trading states, they are typically forced to trade off such rules as part of a common tax, tariff and trade regime, e.g. as defined by a free trade pact. _____ favoring local investors over global ones is typically discouraged in such pacts, and the idea of a separate _____ rapidly becomes a fiction or fantasy, as real decisions reflect the real need for nations to compete for investment, even from their own local investors.

a. AAB
b. ABN Amro
c. A Random Walk Down Wall Street
d. Investment policy

32. _____ of a business involves analyzing its financial statements and health, its management and competitive advantages, and its competitors and markets. The term is used to distinguish such analysis from other types of investment analysis, such as quantitative analysis and technical analysis.

_____ is performed on historical and present data, but with the goal of making financial forecasts.

a. Growth stocks
b. 4-4-5 Calendar
c. Stock valuation
d. Fundamental analysis

33. In finance, _____ refers to the value of a security which is intrinsic to or contained in the security itself. It is also frequently called fundamental value. It is ordinarily calculated by summing the future income generated by the asset, and discounting it to the present value.

a. Accretion
b. Alpha
c. Amortization
d. Intrinsic value

34. _____ is the strategy of making buy or sell decisions of financial assets (often stocks) by attempting to predict future market price movements. The prediction may be based on an outlook of market or economic conditions resulting from technical or fundamental analysis. This is an investment strategy based on the outlook for an aggregate market, rather than for a particular financial asset.

a. Divestment
b. Late trading
c. Market timing
d. Portable alpha

35. _____ is a security analysis discipline for forecasting the future direction of prices through the study of past market data, primarily price and volume. In its purest form, _____ considers only the actual price and volume behavior of the market or instrument. Technical analysts may employ models and trading rules based on price and volume transformations, such as the relative strength index, moving averages, regressions, inter-market and intra-market price correlations, cycles or, classically, through recognition of chart patterns.

a. Support and resistance
b. Point and figure
c. Dow theory
d. Technical analysis

Chapter 2. Buying and Selling Securities

1. _____, in bookkeeping, refers to assets, liabilities, income, and expenses recorded on individual pages of the so called book of final entry or ledger. Changes in _____ value are made by chronologically posting debit (DR) and credit (CR) entries to its page. Examples of _____s are cash, _____s receivable, mortgages, loans, land and buildings, common stock, sales, services provided, wages, and payroll overhead.
   a. Alpha
   b. Accretion
   c. Option
   d. Account

2. A '_____' is a 'Charge' that is paid to obtain the right to delay a payment. Essentially, the payer purchases the right to make a given payment in the future instead of in the Present. The '_____', or 'Charge' that must be paid to delay the payment, is simply the difference between what the payment amount would be if it were paid in the present and what the payment amount would be paid if it were paid in the future.
   a. Value at risk
   b. Risk modeling
   c. Risk aversion
   d. Discount

3. _____ are organizations which pool large sums of money and invest those sums in companies. They include banks, insurance companies, retirement or pension funds, hedge funds and mutual funds. Their role in the economy is to act as highly specialized investors on behalf of others.
   a. ABN Amro
   b. A Random Walk Down Wall Street
   c. AAB
   d. Institutional investors

4. A _____ is a fungible, negotiable instrument representing financial value. They are broadly categorized into debt securities (such as banknotes, bonds and debentures), and equity securities; e.g., common stocks. The company or other entity issuing the _____ is called the issuer.
   a. Tracking stock
   b. Book entry
   c. Securities lending
   d. Security

5. A _____ is an order to buy a security at no more (or sell at no less) than a specific price. This gives the customer some control over the price at which the trade is executed, but may prevent the order from being executed ('filled'.)

   A buy _____ can only be executed by the broker at the limit price or lower.
   a. Limit Order
   b. Common stock
   c. Block premium
   d. Commercial mortgage-backed securities

6. A _____ is the price set by a monopolist to discourage economic entry into a market, and is illegal in many countries. The _____ is the price that the entrant would face upon entering as long as the incumbent firm did not decrease output. The _____ is often lower than the average cost of production or just low enough to make entering not profitable. The quantity produced by the incumbent firm to act as a deterrent to entry is usually larger than would be optimal for a monopolist, but might still produce higher economic profits than would be earned under perfect competition. The problem with limit pricing as strategic behavior is that once the entrant has entered the market, the quantity used as a threat to deter entry is no longer the incumbent firm's best response.
   a. 529 plan
   b. 4-4-5 Calendar
   c. 7-Eleven
   d. Limit price

7. A _____ is a buy or sell order to be executed by the broker immediately at current market prices. As long as there are willing sellers and buyers, _____s are filled.

Chapter 2. Buying and Selling Securities

A _____ is the simplest of the order types.

- a. Trading curb
- b. Stockholder
- c. Block premium
- d. Market order

8. A _____ is an order to buy (or sell) a security once the price of the security has climbed above (or dropped below) a specified stop price. When the specified stop price is reached, the _____ is entered as a market order (no limit.)

With a _____, the customer does not have to actively monitor how a stock is performing.

- a. Share price
- b. Wash sale
- c. Stop order
- d. Stock split

9. A _____ is the price in stop order that triggers creation of market order.

In the case of a Sell on Stop order, when the market reaches or falls below the _____ a market sell order will be triggered. For Buy on Stop orders, the _____ triggers the creation of a market buy order when the market price of the stock rises to or above the _____.

- a. Box spread
- b. Stockholder
- c. Whisper numbers
- d. Stop price

10. In lending agreements, _____ is a borrower's pledge of specific property to a lender, to secure repayment of a loan. The _____ serves as protection for a lender against a borrower's risk of default - that is, a borrower failing to pay the principal and interest under the terms of a loan obligation. If a borrower does default on a loan (due to insolvency or other event), that borrower forfeits (gives up) the property pledged as _____ *ollateral* - and the lender then becomes the owner of the _____.

- a. Collateral
- b. Nominal value
- c. Future-oriented
- d. Refinancing risk

11. Generally, in English and American law, a contract of mortgage or pledge as collateral for a debt in which the subject matter is not delivered into the possession of the pledgee or pawnee. The arrangement is common with modern mortgages - the borrower retains legal ownership of the property but provides the lender with a lien over the property until the debt is paid off.

_____ and re-_____, respectively, are commonly used to describe the means by which securities brokers and dealers first extend credit on margin to their customers using pledged securities as collateral, and then pledge the client-owned securities held in the client's margin account as collateral for the brokerage's bank loan.

- a. 7-Eleven
- b. 529 plan
- c. 4-4-5 Calendar
- d. Hypothecation

Chapter 2. Buying and Selling Securities

12. In finance, a _____ is collateral that the holder of a position in securities, options, or futures contracts has to deposit to cover the credit risk of his counterparty (most often his broker.) This risk can arise if the holder has done any of the following:

- borrowed cash from the counterparty to buy securities or options,
- sold securities or options short, or
- entered into a futures contract.

The collateral can be in the form of cash or securities, and it is deposited in a _____ account. On U.S. futures exchanges, '_____' was formally called performance bond.

_____ buying is buying securities with cash borrowed from a broker, using other securities as collateral.

a. Margin
b. Share
c. Procter ' Gamble
d. Credit

13. The collateral can be in the form of cash or securities, and it is deposited in a _____. On U.S. futures exchanges, 'margin' was formally called performance bond.

Margin buying is buying securities with cash borrowed from a broker, using other securities as collateral.

a. Dollar roll
b. Risk-neutral measure
c. Forward contract
d. Margin account

14. A _____ combines the features of a stop order and a limit order. Once the stop price is reached, the _____ becomes a limit order to buy (or to sell) at no more (or less) than a specified price. As with all limit orders, a _____ doesn't get filled if the security's price never reaches the specified limit price.

a. Box spread
b. Stop price
c. Wash sale
d. Stop-limit order

15. The institution most often referenced by the word '_____' is a public or publicly traded _____, the shares of which are traded on a public stock exchange (e.g., the New York Stock Exchange or Nasdaq in the United States) where shares of stock of _____s are bought and sold by and to the general public. Most of the largest businesses in the world are publicly traded _____s. However, the majority of _____s are said to be closely held, privately held or close _____s, meaning that no ready market exists for the trading of shares.

a. Depository Trust Company
b. Federal Home Loan Mortgage Corporation
c. Protect
d. Corporation

16. The _____ requirement is the amount required to be collateralized in order to open a position. Thereafter, the amount required to be kept in collateral until the position is closed is the maintenance requirement. The maintenance requirement is the minimum amount to be collateralized in order to keep an open position.

a. Initial margin
b. Arbitrage
c. Issuer
d. Efficient-market hypothesis

Chapter 2. Buying and Selling Securities

17. The _____ is the amount required to be collateralized in order to open a position. Thereafter, the amount required to be kept in collateral until the position is closed is the maintenance requirement. The maintenance requirement is the minimum amount to be collateralized in order to keep an open position.
   a. Initial margin requirement
   b. A Random Walk Down Wall Street
   c. ABN Amro
   d. AAB

18. In financial accounting, the term _____ is most commonly used to describe any part of shareholders' equity, except for basic share capital. Sometimes, the term is used instead of the term provision; such a use, however, is inconsistent with the terminology suggested by International Accounting Standards Board. For more information about provisions, see provision (accounting.)
   a. FIFO and LIFO accounting
   b. Reserve
   c. Treasury stock
   d. Closing entries

19. The _____ of 1934 is a law governing the secondary trading of securities (stocks, bonds, and debentures) in the United States of America. The Act, 48 Stat. 881 (enacted June 6, 1934), codified at 15 U.S.C. § 78a et seq., was a sweeping piece of legislation. The Act and related statutes form the basis of regulation of the financial markets and their participants in the United States.
   a. 7-Eleven
   b. Securities Exchange Act
   c. 4-4-5 Calendar
   d. 529 plan

20. In finance, _____ is the process of estimating the potential market value of a financial asset or liability. they can be done on assets (for example, investments in marketable securities such as stocks, options, business enterprises, or intangible assets such as patents and trademarks) or on liabilities (e.g., Bonds issued by a company.) _____ s are required in many contexts including investment analysis, capital budgeting, merger and acquisition transactions, financial reporting, taxable events to determine the proper tax liability, and in litigation.
   a. Margin
   b. Valuation
   c. Procter ' Gamble
   d. Share

21. In finance, a _____ is a standardized contract, to buy or sell a specified commodity of standardized quality at a certain date in the future, at a market determined price (the futures price.)

The price is determined by the instantaneous equilibrium between the forces of supply and demand among competing buy and sell orders on the exchange at the time of the purchase or sale of the contract.

In many cases, the items may be such non-traditional 'commodities' as foreign currencies, commercial or government paper [e.g., bonds], or 'baskets' of corporate equity ['stock indices'] or other financial instruments.

   a. Financial future
   b. Heston model
   c. Repurchase agreement
   d. Futures contract

22. _____ refers to a business or organization attempting to acquire goods or services to accomplish the goals of the enterprise. Though there are several organizations that attempt to set standards in the _____ process, processes can vary greatly between organizations. Typically the word '_____' is not used interchangeably with the word 'procurement', since procurement typically includes Expediting, Supplier Quality, and Traffic and Logistics (T'L) in addition to _____.

Chapter 2. Buying and Selling Securities

a. 529 plan
c. 4-4-5 Calendar
b. 7-Eleven
d. Purchasing

23. The variation margin or _____ is not collateral, but a daily offsetting of profits and losses. Futures are marked-to-market every day, so the current price is compared to the previous day's price. The profit or loss on the day of a position is then paid to or debited from the holder by the futures exchange.

a. SPI 200 futures contract
c. Maintenance margin
b. Total return swap
d. Delivery month

24. The _____, sometimes called the maintenance margin requirement, is the ratio set for:

- (Stock Equity - Leveraged Dollars) to Stock Equity

- Stock Equity being the stock price * no. of stocks bought and Leveraged Dollars being the amount borrowed in the margin account.

- E.g. An investor bought 1000 shares of ABC company each priced at $50. If the initial margin requirement were 60%:

- Stock Equity: $50 * 1000 = $50,000

- Leveraged Dollars or amount borrowed: ($50 * 1000)* (1-60%) = $20,000

So the maintenance margin requirement uses the above variables to form a ratio that investors have to abide by in order to keep the account active.

The point is, let's say the maintenance margin requirement is reduced from 60% to 25% - At what price would the investor be getting a margin call? Let P be the price, so 1000P in our case is the Stock Equity.

- (Stock Equity - Leveraged Dollars) divided by Stock Equity = 25%

- (1000P - $20,000)/1000P = 0.25

- (1000P - $20,000) = 250P

- P = $26.67

So if the stock price drops from $50 to $26.67, investors will be called to add additional funds to the account to make up for the loss in stock equity.

Margin requirements are reduced for positions that offset each other.

a. 7-Eleven
c. 4-4-5 Calendar
b. 529 plan
d. Minimum margin requirement

Chapter 2. Buying and Selling Securities

25. In finance, _____ is a measurement of return on an asset or portfolio. It is one of the simplest measures of investment performance.

_____ is the percentage by which the value of a portfolio (or asset) has grown for a particular period.

   a. Market integration
   b. Creditor
   c. Holding period return
   d. Stock market index option

26. In finance, _____ (or gearing) is borrowing money to supplement existing funds for investment in such a way that the potential positive or negative outcome is magnified and/or enhanced. It generally refers to using borrowed funds, or debt, so as to attempt to increase the returns to equity. Deleveraging is the action of reducing borrowings.
   a. Pension fund
   b. Financial endowment
   c. Leverage
   d. Limited partnership

27. In finance, a _____ is a debt security, in which the authorized issuer owes the holders a debt and, depending on the terms of the _____, is obliged to pay interest (the coupon) and/or to repay the principal at a later date, termed maturity.

Thus a _____ is a loan: the issuer is the borrower, the _____ holder is the lender, and the coupon is the interest. _____s provide the borrower with external funds to finance long-term investments, or, in the case of government _____s, to finance current expenditure.

   a. Catastrophe bonds
   b. Bond
   c. Puttable bond
   d. Convertible bond

28. The U.S. _____ is an independent agency of the United States government which holds primary responsibility for enforcing the federal securities laws and regulating the securities industry, the nation's stock and options exchanges, and other electronic securities markets. The SEC was created by section 4 of the SEC of 1934 (now codified as 15 U.S.C. § 78d and commonly referred to as the 1934 Act.)
   a. 4-4-5 Calendar
   b. 529 plan
   c. 7-Eleven
   d. Securities and Exchange Commission

29. In finance, _____ or 'shorting' is the practice of selling a financial instrument that the seller does not own at the time of the sale. _____ is done with intent of later purchasing the financial instrument at a lower price. Short-sellers attempt to profit from an expected decline in the price of a financial instrument.
   a. 4-4-5 Calendar
   b. 529 plan
   c. Short ratio
   d. Short selling

30. The _____ generally prohibits short selling of securities except on an uptick. The rule was defined by U.S. Securities and Exchange Commission (SEC) which summarized it: 'Rule 10a-1(a)(1) provided that, subject to certain exceptions, a listed security may be sold short (A) at a price above the price at which the immediately preceding sale was effected (plus tick), or (B) at the last sale price if it is higher than the last different price (zero-plus tick.) Short sales were not permitted on minus ticks or zero-minus ticks, subject to narrow exceptions.'

The rule went into effect in 1938 and was removed when Rule 201 Regulation SHO became effective in 2007.

a. AAB
b. A Random Walk Down Wall Street
c. ABN Amro
d. Uptick rule

31. _____ is a form of corporation equity ownership represented in the securities. It is dangerous in comparison to preferred shares and some other investment options, in that in the event of bankruptcy, _____ investors receive their funds after preferred stockholders, bondholders, creditors, etc. On the other hand, common shares on average perform better than preferred shares or bonds over time.

a. Stock market bubble
b. Stop-limit order
c. Stock split
d. Common stock

32. A _____ is a payment made by a corporation to its shareholder members. When a corporation earns a profit or surplus, that money can be put to two uses: it can either be re-invested in the business (called retained earnings), or it can be paid to the shareholders as a _____. Many corporations retain a portion of their earnings and pay the remainder as a _____.

a. Special dividend
b. Dividend puzzle
c. Dividend
d. Dividend yield

33. _____ is a securities industry term describing the date on which a trade (bonds, equities, foreign exchange, commodities etc) settles. That is, the actual day on which transfer of cash or assets is completed.

It is not necessarily the same as value date (when the settlement amount is calculated.)

a. Mid price
b. Settlement date
c. Political risk
d. Single-index model

34. The _____ is usually the number of shares outstanding of a publicly traded company that is sold short, divided by the average daily trading volume (daily transaction).

It is one measure of the market's outlook on a given stock; a higher short interest ratio indicates more pessimism, because a higher proportion of a company's total float has already been sold short.

The short interest and _____ can be deceiving, however, when a company has many convertible securities outstanding and is perceived to be at risk, because convertible and options arbitrageurs will often sell the stock short to manage risk with their long positions in these other instruments.

a. Short selling
b. 4-4-5 Calendar
c. 529 plan
d. Short ratio

35. _____ is a fee paid on borrowed assets. It is the price paid for the use of borrowed money, or, money earned by deposited funds. Assets that are sometimes lent with _____ include money, shares, consumer goods through hire purchase, major assets such as aircraft, and even entire factories in finance lease arrangements.

a. Interest
b. Insolvency
c. A Random Walk Down Wall Street
d. AAB

Chapter 3. Security Markets

1. _____ is a measure of the ability of a debtor to pay their debts as and when they fall due. It is usually expressed as a ratio or a percentage of current liabilities.

For a corporation with a published balance sheet there are various ratios used to calculate a measure of liquidity.

- a. Invested capital
- b. Operating profit margin
- c. Accounting liquidity
- d. Operating leverage

2. An _____ is a contract written by a seller that conveys to the buyer the right -- but not the obligation -- to buy (in the case of a call _____) or to sell (in the case of a put _____) a particular asset, such as a piece of property such as, among others, a futures contract. In return for granting the _____, the seller collects a payment (the premium) from the buyer.

For example, buying a call _____ provides the right to buy a specified quantity of a security at a set strike price at some time on or before expiration, while buying a put _____ provides the right to sell.

- a. Annuity
- b. Option
- c. AT'T Mobility LLC
- d. Amortization

3. The _____ is that part of the capital markets that deals with the issuance of new securities. Companies, governments or public sector institutions can obtain funding through the sale of a new stock or bond issue. This is typically done through a syndicate of securities dealers.

- a. Primary market
- b. Peer group analysis
- c. Sector rotation
- d. Volatility clustering

4. The _____ is the financial market where previously issued securities and financial instruments such as stock, bonds, options, and futures are bought and sold. The term '_____' is also used refer to the market for any used goods or assets, or an alternative use for an existing product or asset where the customer base is the second market

With primary issuances of securities or financial instruments, or the primary market, investors purchase these securities directly from issuers such as corporations issuing shares in an IPO or private placement, or directly from the federal government in the case of treasuries.

- a. Secondary market
- b. Delta neutral
- c. Financial market
- d. Performance attribution

5. A _____ is a fungible, negotiable instrument representing financial value. They are broadly categorized into debt securities (such as banknotes, bonds and debentures), and equity securities; e.g., common stocks. The company or other entity issuing the _____ is called the issuer.
- a. Book entry
- b. Securities lending
- c. Tracking stock
- d. Security

6. The _____ is a stock exchange based in New York City, New York. It is the largest stock exchange in the world by dollar value of its listed companies securities. As of October 2008, the combined capitalization of all domestic _____ listed companies was $10.1 trillion.

Chapter 3. Security Markets

a. 529 plan
c. 7-Eleven
b. New York Stock Exchange
d. 4-4-5 Calendar

7. A _____, securities exchange or (in Europe) bourse is a corporation or mutual organization which provides 'trading' facilities for stock brokers and traders, to trade stocks and other securities. _____s also provide facilities for the issue and redemption of securities as well as other financial instruments and capital events including the payment of income and dividends. The securities traded on a _____ include: shares issued by companies, unit trusts and other pooled investment products and bonds.

a. 4-4-5 Calendar
c. 7-Eleven
b. 529 plan
d. Stock Exchange

8. A '_____' is a 'Charge' that is paid to obtain the right to delay a payment. Essentially, the payer purchases the right to make a given payment in the future instead of in the Present. The '_____', or 'Charge' that must be paid to delay the payment, is simply the difference between what the payment amount would be if it were paid in the present and what the payment amount would be paid if it were paid in the future.

a. Risk modeling
c. Value at risk
b. Risk aversion
d. Discount

9. In finance, a _____ is a debt security, in which the authorized issuer owes the holders a debt and, depending on the terms of the _____, is obliged to pay interest (the coupon) and/or to repay the principal at a later date, termed maturity.

Thus a _____ is a loan: the issuer is the borrower, the _____ holder is the lender, and the coupon is the interest. _____s provide the borrower with external funds to finance long-term investments, or, in the case of government _____s, to finance current expenditure.

a. Puttable bond
c. Catastrophe bonds
b. Bond
d. Convertible bond

10. The _____ is one of several stock market indices, created by nineteenth-century Wall Street Journal editor and Dow Jones ' Company co-founder Charles Dow. Dow compiled the index to gauge the performance of the industrial sector of the American stock market. It is the second-oldest U.S. market index, after the Dow Jones Transportation Average, which Dow also created.

a. 7-Eleven
c. 529 plan
b. Dow Jones Industrial Average
d. 4-4-5 Calendar

11. A _____ is a member of an exchange who is an employee of a member firm and executes orders, as agent, on the floor of the exchange for clients. The _____ receives an order via teletype machine from his firm's trading department and then proceeds to the appropriate trading post on the exchange floor. There he joins other brokers and the specialist in the security being bought or sold and executes the trade at the best competitive price available.

a. Business valuation standards
c. Floor broker
b. Multivariate normal distribution
d. Case-Shiller Home Price Indices

12. A _____ is the highest price that a buyer (i.e., bidder) is willing to pay for a good. It is usually referred to simply as the 'bid.'

In bid and ask, the _____ stands in contrast to the ask price or 'offer', and the difference between the two is called the bid/ask spread.

An unsolicited bid or offer is when a person or company receives a bid even though they are not looking to sell.

a. Political risk
b. Mid price
c. Settlement date
d. Bid price

13. A _____ is an order to buy a security at no more (or sell at no less) than a specific price. This gives the customer some control over the price at which the trade is executed, but may prevent the order from being executed ('filled'.)

A buy _____ can only be executed by the broker at the limit price or lower.

a. Commercial mortgage-backed securities
b. Limit order
c. Common stock
d. Block premium

14. A _____ is a buy or sell order to be executed by the broker immediately at current market prices. As long as there are willing sellers and buyers, _____s are filled.

A _____ is the simplest of the order types.

a. Stockholder
b. Block premium
c. Trading curb
d. Market order

15. A _____ is a process of buying and selling goods when potential buyers submit their bids and potential sellers simultaneously submit their ask prices to an auctioneer, and then an auctioneer chooses some price p that clears the market: all the sellers who asked less than p sell and all buyers who bid more than p buy at this price p.

a. 7-Eleven
b. 529 plan
c. 4-4-5 Calendar
d. Double auction

16. _____ are securities that can be easily converted into cash. Such securities will generally have highly liquid markets allowing the security to be sold at a reasonable price very quickly.This is a usual feature in real estate .

a. Securities lending
b. Tracking stock
c. Book entry
d. Marketable

17. The phrase _____ refers to the aspect of corporate strategy, corporate finance and management dealing with the buying, selling and combining of different companies that can aid, finance, or help a growing company in a given industry grow rapidly without having to create another business entity.

An acquisition, also known as a takeover, is the buying of one company (the 'target') by another. An acquisition may be friendly or hostile.

a. 7-Eleven
b. 4-4-5 Calendar
c. 529 plan
d. Mergers and acquisitions

Chapter 3. Security Markets

18. In finance, a _____ is a standardized contract, to buy or sell a specified commodity of standardized quality at a certain date in the future, at a market determined price (the futures price.)

The price is determined by the instantaneous equilibrium between the forces of supply and demand among competing buy and sell orders on the exchange at the time of the purchase or sale of the contract.

In many cases, the items may be such non-traditional 'commodities' as foreign currencies, commercial or government paper [e.g., bonds], or 'baskets' of corporate equity ['stock indices'] or other financial instruments.

a. Heston model
b. Financial future
c. Repurchase agreement
d. Futures contract

19. A _____ is a central financial exchange where people can trade standardized futures contracts; that is, a contract to buy specific quantities of a commodity or financial instrument at a specified price with delivery set at a specified time in the future.

Though the origins of futures trading can supposedly be traced to Ancient Greek or Phoenician times, the first modern organized _____ began in 1710 at the Dojima Rice Exchange in Osaka, Japan.

The United States followed in the early 1800s.

a. 4-4-5 Calendar
b. 529 plan
c. 7-Eleven
d. Futures exchange

20. The _____ is an American stock exchange. It is the largest electronic screen-based equity securities trading market in the United States. With approximately 3,200 companies, it has more trading volume per day than any other stock exchange in the world.

a. 4-4-5 Calendar
b. 7-Eleven
c. 529 plan
d. Nasdaq

21. In the United States, the Financial Industry Regulatory Authority (FINRA) is a self-regulatory organization (SRO) under the Securities Exchange Act of 1934, successor to the _____, Inc.

FINRA is responsible for regulatory oversight of all securities firms that do business with the public; professional training, testing and licensing of registered persons; arbitration and mediation; market regulation by contract for The NASDAQ Stock Market, Inc., the American Stock Exchange LLC, and the International Securities Exchange, LLC; and industry utilities, such as Trade Reporting Facilities and other over-the-counter operations.

a. 529 plan
b. 4-4-5 Calendar
c. 7-Eleven
d. National Association of Securities Dealers

22. In finance, _____ trading is the trading of exchange listed securities in the over-the-counter (OTC) market. Bernard Madoff was engaged in _____ trading.

a. 529 plan
b. 7-Eleven
c. 4-4-5 Calendar
d. Third market

23. A _____ or market-based mechanism is any of a wide variety of ways to match up buyers and sellers.

An example of a _____ uses announced bid and ask prices. Generally speaking, when two parties wish to engage in a trade, the purchaser will announce a price he is willing to pay (the bid price) and seller will announce a price he is willing to accept (the ask price).

a. 7-Eleven
b. 4-4-5 Calendar
c. 529 plan
d. Price mechanism

24. The _____ for securities is the difference between the price quoted by a market maker for an immediate sale and an immediate purchase The size of the bid-offer spread in a given commodity is a measure of the liquidity of the market.

The trader initiating the transaction is said to demand liquidity, and the other party to the transaction supplies liquidity.

a. Defined contribution plan
b. Capital outflow
c. Trade-off
d. Bid/offer spread

25. _____ is a SEC regulation requiring brokers to guarantee customers the best available ask price when buying securities, and the best available bid price when selling securities. This resulted in the making of the Options linkage plan.

a. 4-4-5 Calendar
b. 529 plan
c. 7-Eleven
d. National Best Bid and Offer

26. In financial accounting, the term _____ is most commonly used to describe any part of shareholders' equity, except for basic share capital. Sometimes, the term is used instead of the term provision; such a use, however, is inconsistent with the terminology suggested by International Accounting Standards Board. For more information about provisions, see provision (accounting.)

a. FIFO and LIFO accounting
b. Closing entries
c. Treasury stock
d. Reserve

27. In economics and related disciplines, a _____ is a cost incurred in making an economic exchange. For example, most people, when buying or selling a stock, must pay a commission to their broker; that commission is a _____ of doing the stock deal. Or consider buying a banana from a store; to purchase the banana, your costs will be not only the price of the banana itself, but also the energy and effort it requires to find out which of the various banana products you prefer, where to get them and at what price, the cost of traveling from your house to the store and back, the time waiting in line, and the effort of the paying itself; the costs above and beyond the cost of the banana are the _____s.

a. Marginal cost
b. Variable costs
c. Transaction cost
d. Fixed costs

28. In economics, business, and accounting, a _____ is the value of money that has been used up to produce something, and hence is not available for use anymore. In business, the _____ may be one of acquisition, in which case the amount of money expended to acquire it is counted as _____. In this case, money is the input that is gone in order to acquire the thing.

Chapter 3. Security Markets

a. Cost
c. Fixed costs
b. Sliding scale fees
d. Marginal cost

29. The _____ requirement is the amount required to be collateralized in order to open a position. Thereafter, the amount required to be kept in collateral until the position is closed is the maintenance requirement. The maintenance requirement is the minimum amount to be collateralized in order to keep an open position.
   a. Initial margin
   c. Issuer
   b. Arbitrage
   d. Efficient-market hypothesis

30. The _____ is the amount required to be collateralized in order to open a position. Thereafter, the amount required to be kept in collateral until the position is closed is the maintenance requirement. The maintenance requirement is the minimum amount to be collateralized in order to keep an open position.
   a. Initial margin requirement
   c. A Random Walk Down Wall Street
   b. ABN Amro
   d. AAB

31. In finance, a _____ is collateral that the holder of a position in securities, options, or futures contracts has to deposit to cover the credit risk of his counterparty (most often his broker.) This risk can arise if the holder has done any of the following:

   - borrowed cash from the counterparty to buy securities or options,
   - sold securities or options short, or
   - entered into a futures contract.

The collateral can be in the form of cash or securities, and it is deposited in a _____ account. On U.S. futures exchanges, '_____' was formally called performance bond.

_____ buying is buying securities with cash borrowed from a broker, using other securities as collateral.

   a. Procter ' Gamble
   c. Credit
   b. Margin
   d. Share

32. _____ are organizations which pool large sums of money and invest those sums in companies. They include banks, insurance companies, retirement or pension funds, hedge funds and mutual funds. Their role in the economy is to act as highly specialized investors on behalf of others.
   a. ABN Amro
   c. Institutional investors
   b. A Random Walk Down Wall Street
   d. AAB

33. The _____ is an electronic quotation system in the United States that displays real-time quotes, last-sale prices, and volume information for many over-the-counter (OTC) equity securities that are not listed on the NASDAQ stock exchange or a national securities exchange. Broker-dealers who subscribe to the system can use the _____ to look up prices or enter quotes for OTC securities.
   a. Insolvency
   c. AT'T Inc.
   b. OTC Bulletin Board
   d. Internal control

Chapter 3. Security Markets

34. The U.S. _____ is an independent agency of the United States government which holds primary responsibility for enforcing the federal securities laws and regulating the securities industry, the nation's stock and options exchanges, and other electronic securities markets. The SEC was created by section 4 of the SEC of 1934 (now codified as 15 U.S.C. §78d and commonly referred to as the 1934 Act.)
   a. 529 plan
   b. 7-Eleven
   c. 4-4-5 Calendar
   d. Securities and Exchange Commission

35. An _____ is the term used in financial circles for a type of computer system that facilitates trading of financial products outside of stock exchanges. The primary products that are traded on an _____ are stocks and currencies. They came into existence in 1998 when the SEC authorized their creation.
   a. Intellidex
   b. Electronic communication network
   c. Open outcry
   d. Insider trading

36. _____ trading refers to direct institution-to-institution trading without using the service of broker-dealers. It is impossible to estimate the volume of _____ activity because trades are not subject to reporting requirements. Studies have suggested that several millions shares are traded per day.
   a. 529 plan
   b. 4-4-5 Calendar
   c. 7-Eleven
   d. Fourth market

37. _____ is a standard to measure global business processes that are maintained in multiple business applications and serviced by various outsourcing companies.

Internationally, _____ is assessed, managed and monitored by ICIM, a Chicago-based decision science company.

As all standards, this is also an assessment. However, the difference is that it measures companies on three aspects:

   1. Process activity and flow standards
   2. Process performance standards
   3. Process management standards.

   a. 529 plan
   b. 4-4-5 Calendar
   c. 7-Eleven
   d. POSIT

38. An _____ is a company whose main business is holding securities of other companies purely for investment purposes. The _____ invests money on behalf of its shareholders who in turn share in the profits and losses.
   a. AAB
   b. Investment company
   c. Unit investment trust
   d. A Random Walk Down Wall Street

39. A _____ is a payment made by a corporation to its shareholder members. When a corporation earns a profit or surplus, that money can be put to two uses: it can either be re-invested in the business (called retained earnings), or it can be paid to the shareholders as a _____. Many corporations retain a portion of their earnings and pay the remainder as a _____.

Chapter 3. Security Markets

a. Dividend puzzle
c. Dividend

b. Special dividend
d. Dividend yield

40. The _____ on a company stock is the company's annual dividend payments divided by its market cap, or the dividend per share divided by the price per share. It is often expressed as a percentage.

Dividend payments on preferred shares are stipulated by the prospectus.

a. Dividend imputation
c. Dividend reinvestment plan

b. Special dividend
d. Dividend yield

41. The _____ of a stock is a measure of the price paid for a share relative to the annual income or profit earned by the firm per share. It is a financial ratio used for valuation: a higher _____ means that investors are paying more for each unit of income, so the stock is more expensive compared to one with lower _____.

The _____ has units of years, which can be interpreted as 'number of years of earnings to pay back purchase price'.

a. Return of capital
c. Sustainable growth rate

b. Quick ratio
d. P/E ratio

42. In finance, the term _____ describes the amount in cash that returns to the owners of a security. Normally it does not include the price variations, at the difference of the total return. _____ applies to various stated rates of return on stocks (common and preferred, and convertible), fixed income instruments (bonds, notes, bills, strips, zero coupon), and some other investment type insurance products (e.g. annuities.)

a. Macaulay duration
c. Yield to maturity

b. 4-4-5 Calendar
d. Yield

43. The _____ is overseen by the _____ Association.

Tape C contains over-the-counter stocks listed on the NASDAQ National Market or NASDAQ Small Cap Market, and is overseen by the OTC/UTP Operating Committee.

a. Liquidating dividend
c. January effect

b. Peer group analysis
d. Consolidated tape

44. A _____ is the price of a single share of a no. of saleable stocks of the company. Once the stock is purchased, the owner becomes a shareholder of the company that issued the share.

a. Share price
c. Whisper numbers

b. Trading curb
d. Stock split

45. In banking and finance, _____ denotes all activities from the time a commitment is made for a transaction until it is settled. _____ is necessary because the speed of trades is much faster than the cycle time for completing the underlying transaction.

In its widest sense _____ involves the management of post-trading, pre-settlement credit exposures, to ensure that trades are settled in accordance with market rules, even if a buyer or seller should become insolvent prior to settlement.

a. Clearing
c. Share

b. Procter ' Gamble
d. Clearing house

46. The institution most often referenced by the word '_____' is a public or publicly traded _____, the shares of which are traded on a public stock exchange (e.g., the New York Stock Exchange or Nasdaq in the United States) where shares of stock of _____s are bought and sold by and to the general public. Most of the largest businesses in the world are publicly traded _____s. However, the majority of _____s are said to be closely held, privately held or close _____s, meaning that no ready market exists for the trading of shares.

a. Federal Home Loan Mortgage Corporation
c. Protect

b. Depository Trust Company
d. Corporation

47. Established in 1973, The _____ was created to alleviate the rising volumes of paperwork and the lack of security that developed after rapid growth in the volume of transactions in the U.S. securities industry in the late 1960s.

Before _____ and NSCC were formed, brokers physically exchanged certificates, employing hundreds of messengers to carry certificates and checks. The mechanisms brokers used to transfer securities and keep records relied heavily on pen and paper.

a. Protect
c. Federal Home Loan Mortgage Corporation

b. Wells Fargo ' Co.
d. Depository Trust Company

48. The _____ of 1970 codified at 15 U.S.C. § 78aaa through 15 U.S.C. § 78lll, established the Securities Investor Protection Corporation (SIPC). Most brokers and dealers registered under the Securities Exchange Act of 1934 are required to be members of the SIPC.

The SIPC maintains a fund that is intended to protect investors against the misappropriation of their funds and of most types of securities in the event of the failure of their broker.

a. Fiduciary
c. McFadden Act

b. Quiet period
d. Securities Investor Protection Act

49. The _____ is a federally mandated non-profit corporation in the United States that protects securities investors from harm if a broker-dealer company fails. Investors are not insured for any potential loss while invested in the market.

Congress created _____ in 1970 through the Securities Investor Protection Act (15 U.S.C.

a. Securities Investor Protection Corporation
c. Rule 144A

b. Prudent man rule
d. SIPC

Chapter 3. Security Markets

50. A _____ is a corporation, especially a commercial bank, organized to perform the fiduciary functions of trusts and agencies. It is normally owned by one of three types of structures: an independent partnership, a bank, or a law firm, each of which specializes in being a trustee of various kinds of trusts and in managing estates.
    a. Mutual fund
    b. Person-to-person lending
    c. Savings and loan association
    d. Trust Company

51. _____, in microeconomics, are the cost advantages that a business obtains due to expansion. _____ may be utilized by any size firm expanding its scale of operation.
    a. Economies of scale
    b. Uniform Commercial Code
    c. Articles of incorporation
    d. Employee Retirement Income Security Act

52. The _____ of 1934 is a law governing the secondary trading of securities (stocks, bonds, and debentures) in the United States of America. The Act, 48 Stat. 881 (enacted June 6, 1934), codified at 15 U.S.C. § 78a et seq., was a sweeping piece of legislation. The Act and related statutes form the basis of regulation of the financial markets and their participants in the United States.
    a. 529 plan
    b. Securities Exchange Act
    c. 4-4-5 Calendar
    d. 7-Eleven

53. _____ is a measurement of corporate or economic size equal to the share price times the number of shares outstanding of a public company. As owning stock represents owning the company, including all its equity, capitalization could represent the public opinion of a company's net worth and is a determining factor in stock valuation. Likewise, the capitalization of stock markets or economic regions may be compared to other economic indicators.
    a. Market capitalization
    b. Just-in-time
    c. Proxy fight
    d. Synthetic CDO

54. _____ is defined by The Wall Street Journal, as a form of barter that involves a company selling 'an unused asset to another company while at the same time agreeing to buy back the same or similar assets at about the same price.' Round trips are characteristic of the New Economy companies. They played a crucial part in temporarily inflating the market capitalization of energy traders such as Enron, CMS Energy, Reliant Energy, and Dynegy.

Other companies making unconventional _____ deals include AOL with Sun Microsystems and Global Crossing with Qwest Communications.

    a. Round-tripping
    b. Net pay
    c. Residual value
    d. Days Sales Outstanding

55. Congress enacted the _____, in the aftermath of the stock market crash of 1929 and during the ensuing Great Depression. It requires that any offer or sale of securities using the means and instrumentalities of interstate commerce be registered pursuant to the 1933 Act, unless an exemption from registration exists under the law.
    a. 529 plan
    b. Securities Act of 1933
    c. 4-4-5 Calendar
    d. 7-Eleven

56.

A _____ is a type of financial intermediary and a type of bank. Commercial banking is also known as business banking. It is a bank that provides checking accounts, savings accounts, and money market accounts and that accepts time deposits.

a. 529 plan
c. 7-Eleven
b. 4-4-5 Calendar
d. Commercial bank

57. The _____ of 1933 established the Federal Deposit Insurance Corporation (FDIC) in the United States and included banking reforms, some of which were designed to control speculation. Some provisions such as Regulation Q, which allowed the Federal Reserve to regulate interest rates in savings accounts, were repealed by the Depository Institutions Deregulation and Monetary Control Act of 1980. Provisions that prohibit a bank holding company from owning other financial companies were repealed on November 12, 1999, by the Gramm-Leach-Bliley Act.

a. 7-Eleven
c. 529 plan
b. 4-4-5 Calendar
d. Glass-Steagall Act

58. An _____ is an individual or firm that advises clients on investment matters on a professional basis.

They tend to fall into two distinct categories:

- _____s offering direct financial advice to individuals or businesses, or
- _____s offering asset management for (typically) corporate clients, hedge funds and/or mutual funds.

Depending on the nature of the relationship, _____s charge fees calculated as a percentage (e.g., 1%) of assets under management, on an annual basis, an hourly or on a 'flat fee' basis.

In the United States whether a firm should be registered as an _____ with the SEC or a state is typically determined by the amount of assets receiving continuous and regular supervisory or management services (AUM.) In order for a firm to register with the SEC, the firm must have over $25 million of AUM at the time of registration or within 120 days of the effective date of the registration.

a. A Random Walk Down Wall Street
c. Investment Advisor
b. AAB
d. ABN Amro

59. A _____ is an institution, firm or individual who mediates between two or more parties in a financial context. Typically the first party is a provider of a product or service and the second party is a consumer or customer.

In the U.S., a _____ is typically an institution that facilitates the channelling of funds between lenders and borrowers indirectly.

a. Net asset value
c. Mutual fund
b. Financial intermediary
d. Savings and loan association

Chapter 3. Security Markets

60. A _____ is a state law in the United States that regulates the offering and sale of securities to protect the public from fraud. Though the specific provisions of these laws vary among states, they all require the registration of all securities offerings and sales, as well as of stock brokers and brokerage firms. Each state's _____ is administered by its appropriate regulatory agency, and most also provide private causes of action for private investors who have been injured by securities fraud.

   a. Court of Audit of Belgium   b. Blue sky law
   c. Bundesrechnungshof   d. Patent

61. The _____ is a model statute designed to guide each state in drafting its state securities law. It was created by the National Conference of Commissioners on Uniform State Laws (NCCUSL.)

The purpose of the _____ is to provide model legislation that can be adopted by a state to deal with securities fraud at the state level, supplementing enforcement and regulation efforts of the U.S. Securities and Exchange Commission (SEC.)

   a. Employee Retirement Income Security Act   b. Uniform Securities Act
   c. Economies of scale   d. External risks

Chapter 4. Efficient Markets, Investment Value, and Market Price

1. Modern portfolio theory (MPT) proposes how rational investors will use diversification to optimize their portfolios, and how a risky asset should be priced. The basic concepts of the theory are Markowitz diversification, the _____, capital asset pricing model, the alpha and beta coefficients, the Capital Market Line and the Securities Market Line.

   MPT models an asset's return as a random variable, and models a portfolio as a weighted combination of assets so that the return of a portfolio is the weighted combination of the assets' returns.

   a. ABN Amro
   b. Efficient frontier
   c. AAB
   d. A Random Walk Down Wall Street

2. In economics and contract theory, _____ deals with the study of decisions in transactions where one party has more or better information than the other. This creates an imbalance of power in transactions which can sometimes cause the transactions to go awry. Examples of this problem are adverse selection and moral hazard.
   a. A Random Walk Down Wall Street
   b. AAB
   c. ABN Amro
   d. Information asymmetry

3. _____ is the value of a property to a particular investor. In the U.S., it is equal to market value for the investor who has the capacity to put the property to good use -- its highest-and-best-use, its most valuable use. For other investors with limited capacity or vision, _____ is lower because they cannot put the property to use in a way that is maximally productive.
   a. AAB
   b. A Random Walk Down Wall Street
   c. ABN Amro
   d. Investment value

4. A _____, is a mathematical formalization of a trajectory that consists of taking successive random steps. The results of _____ analysis have been applied to computer science, physics, ecology, economics and a number of other fields as a fundamental model for random processes in time. For example, the path traced by a molecule as it travels in a liquid or a gas, the search path of a foraging animal, the price of a fluctuating stock and the financial status of a gambler can all be modeled as _____s.
   a. Random walk
   b. 529 plan
   c. 7-Eleven
   d. 4-4-5 Calendar

5. The _____ is a random-based mobility model used in mobility management schemes for mobile communication systems. The mobility model is designed to describe the movement pattern of mobile users, and how their location, velocity and acceleration change over time. Mobility models are used for simulation purposes when new network protocols are evaluated.
   a. 529 plan
   b. 4-4-5 Calendar
   c. 7-Eleven
   d. Random waypoint model

6. _____ of a business involves analyzing its financial statements and health, its management and competitive advantages, and its competitors and markets. The term is used to distinguish such analysis from other types of investment analysis, such as quantitative analysis and technical analysis.

   _____ is performed on historical and present data, but with the goal of making financial forecasts.

   a. Growth stocks
   b. Fundamental analysis
   c. Stock valuation
   d. 4-4-5 Calendar

Chapter 4. Efficient Markets, Investment Value, and Market Price

7. _____ is a security analysis discipline for forecasting the future direction of prices through the study of past market data, primarily price and volume. In its purest form, _____ considers only the actual price and volume behavior of the market or instrument. Technical analysts may employ models and trading rules based on price and volume transformations, such as the relative strength index, moving averages, regressions, inter-market and intra-market price correlations, cycles or, classically, through recognition of chart patterns.
    a. Support and resistance
    b. Technical analysis
    c. Point and figure
    d. Dow theory

8. A _____ is a fungible, negotiable instrument representing financial value. They are broadly categorized into debt securities (such as banknotes, bonds and debentures), and equity securities; e.g., common stocks. The company or other entity issuing the _____ is called the issuer.
    a. Book entry
    b. Tracking stock
    c. Securities lending
    d. Security

9. In economics and related disciplines, a _____ is a cost incurred in making an economic exchange. For example, most people, when buying or selling a stock, must pay a commission to their broker; that commission is a _____ of doing the stock deal. Or consider buying a banana from a store; to purchase the banana, your costs will be not only the price of the banana itself, but also the energy and effort it requires to find out which of the various banana products you prefer, where to get them and at what price, the cost of traveling from your house to the store and back, the time waiting in line, and the effort of the paying itself; the costs above and beyond the cost of the banana are the _____s.
    a. Fixed costs
    b. Marginal cost
    c. Variable costs
    d. Transaction cost

10. In economics, business, and accounting, a _____ is the value of money that has been used up to produce something, and hence is not available for use anymore. In business, the _____ may be one of acquisition, in which case the amount of money expended to acquire it is counted as _____. In this case, money is the input that is gone in order to acquire the thing.
    a. Sliding scale fees
    b. Marginal cost
    c. Cost
    d. Fixed costs

11. _____ refers to a portfolio management strategy where the manager makes specific investments with the goal of outperforming an investment benchmark index. Investors or mutual funds that do not aspire to create a return in excess of a benchmark index will often invest in an index fund that replicates as closely as possible the investment weighting and returns of that index; this is called passive management. _____ is the opposite of passive management, because in passive management the manager does not seek to outperform the benchmark index.
    a. AAB
    b. ABN Amro
    c. A Random Walk Down Wall Street
    d. Active management

12. In business and accounting, _____s are everything of value that is owned by a person or company. The balance sheet of a firm records the monetary value of the _____s owned by the firm. The two major _____ classes are tangible _____s and intangible _____s.
    a. EBITDA
    b. Income
    c. Accounts payable
    d. Asset

Chapter 4. Efficient Markets, Investment Value, and Market Price

13. In finance, _____ is the process of estimating the potential market value of a financial asset or liability. they can be done on assets (for example, investments in marketable securities such as stocks, options, business enterprises, or intangible assets such as patents and trademarks) or on liabilities (e.g., Bonds issued by a company.) _____s are required in many contexts including investment analysis, capital budgeting, merger and acquisition transactions, financial reporting, taxable events to determine the proper tax liability, and in litigation.

   a. Procter ' Gamble
   b. Share
   c. Margin
   d. Valuation

14. The term _____ has three unrelated technical definitions, and is also used in a variety of non-technical ways.

   - In financial economics, it refers to any asset used to make money, as opposed to assets used for personal enjoyment or consumption. This is an important distinction because two people can disagree sharply about the value of personal assets, one person might think a sports car is more valuable than a pickup truck, another person might have the opposite taste. But if an asset is held for the purpose of making money, taste has nothing to do with it, only differences of opinion about how much money the asset will produce. With the further assumption that people agree on the probability distribution of future cash flows, it is possible to have an objective _____ pricing model. Even without the assumption of agreement, it is possible to set rational limits on _____ value.
   - In governmental accounting, it is defined as any asset used in operations with an initial useful life extending beyond one reporting period. Generally, government managers have a 'stewardship' duty to maintain _____s under their control. See International Public Sector Accounting Standards for details.
   - In US tax accounting, it is defined as any property other than a list of exceptions. The main exceptions are anything held for sale, and any real estate or depreciable property used in business. Almost everything you own and use for personal purposes, pleasure or investment is a _____. If something is a _____ for tax purposes, gains or losses on sale or disposition are capital gains or capital losses. For individuals, however, capital losses on property held for personal use are generally not deductible. See the IRS publication Tax Facts about Capital Gains and Losses for details.

A well-known financial accounting textbook advises that the term be avoided except in tax accounting because it is used in so many different senses, not all of them well-defined. For example it is often used as a synonym for fixed assets or for investments in securities.

A common non-technical usage occurs when people ask that employees or the environment or something else be treated as a _____.

   a. Political risk
   b. Settlement date
   c. Capital Asset
   d. Solvency

15. In finance, the _____ is used to determine a theoretically appropriate required rate of return of an asset, if that asset is to be added to an already well-diversified portfolio, given that asset's non-diversifiable risk. The model takes into account the asset's sensitivity to non-diversifiable risk (also known as systemic risk or market risk), often represented by the quantity beta (β) in the financial industry, as well as the expected return of the market and the expected return of a theoretical risk-free asset.

The model was introduced by Jack Treynor (1961, 1962), William Sharpe (1964), John Lintner (1965a,b) and Jan Mossin (1966) independently, building on the earlier work of Harry Markowitz on diversification and modern portfolio theory.

a. Capital Asset Pricing Model
b. Random walk hypothesis
c. Hull-White model
d. Cox-Ingersoll-Ross model

16. An _____ or index tracker is a collective investment scheme (usually a mutual fund or exchange-traded fund) that aims to replicate the movements of an index of a specific financial market regardless of market conditions.

Tracking can be achieved by trying to hold all of the securities in the index, in the same proportions as the index. Other methods include statistically sampling the market and holding 'representative' securities.

a. AAB
b. A Random Walk Down Wall Street
c. Index fund
d. Investment company

17. A _____ is a portfolio consisting of a weighted sum of every asset in the market, with weights in the proportions that they exist in the market (with the necessary assumption that these assets are infinitely divisible.)

Neha Tyagi's critique (1977) states that this is only a theoretical concept, as to create a _____ for investment purposes in practice would necessarily include every single possible available asset, including real estate, precious metals, stamp collections, jewelry, and anything with any worth, as the theoretical market being referred to would be the world market. As a result, proxies for the market are used in practice by investors.

a. Delta neutral
b. Market price
c. Central Securities Depository
d. Market portfolio

18. _____ is a financial strategy in which a fund manager makes as few portfolio decisions as possible, in order to minimize transaction costs, including the incidence of capital gains tax. One popular method is to mimic the performance of an externally specified index--called 'index funds'. The ethos of an index fund is aptly summed up in the injunction to an index fund manager: 'Don't just do something, sit there!'

_____ is most common on the equity market, where index funds track a stock market index, but it is becoming more common in other investment types, including bonds, commodities and hedge funds.

a. Trust company
b. Net asset value
c. Savings and loan association
d. Passive management

19. An _____ is a statistical method to assess the impact of an event on the value of a firm. For example, the announcement of a merger between two firms can be analyzed to see whether investors believe the merger will create or destroy value. Event studies have been used in a large variety of studies, including [mergers and acquisitions], earnings announcements, debt or equity issues, corporate reorganisations, investment decisions and corporate social responsibility (MacKinlay 1997; McWilliams ' Siegel, 1997.)

a. ABN Amro
b. AAB
c. Event study
d. A Random Walk Down Wall Street

20. The _____ is the tendency of the stock market to rise between December 31 and the end of the first week in January. There are many theories for why this happens, the main one being that it occurs because many investors choose to sell some of their stock right before the end of the year in order to claim a capital loss for tax purposes. Once the tax calendar rolls over to a new year on January 1st these same investors quickly reinvest their money in the market, causing stock prices to rise.

a. Sector rotation
b. Death spiral financing
c. Revaluation
d. January effect

21.

In finance, the _____ can be the expected rate of return above the risk-free interest rate. When measuring risk, a common sense approach is to compare the risk-free return on T-bills and the very risky return on other investments. The difference between these two returns can be interpreted as a measure of the excess return on the average risky asset. This excess return is known as the _____.

a. Risk aversion
b. Risk modeling
c. Risk premium
d. Risk adjusted return on capital

22. _____ is the process whereby an organization establishes the parameters within which programs, investments, and acquisitions are reaching the desired results. Performance Reference Model of the Federal Enterprise Architecture, 2005.

This process of measuring performance ofter requires the use of statistical evidence to determine progress toward specific defined organizational objectives.

There are many types of measurements.

a. Corporate Transparency
b. Decentralization
c. Performance measurement
d. Cash cow

Chapter 5. Taxes

1. _____ refers to a tax levied by various jurisdictions on the profits made by companies or associations. It is a tax on the value of the corporation's profits.

The measure of taxable profits varies from country to country.

   a. Trade finance
   b. Proxy fight
   c. Corporate tax
   d. First-mover advantage

2. A _____ is a type of business entity in which partners (owners) share with each other the profits or losses of the business undertaking in which all have invested. _____s are often favored over corporations for taxation purposes, as the _____ structure does not generally incur a tax on profits before it is distributed to the partners (i.e. there is no dividend tax levied.) However, depending on the _____ structure and the jurisdiction in which it operates, owners of a _____ may be exposed to greater personal liability than they would as shareholders of a corporation.
   a. Fiduciary
   b. Clayton Antitrust Act
   c. National Securities Markets Improvement Act of 1996
   d. Partnership

3. A sole _____, or simply _____ is a type of business entity which legally has no separate existence from its owner. Hence, the limitations of liability enjoyed by a corporation and limited liability partnerships do not apply to sole proprietors. All debts of the business are debts of the owner.
   a. Just-in-time
   b. Free cash flow
   c. Proprietorship
   d. Product life cycle

4. _____, refers to consumption opportunity gained by an entity within a specified time frame, which is generally expressed in monetary terms. However, for households and individuals, '_____ is the sum of all the wages, salaries, profits, interests payments, rents and other forms of earnings received... in a given period of time.' For firms, _____ generally refers to net-profit: what remains of revenue after expenses have been subtracted.
   a. Income
   b. OIBDA
   c. Annual report
   d. Accrual

5. An _____ is a tax levied on the financial income of people, corporations, or other legal entities. Various _____ systems exist, with varying degrees of tax incidence. Income taxation can be progressive, proportional, or regressive.
   a. AAB
   b. ABN Amro
   c. A Random Walk Down Wall Street
   d. Income tax

6. In finance, a _____ is a debt security, in which the authorized issuer owes the holders a debt and, depending on the terms of the _____, is obliged to pay interest (the coupon) and/or to repay the principal at a later date, termed maturity.

Thus a _____ is a loan: the issuer is the borrower, the _____ holder is the lender, and the coupon is the interest. _____s provide the borrower with external funds to finance long-term investments, or, in the case of government _____s, to finance current expenditure.

   a. Puttable bond
   b. Convertible bond
   c. Catastrophe bonds
   d. Bond

Chapter 5. Taxes

7. A _____ is a profit that results from investments into a capital asset, such as stocks, bonds or real estate, which exceeds the purchase price. It is the difference between a higher selling price and a lower purchase price, resulting in a financial gain for the seller. Conversely, a capital loss arises if the proceeds from the sale of a capital asset are less than the purchase price.
    a. Capital gain
    b. Capital gains tax
    c. Payroll tax
    d. Tax brackets

8. A _____ is a payment made by a corporation to its shareholder members. When a corporation earns a profit or surplus, that money can be put to two uses: it can either be re-invested in the business (called retained earnings), or it can be paid to the shareholders as a _____. Many corporations retain a portion of their earnings and pay the remainder as a _____.
    a. Special dividend
    b. Dividend yield
    c. Dividend puzzle
    d. Dividend

9. A _____ is an international bond that is denominated in a currency not native to the country where it is issued. It can be categorised according to the currency in which it is issued. London is one of the centers of the _____ market, but _____s may be traded throughout the world - for example in Singapore or Tokyo.
    a. Education production function
    b. Economic entity
    c. Interest rate option
    d. Eurobond

10. _____ is a fee paid on borrowed assets. It is the price paid for the use of borrowed money, or, money earned by deposited funds. Assets that are sometimes lent with _____ include money, shares, consumer goods through hire purchase, major assets such as aircraft, and even entire factories in finance lease arrangements.
    a. Insolvency
    b. Interest
    c. AAB
    d. A Random Walk Down Wall Street

11. _____ is typically a higher ranking stock than voting shares, and its terms are negotiated between the corporation and the investor.

    _____ usually carry no voting rights, but may carry superior priority over common stock in the payment of dividends and upon liquidation. _____ may carry a dividend that is paid out prior to any dividends to common stock holders.
    a. Trade-off theory
    b. Preferred stock
    c. Follow-on offering
    d. Second lien loan

12. An _____ is a company whose main business is holding securities of other companies purely for investment purposes. The _____ invests money on behalf of its shareholders who in turn share in the profits and losses.
    a. AAB
    b. Investment company
    c. A Random Walk Down Wall Street
    d. Unit investment trust

13. A _____ is an exemption from all or certain taxes of a state or nation in which part of the taxes that would normally be collected from an individual or an organization are instead foregone.

Chapter 5. Taxes

Normally a _____ is provided to an individual or organization which falls within a class which the government wishes to promote economically, such as charitable organizations. _____s are usually meant to either reduce the tax burden on a particular segment of society in the interests of fairness or to promote some type of economic activity through reducing the tax burden on those organizations or individuals who are involved in that activity.

a. Federal Open Market Committee
b. Tax exemption
c. Tax compliance solution
d. Tax incidence

14. A _____ is a pool of assets forming an independent legal entity that are bought with the contributions to a pension plan for the exclusive purpose of financing pension plan benefits.

_____s are important shareholders of listed and private companies. They are especially important to the stock market where large institutional investors like the Ontario Teachers' Pension Plan dominate.

a. Limited liability company
b. Leveraged buyout
c. Leverage
d. Pension fund

15. In the United States, a _____ is a bond issued by a city or other local government, or their agencies. Potential issuers of these bonds include cities, counties, redevelopment agencies, school districts, publicly owned airports and seaports, and any other governmental entity (or group of governments) below the state level. They may be general obligations of the issuer or secured by specified revenues.

a. Senior debt
b. Puttable bond
c. Premium bond
d. Municipal bond

16. A _____ is a fungible, negotiable instrument representing financial value. They are broadly categorized into debt securities (such as banknotes, bonds and debentures), and equity securities; e.g., common stocks. The company or other entity issuing the _____ is called the issuer.

a. Tracking stock
b. Book entry
c. Security
d. Securities lending

17. Realization is generally understood in financial circles as the point at which revenue is recognized, typically through a transaction which involves the exchange of an asset, product, or service for cash or its equivalents.

This approach gives the accounting division a strictly objective basis for changing the books. For example, a homeowner may believe that his house has grown in value during a strong market, or fallen in value during a weak market, but until the house is actually sold for a specific price to a specific buyer, the change in value can only be estimated and is considered _____.

a. Unrealized
b. ABN Amro
c. A Random Walk Down Wall Street
d. AAB

Chapter 5. Taxes

18. _____ is a sale of a security (stock, bonds, options) at a loss and repurchasing the same or substantially identical stock soon afterwards. The idea is to make an unrealised loss claimable as a tax deduction, by offsetting against other capital gains in the current or future tax years. The security is repurchased in the hope that it will recover its previous value.
   a. Stop-limit order
   b. Block premium
   c. Program trading
   d. Wash sale

19. _____s are full-fledged pension plans for self-employed people in the United States. They are sometimes called HR10 plans and are not Individual Retirement Accounts (IRA.)

Since a _____ is a full-fledged pension, there is a Keogh for every employer-sponsored pension-plan design.

   a. Keogh plan
   b. 529 plan
   c. 7-Eleven
   d. 4-4-5 Calendar

20. _____ is an income tax in the United States that is levied by each individual state. Seven states choose to impose no income tax. These states are Alaska, Florida, Nevada, South Dakota, Texas, Washington, and Wyoming.
   a. State income tax
   b. 7-Eleven
   c. 4-4-5 Calendar
   d. 529 plan

21. In economics, _____ is a rise in the general level of prices of goods and services in an economy over a period of time. The term '_____' once referred to increases in the money supply (monetary _____); however, economic debates about the relationship between money supply and price levels have led to its primary use today in describing price _____. _____ can also be described as a decline in the real value of money--a loss of purchasing power in the medium of exchange which is also the monetary unit of account.
   a. Inflation
   b. AAB
   c. ABN Amro
   d. A Random Walk Down Wall Street

22. An _____ is a retirement plan account that provides some tax advantages for retirement savings in the United States.
   a. A Random Walk Down Wall Street
   b. Individual Retirement Arrangement
   c. ABN Amro
   d. AAB

23. _____, in bookkeeping, refers to assets, liabilities, income, and expenses recorded on individual pages of the so called book of final entry or ledger. Changes in _____ value are made by chronologically posting debit (DR) and credit (CR) entries to its page. Examples of _____s are cash, _____s receivable, mortgages, loans, land and buildings, common stock, sales, services provided, wages, and payroll overhead.
   a. Accretion
   b. Alpha
   c. Account
   d. Option

Chapter 6. Inflation

1. A _____ is a theoretical price index that measures relative cost of living over time. It is an index that measures differences in the price of goods and services, and allows for substitutions to other items as prices change.

There are many different methodologies that have been developed to approximate _____es, including methods that allow for substitution among items as relative prices change.

    a. 529 plan
    c. 4-4-5 Calendar
    b. Cost-of-living index
    d. 7-Eleven

2. In economics, _____ is a rise in the general level of prices of goods and services in an economy over a period of time. The term '_____' once referred to increases in the money supply (monetary _____); however, economic debates about the relationship between money supply and price levels have led to its primary use today in describing price _____. _____ can also be described as a decline in the real value of money--a loss of purchasing power in the medium of exchange which is also the monetary unit of account.

    a. ABN Amro
    c. A Random Walk Down Wall Street
    b. Inflation
    d. AAB

3. A _____ is a measure of the average price of consumer goods and services purchased by households. The _____ can be used to index (i.e., adjust for the effects of inflation) wages, salaries, pensions, or regulated or contracted prices. The _____ is, along with the population census and the National Income and Product Accounts, one of the most closely watched national economic statistics.

    a. Consumer Price Index
    c. 529 plan
    b. Divisia index
    d. 4-4-5 Calendar

4. _____ in economics is a persistent decrease in the general price level of goods and services - a negative inflation rate. When the inflation rate slows down (decreases, but remains positive), this is known as disinflation.

Inflation destroys real value in money.

    a. Mercantilism
    c. Fixed exchange rate
    b. Recession
    d. Deflation

5. The _____, in mathematics, is a type of mean or average, which indicates the central tendency or typical value of a set of numbers. It is similar to the arithmetic mean, which is what most people think of with the word 'average,' except that instead of adding the set of numbers and then dividing the sum by the count of numbers in the set, n, the numbers are multiplied and then the nth root of the resulting product is taken.

For instance, the _____ of two numbers, say 2 and 8, is just the square root (i.e., the second root) of their product, 16, which is 4.

    a. Standard deviation
    c. Kurtosis
    b. Statistics
    d. Geometric mean

6. A _____ is a normalized average (typically a weighted average) of prices for a given class of goods or services in a given region, during a given interval of time. It is a statistic designed to help to compare how these prices, taken as a whole, differ between time periods or geographical locations.

a. Discounts and allowances
c. Price discrimination
b. Transfer pricing
d. Price Index

7. _____ is a mathematical science pertaining to the collection, analysis, interpretation or explanation, and presentation of data. It also provides tools for prediction and forecasting based on data. It is applicable to a wide variety of academic disciplines, from the natural and social sciences to the humanities, government and business.
   a. Sample size
   b. Covariance
   c. Mean
   d. Statistics

8. In statistics, _____ has two related meanings:

   - the arithmetic _____
   - the expected value of a random variable, which is also called the population _____.

It is sometimes stated that the '_____' is average. This is incorrect if '_____' is taken in the specific sense of 'arithmetic _____' as there are different types of averages: the _____, median, and mode. Other simple statistical analyses use measures of spread, such as range, interquartile range, or standard deviation. For a real-valued random variable X, the _____ is the expectation of X. Note that not every probability distribution has a defined _____; see the Cauchy distribution for an example.

   a. Harmonic mean
   b. Sample size
   c. Mean
   d. Probability distribution

9. _____ is a fee paid on borrowed assets. It is the price paid for the use of borrowed money , or, money earned by deposited funds . Assets that are sometimes lent with _____ include money, shares, consumer goods through hire purchase, major assets such as aircraft, and even entire factories in finance lease arrangements.
   a. Insolvency
   b. AAB
   c. Interest
   d. A Random Walk Down Wall Street

10. An _____ is the price a borrower pays for the use of money they do not own, and the return a lender receives for deferring the use of funds, by lending it to the borrower. _____s are normally expressed as a percentage rate over the period of one year.

   _____s targets are also a vital tool of monetary policy and are used to control variables like investment, inflation, and unemployment.

   a. Interest rate
   b. ABN Amro
   c. AAB
   d. A Random Walk Down Wall Street

11. In finance and economics _____ refers to the rate of interest before adjustment for inflation (in contrast with the real interest rate); or, for interest balls stated' without adjustment for the full effect of compounding (also referred to as the nominal annual rate.) An interest rate is called nominal if the frequency of compounding (e.g. a month) is not identical to the basic time unit (normally a year.)

The real interest rate includes compensation for the lender's lost value due to inflation, whereas the _____ excludes inflation.

Chapter 6. Inflation

a. Shanghai Interbank Offered Rate
b. SIBOR
c. Cash accumulation equation
d. Nominal interest rate

12. _____ is a technique to adjust income payments by means of a price index, in order to maintain the purchasing power of the public after inflation.

Applying a cost-of-living escalation COLA clause to a stream of periodic payments protects the real value of those payments and effectively transfers the risk of inflation from the payee to the payor, who must pay more each year to reflect the increases in prices. Thus, inflation _____ is often applied to pension payments, rents and other situations which are not subject to regular re-pricing in the market.

a. Indexation
b. A Random Walk Down Wall Street
c. ABN Amro
d. AAB

13. In finance, a _____ is the party in a loan agreement which receives money or other instrument from a lender and promises to repay the lender in a specified time.

a. Line of credit
b. Debt management plan
c. Cash credit
d. Borrower

14. _____ refers to a business or organization attempting to acquire goods or services to accomplish the goals of the enterprise. Though there are several organizations that attempt to set standards in the _____ process, processes can vary greatly between organizations. Typically the word '_____' is not used interchangeably with the word 'procurement', since procurement typically includes Expediting, Supplier Quality, and Traffic and Logistics (T'L) in addition to _____.

a. 7-Eleven
b. 529 plan
c. 4-4-5 Calendar
d. Purchasing

15. _____ is the value of goods/services compared to the amount paid with a currency. Currency can be either a commodity money, like gold or silver, or fiat currency like US dollars which are the world reserve currency. As Adam Smith noted, having money gives one the ability to 'command' others' labor, so _____ to some extent is power over other people, to the extent that they are willing to trade their labor or goods for money or currency.

a. Purchasing power
b. 529 plan
c. 7-Eleven
d. 4-4-5 Calendar

16. In finance, a _____ is a debt security, in which the authorized issuer owes the holders a debt and, depending on the terms of the _____, is obliged to pay interest (the coupon) and/or to repay the principal at a later date, termed maturity.

Thus a _____ is a loan: the issuer is the borrower, the _____ holder is the lender, and the coupon is the interest. _____s provide the borrower with external funds to finance long-term investments, or, in the case of government _____s, to finance current expenditure.

a. Catastrophe bonds
b. Convertible bond
c. Puttable bond
d. Bond

17. A _____ is a bond issued by a national government denominated in the country's own currency. Bonds issued by national governments in foreign currencies are normally referred to as sovereign bonds. The first ever _____ was issued by the British government in 1693 to raise money to fund a war against France.
   a. Zero-coupon bond
   b. Government bond
   c. Municipal bond
   d. Collateralized debt obligations

18. A _____ is a fungible, negotiable instrument representing financial value. They are broadly categorized into debt securities (such as banknotes, bonds and debentures), and equity securities; e.g., common stocks. The company or other entity issuing the _____ is called the issuer.
   a. Book entry
   b. Security
   c. Securities lending
   d. Tracking stock

19. In economics, _____ is the removal of intermediaries in a supply chain: 'cutting out the middleman'. Instead of going through traditional distribution channels, which had some type of intermediate (such as a distributor, wholesaler, broker, or agent), companies may now deal with every customer directly, for example via the Internet. One important factor is a drop in the cost of servicing customers directly.
   a. 4-4-5 Calendar
   b. 529 plan
   c. 7-Eleven
   d. Disintermediation

20. A _____ is an exchange of promises between two or more parties to do an act which is enforceable in a court of law. It is where an unqualified offer meets a qualified acceptance and the parties reach Consensus ad Idem. The parties must have the necessary capacity to _____ and the _____ must not be either trifling, indeterminate, impossible or illegal.
   a. 7-Eleven
   b. Contract
   c. 529 plan
   d. 4-4-5 Calendar

21. The _____ is a term coined by economists Rajnish Mehra and Edward C. Prescott. It is based on the observation that in order to reconcile the much higher return on equity stock compared to government bonds in the United States, individuals must have implausibly high risk aversion according to standard economics models. Similar situations prevail in many other industrialized countries.
   a. A Random Walk Down Wall Street
   b. AAB
   c. ABN Amro
   d. Equity premium puzzle

22. _____ mature in one year or less. Like zero-coupon bonds, they do not pay interest prior to maturity; instead they are sold at a discount of the par value to create a positive yield to maturity. Many regard _____ as the least risky investment available to U.S. investors.
   a. Treasury securities
   b. Treasury bills
   c. 4-4-5 Calendar
   d. Treasury Inflation Protected Securities

23. A _____ refers to any type debt instrument, such as a loan, bond, mortgage that does not have a fixed rate of interest over the life of the instrument. Such debt typically uses an index or other base rate for establishing the interest rate for each relevant period. One of the most common rates to use as the basis for applying interest rates is the London Inter-bank Offered Rate, or LIBOR
   a. Cost of living
   b. Disposal tax effect
   c. Foreign exchange hedge
   d. Floating interest rate

24. An _____ can be defined as a contract which provides an income stream in return for an initial payment.

An immediate _____ is an _____ for which the time between the contract date and the date of the first payment is not longer than the time interval between payments. A common use for an immediate _____ is to provide a pension to a retired person or persons.

a. AT'T Inc.
c. Intrinsic value
b. Annuity
d. Amortization

Chapter 7. The Portfolio Selection Problem

1. The _____ is the weighted-average most likely outcome in gambling, probability theory, economics or finance.

In gambling and probability theory, there is usually a discrete set of possible outcomes. In this case, _____ is a measure of the relative balance of win or loss weighted by their chances of occurring.

a. AAB
c. ABN Amro
b. A Random Walk Down Wall Street
d. Expected return

2. _____ proposes how rational investors will use diversification to optimize their portfolios, and how a risky asset should be priced. The basic concepts of the theory are Markowitz diversification, the efficient frontier, capital asset pricing model, the alpha and beta coefficients, the Capital Market Line and the Securities Market Line.

_____ models an asset's return as a random variable, and models a portfolio as a weighted combination of assets so that the return of a portfolio is the weighted combination of the assets' returns.

a. Market value
c. Payback period
b. Consumer basket
d. Modern portfolio theory

3. In finance, _____ is a measurement of return on an asset or portfolio. It is one of the simplest measures of investment performance.

_____ is the percentage by which the value of a portfolio (or asset) has grown for a particular period.

a. Stock market index option
c. Creditor
b. Market integration
d. Holding period return

4. In mathematics, _____ are used in the study of chance and probability. They were developed to assist in the analysis of games of chance, stochastic events, and the results of scientific experiments by capturing only the mathematical properties necessary to answer probabilistic questions. Further formalizations have firmly grounded the entity in the theoretical domains of mathematics by making use of measure theory.

a. Standard deviation
c. Monte Carlo methods
b. Variance
d. Random variables

5. In finance, _____, also known as return on investment is the ratio of money gained or lost on an investment relative to the amount of money invested. The amount of money gained or lost may be referred to as interest, profit/loss, gain/loss, or net income/loss. The money invested may be referred to as the asset, capital, principal, or the cost basis of the investment.

a. Doctrine of the Proper Law
c. Stock or scrip dividends
b. Composiition of Creditors
d. Rate of return

6. In probability and statistics, the _____ of a collection of numbers is a measure of the dispersion of the numbers from their expected (mean) value. It can apply to a probability distribution, a random variable, a population or a data set. The _____ is usually denoted with the letter σ (lowercase sigma.)

a. Mean
c. Sample size
b. Kurtosis
d. Standard deviation

Chapter 7. The Portfolio Selection Problem

7. In economics, the _____ of a good or of a service is the utility of the specific use to which an agent would put a given increase in that good or service, or of the specific use that would be abandoned in response to a given decrease. In other words, _____ is the utility of the marginal use -- which, on the assumption of economic rationality, would be the least urgent use of the good or service, from the best feasible combination of actions in which its use is included. Under the mainstream assumptions, the _____ of a good or service is the posited quantified change in utility obtained by increasing or by decreasing use of that good or service.
   a. Marginal utility
   b. 529 plan
   c. 7-Eleven
   d. 4-4-5 Calendar

8. _____ is a concept in economics, finance, and psychology related to the behaviour of consumers and investors under uncertainty. _____ is the reluctance of a person to accept a bargain with an uncertain payoff rather than another bargain with a more certain, but possibly lower, expected payoff.

The inverse of a person's _____ is sometimes called their risk tolerance

   a. Risk aversion
   b. Risk adjusted return on capital
   c. Risk premium
   d. Discount factor

9. In economics, _____ is a measure of the relative satisfaction from or desirability of consumption of various goods and services. Given this measure, one may speak meaningfully of increasing or decreasing _____, and thereby explain economic behavior in terms of attempts to increase one's _____. For illustrative purposes, changes in _____ are sometimes expressed in units called utils.
   a. Utility
   b. Utility function
   c. AAB
   d. A Random Walk Down Wall Street

10. The _____ is the guaranteed payoff at which a person is 'indifferent' between accepting the guaranteed payoff and a higher but uncertain payoff. (It is the amount of the higher payout minus the risk premium).
    a. 4-4-5 Calendar
    b. 7-Eleven
    c. 529 plan
    d. Certainty equivalent

11. In microeconomic theory, an _____ is a graph showing different bundles of goods, each measured as to quantity, between which a consumer is indifferent. That is, at each point on the curve, the consumer has no preference for one bundle over another. In other words, they are all equally preferred. One can equivalently refer to each point on the _____ as rendering the same level of utility (satisfaction) for the consumer.
    a. Indifference curve
    b. A Random Walk Down Wall Street
    c. ABN Amro
    d. AAB

12.

In finance, the _____ can be the expected rate of return above the risk-free interest rate. When measuring risk, a common sense approach is to compare the risk-free return on T-bills and the very risky return on other investments. The difference between these two returns can be interpreted as a measure of the excess return on the average risky asset. This excess return is known as the _____.

Chapter 7. The Portfolio Selection Problem

a. Risk modeling
c. Risk premium
b. Risk aversion
d. Risk adjusted return on capital

13. Behavioral economics and _____ are closely related fields that have evolved to be a separate branch of economic and financial analysis which applies scientific research on human and social, cognitive and emotional factors to better understand economic decisions by, say, consumers, borrowers, investors, and how they affect market prices, returns and the allocation of resources.

The field is primarily concerned with the bounds of rationality (selfishness, self-control) of economic agents. Behavioral models typically integrate insights from psychology with neo-classical economic theory.

a. Medium of exchange
c. Market structure
b. Recession
d. Behavioral finance

14. A _____ is a fungible, negotiable instrument representing financial value. They are broadly categorized into debt securities (such as banknotes, bonds and debentures), and equity securities; e.g., common stocks. The company or other entity issuing the _____ is called the issuer.

a. Book entry
c. Tracking stock
b. Securities lending
d. Security

15. The _____ is an important family of continuous probability distributions, applicable in many fields. Each member of the family may be defined by two parameters, location and scale: the mean and variance respectively. The standard _____ is the _____ with a mean of zero and a variance of one

a. Random variables
c. Normal distribution
b. Correlation
d. Probability distribution

16. In probability theory and statistics, a _____ identifies either the probability of each value of an unidentified random variable (when the variable is discrete), or the probability of the value falling within a particular interval (when the variable is continuous.) The _____ describes the range of possible values that a random variable can attain and the probability that the value of the random variable is within any (measurable) subset of that range. The Normal distribution, often called the 'bell curve'

When the random variable takes values in the set of real numbers, the _____ is completely described by the cumulative distribution function, whose value at each real x is the probability that the random variable is smaller than or equal to x.

a. Standard deviation
c. Probability distribution
b. Correlation
d. P-value

17. In probability theory and statistics, _____ indicates the strength and direction of a linear relationship between two random variables. That is in contrast with the usage of the term in colloquial speech, which denotes any relationship, not necessarily linear. In general statistical usage, _____ or co-relation refers to the departure of two random variables from independence.

a. Variance
c. Geometric mean
b. Probability distribution
d. Correlation

Chapter 7. The Portfolio Selection Problem

18. In probability theory and statistics, _____ is a measure of how much two variables change together (variance is a special case of the _____ when the two variables are identical.)

If two variables tend to vary together (that is, when one of them is above its expected value, then the other variable tends to be above its expected value too), then the _____ between the two variables will be positive. On the other hand, when one of them is above its expected value the other variable tends to be below its expected value, then the _____ between the two variables will be negative.

   a. Probability distribution
   b. Frequency distribution
   c. Stratified sampling
   d. Covariance

19. In probability theory and statistics, the _____ of a random variable, probability distribution averaging the squared distance of its possible values from the expected value (mean.) Whereas the mean is a way to describe the location of a distribution, the _____ is a way to capture its scale or degree of being spread out. The unit of _____ is the square of the unit of the original variable.
   a. Semivariance
   b. Harmonic mean
   c. Monte Carlo methods
   d. Variance

20. In probability theory and statistics, a _____ is described as the number separating the higher half of a sample, a population, or a probability distribution from the lower half. The _____ of a finite list of numbers can be found by arranging all the observations from lowest value to highest value and picking the middle one. If there is an even number of observations, the _____ is not unique, so one often takes the mean of the two middle values.
   a. Standard deviation
   b. Variance
   c. Geometric mean
   d. Median

21. _____ is a form of corporation equity ownership represented in the securities. It is dangerous in comparison to preferred shares and some other investment options, in that in the event of bankruptcy, _____ investors receive their funds after preferred stockholders, bondholders, creditors, etc. On the other hand, common shares on average perform better than preferred shares or bonds over time.
   a. Common stock
   b. Stock market bubble
   c. Stock split
   d. Stop-limit order

22. _____ is an estimate of the fair value of corporations and their stocks, by using fundamental economic criteria. This theoretical valuation has to be perfected with market criteria, as the final purpose is to determine potential market prices.
   a. Security Analysis
   b. 4-4-5 Calendar
   c. Growth stocks
   d. Stock valuation

23. In finance, _____ is the process of estimating the potential market value of a financial asset or liability. they can be done on assets (for example, investments in marketable securities such as stocks, options, business enterprises, or intangible assets such as patents and trademarks) or on liabilities (e.g., Bonds issued by a company.) _____s are required in many contexts including investment analysis, capital budgeting, merger and acquisition transactions, financial reporting, taxable events to determine the proper tax liability, and in litigation.
   a. Procter ' Gamble
   b. Share
   c. Margin
   d. Valuation

Chapter 8. Portfolio Analysis

1. _____ is a measure of the ability of a debtor to pay their debts as and when they fall due. It is usually expressed as a ratio or a percentage of current liabilities.

For a corporation with a published balance sheet there are various ratios used to calculate a measure of liquidity.

   a. Operating leverage
   b. Accounting liquidity
   c. Invested capital
   d. Operating profit margin

2. In probability theory and statistics, _____ indicates the strength and direction of a linear relationship between two random variables. That is in contrast with the usage of the term in colloquial speech, which denotes any relationship, not necessarily linear. In general statistical usage, _____ or co-relation refers to the departure of two random variables from independence.

   a. Variance
   b. Geometric mean
   c. Probability distribution
   d. Correlation

3. _____ in finance is a risk management technique, related to hedging, that mixes a wide variety of investments within a portfolio. Because the fluctuations of a single security have less impact on a diverse portfolio, _____ minimizes the risk from any one investment.

A simple example of _____ is the following: On a particular island the entire economy consists of two companies: one that sells umbrellas and another that sells sunscreen.

   a. Diversification
   b. 4-4-5 Calendar
   c. 7-Eleven
   d. 529 plan

4. _____ is a technique to adjust income payments by means of a price index, in order to maintain the purchasing power of the public after inflation.

Applying a cost-of-living escalation COLA clause to a stream of periodic payments protects the real value of those payments and effectively transfers the risk of inflation from the payee to the payor, who must pay more each year to reflect the increases in prices. Thus, inflation _____ is often applied to pension payments, rents and other situations which are not subject to regular re-pricing in the market.

   a. A Random Walk Down Wall Street
   b. AAB
   c. ABN Amro
   d. Indexation

5. A _____ is a firm that quotes both a buy and a sell price in a financial instrument or commodity, hoping to make a profit on the bid/offer spread, or turn.

In foreign exchange trading, where most deals are conducted over-the-counter and are, therefore, completely virtual, the _____ sells to and buys from its clients. Hence, the client's loss and the spread is the _____ firm's profit, which gets thus compensated for the effort of providing liquidity in a competitive market.

   a. 7-Eleven
   b. 529 plan
   c. 4-4-5 Calendar
   d. Market maker

Chapter 8. Portfolio Analysis

6. _____ is the risk that the value of an investment will decrease due to moves in market factors. The five standard _____ factors are:

- Equity risk, the risk that stock prices will change.
- Interest rate risk, the risk that interest rates will change.
- Currency risk, the risk that foreign exchange rates will change.
- Commodity risk, the risk that commodity prices (e.g. grains, metals) will change.

As with other forms of risk, _____ may be measured in a number of ways. Traditionally, this is done using a Value at Risk methodology. Value at risk is well established as a risk management technique, but it contains a number of limiting assumptions that constrain its accuracy.

a. Transaction risk
c. Currency risk
b. Tracking error
d. Market risk

7. In business and finance, a _____ (also referred to as equity _____) of stock means a _____ of ownership in a corporation (company.) In the plural, stocks is often used as a synonym for _____s especially in the United States, but it is less commonly used that way outside of North America.

In the United Kingdom, South Africa, and Australia, stock can also refer to completely different financial instruments such as government bonds or, less commonly, to all kinds of marketable securities.

a. Margin
c. Procter ' Gamble
b. Bucket shop
d. Share

Chapter 9. Riskfree Lending and Borrowing

1. In business and accounting, _____s are everything of value that is owned by a person or company. The balance sheet of a firm records the monetary value of the _____s owned by the firm. The two major _____ classes are tangible _____s and intangible _____s.
   a. EBITDA
   b. Income
   c. Accounts payable
   d. Asset

2. _____ is a fee paid on borrowed assets. It is the price paid for the use of borrowed money, or, money earned by deposited funds. Assets that are sometimes lent with _____ include money, shares, consumer goods through hire purchase, major assets such as aircraft, and even entire factories in finance lease arrangements.
   a. AAB
   b. Insolvency
   c. Interest
   d. A Random Walk Down Wall Street

3. An _____ is the price a borrower pays for the use of money they do not own, and the return a lender receives for deferring the use of funds, by lending it to the borrower. _____s are normally expressed as a percentage rate over the period of one year.

   _____s targets are also a vital tool of monetary policy and are used to control variables like investment, inflation, and unemployment.

   a. AAB
   b. A Random Walk Down Wall Street
   c. ABN Amro
   d. Interest rate

4. _____ is the risk (variability in value) borne by an interest-bearing asset, such as a loan or a bond, due to variability of interest rates. In general, as rates rise, the price of a fixed rate bond will fall, and vice versa. _____ is commonly measured by the bond's duration.
   a. Official bank rate
   b. International Fisher effect
   c. A Random Walk Down Wall Street
   d. Interest rate Risk

5. A _____ is a fungible, negotiable instrument representing financial value. They are broadly categorized into debt securities (such as banknotes, bonds and debentures), and equity securities; e.g., common stocks. The company or other entity issuing the _____ is called the issuer.
   a. Book entry
   b. Securities lending
   c. Security
   d. Tracking stock

6. In the global money market, _____ is an unsecured promissory note with a fixed maturity of one to 270 days. _____ is a money-market security issued (sold) by large banks and corporations to get money to meet short term debt obligations (for example, payroll), and is only backed by an issuing bank or corporation's promise to pay the face amount on the maturity date specified on the note. Since it is not backed by collateral, only firms with excellent credit ratings from a recognized rating agency will be able to sell their _____ at a reasonable price.
   a. Book building
   b. Financial distress
   c. Trade-off theory
   d. Commercial paper

7. In finance, the _____ is the global financial market for short-term borrowing and lending. It provides short-term liquidity funding for the global financial system. The _____ is where short-term obligations such as Treasury bills, commercial paper and bankers' acceptances are bought and sold.

Chapter 9. Riskfree Lending and Borrowing

a. Cramdown
b. Consumer debt
c. Money market
d. Debt-for-equity swap

8. _____ is a term applied in many countries to a reference interest rate used by banks. The term originally indicated the rate of interest at which banks lent to favored customers, i.e., those with high credibility, though this is no longer always the case. Some variable interest rates may be expressed as a percentage above or below _____.
a. Time deposit
b. Reserve requirement
c. Credit bureau
d. Prime rate

9. In economics, the concept of the _____ refers to the decision-making time frame of a firm in which at least one factor of production is fixed. Costs which are fixed in the _____ have no impact on a firms decisions. For example a firm can raise output by increasing the amount of labour through overtime.
a. 529 plan
b. Long-run
c. 4-4-5 Calendar
d. Short-run

10. _____ mature in one year or less. Like zero-coupon bonds, they do not pay interest prior to maturity; instead they are sold at a discount of the par value to create a positive yield to maturity. Many regard _____ as the least risky investment available to U.S. investors.
a. Treasury securities
b. Treasury Inflation Protected Securities
c. 4-4-5 Calendar
d. Treasury bills

11. In finance, the term _____ describes the amount in cash that returns to the owners of a security. Normally it does not include the price variations, at the difference of the total return. _____ applies to various stated rates of return on stocks (common and preferred, and convertible), fixed income instruments (bonds, notes, bills, strips, zero coupon), and some other investment type insurance products (e.g. annuities.)
a. 4-4-5 Calendar
b. Macaulay duration
c. Yield
d. Yield to maturity

12. In finance, the _____ is the difference between the quoted rates of return on two different investments, usually of different credit quality.

It is a compound of yield and spread.

The '_____ of X over Y' is simply the percentage return on investment (ROI) from financial instrument X minus the percentage return on investment from financial instrument Y (per annum.)

a. Debtor-in-possession financing
b. Yield spread
c. Duty of loyalty
d. Portfolio insurance

13. In economics, business, and accounting, a _____ is the value of money that has been used up to produce something, and hence is not available for use anymore. In business, the _____ may be one of acquisition, in which case the amount of money expended to acquire it is counted as _____. In this case, money is the input that is gone in order to acquire the thing.
a. Sliding scale fees
b. Cost
c. Fixed costs
d. Marginal cost

Chapter 10. The Capital Asset Pricing Model

1. In business and accounting, _____s are everything of value that is owned by a person or company. The balance sheet of a firm records the monetary value of the _____s owned by the firm. The two major _____ classes are tangible _____s and intangible _____s.

   a. EBITDA
   b. Income
   c. Accounts payable
   d. Asset

2. In finance, _____ is the process of estimating the potential market value of a financial asset or liability. they can be done on assets (for example, investments in marketable securities such as stocks, options, business enterprises, or intangible assets such as patents and trademarks) or on liabilities (e.g., Bonds issued by a company.) _____s are required in many contexts including investment analysis, capital budgeting, merger and acquisition transactions, financial reporting, taxable events to determine the proper tax liability, and in litigation.

   a. Procter ' Gamble
   b. Margin
   c. Valuation
   d. Share

3. The term _____ has three unrelated technical definitions, and is also used in a variety of non-technical ways.

   - In financial economics, it refers to any asset used to make money, as opposed to assets used for personal enjoyment or consumption. This is an important distinction because two people can disagree sharply about the value of personal assets, one person might think a sports car is more valuable than a pickup truck, another person might have the opposite taste. But if an asset is held for the purpose of making money, taste has nothing to do with it, only differences of opinion about how much money the asset will produce. With the further assumption that people agree on the probability distribution of future cash flows, it is possible to have an objective _____ pricing model. Even without the assumption of agreement, it is possible to set rational limits on _____ value.
   - In governmental accounting, it is defined as any asset used in operations with an initial useful life extending beyond one reporting period. Generally, government managers have a 'stewardship' duty to maintain _____s under their control. See International Public Sector Accounting Standards for details.
   - In US tax accounting, it is defined as any property other than a list of exceptions. The main exceptions are anything held for sale, and any real estate or depreciable property used in business. Almost everything you own and use for personal purposes, pleasure or investment is a _____. If something is a _____ for tax purposes, gains or losses on sale or disposition are capital gains or capital losses. For individuals, however, capital losses on property held for personal use are generally not deductible. See the IRS publication Tax Facts about Capital Gains and Losses for details.

   A well-known financial accounting textbook advises that the term be avoided except in tax accounting because it is used in so many different senses, not all of them well-defined. For example it is often used as a synonym for fixed assets or for investments in securities.

   A common non-technical usage occurs when people ask that employees or the environment or something else be treated as a _____.

   a. Capital Asset
   b. Settlement date
   c. Political risk
   d. Solvency

Chapter 10. The Capital Asset Pricing Model

4. In finance, the _____ is used to determine a theoretically appropriate required rate of return of an asset, if that asset is to be added to an already well-diversified portfolio, given that asset's non-diversifiable risk. The model takes into account the asset's sensitivity to non-diversifiable risk (also known as systemic risk or market risk), often represented by the quantity beta (β) in the financial industry, as well as the expected return of the market and the expected return of a theoretical risk-free asset.

The model was introduced by Jack Treynor (1961, 1962), William Sharpe (1964), John Lintner (1965a,b) and Jan Mossin (1966) independently, building on the earlier work of Harry Markowitz on diversification and modern portfolio theory.

a. Capital Asset Pricing Model
b. Cox-Ingersoll-Ross model
c. Hull-White model
d. Random walk hypothesis

5. _____ is the branch of economics that incorporates value judgments (that is, normative judgements) about what the economy ought to be like or what particular policy actions ought to be recommended to achieve a desirable goal. _____ looks at the desirability of certain aspects of the economy. It underlies expressions of support for particular economic policies.

a. Normative economics
b. Reverse stock split
c. Financial risk
d. Fund Accounting

6. _____ is the branch of economics that concerns the description and explanation of economic phenomena (Wong, 1987, p. 920). It focuses on facts and cause-and-effect relationships and includes the development and testing of economics theories.

a. 4-4-5 Calendar
b. Positive economics
c. 7-Eleven
d. 529 plan

7. The _____ is the market for securities, where companies and governments can raise longterm funds. The _____ includes the stock market and the bond market. Financial regulators, such as the U.S. Securities and Exchange Commission, oversee the _____s in their designated countries to ensure that investors are protected against fraud.

a. Forward market
b. Delta neutral
c. Capital market
d. Spot rate

8. _____ proposes how rational investors will use diversification to optimize their portfolios, and how a risky asset should be priced. The basic concepts of the theory are Markowitz diversification, the efficient frontier, capital asset pricing model, the alpha and beta coefficients, the Capital Market Line and the Securities Market Line.

_____ models an asset's return as a random variable, and models a portfolio as a weighted combination of assets so that the return of a portfolio is the weighted combination of the assets' returns.

a. Market value
b. Modern portfolio theory
c. Payback period
d. Consumer basket

Chapter 10. The Capital Asset Pricing Model

9. A _____ is heuristic and has the following assumptions :

- Rationality of all market actors (Rationality in meaning of the actor's utility maximization)
- No transaction costs (particularly no information costs and no taxes)
- Price taking behavior - there is a sufficiently large number of participants such that no individual can affect the market
- given rare resources
- freedom of decision to do something or to let it be (no external effects)

Share and foreign exchange markets are commonly seen to be the most similar to the _____. The real estate market is an example of a very imperfect market. a free market economy is also related to this _____ system as the public have free will

Other characteristics of a _____ include:-

- No barriers to entry to (or exit from) the market
- Perfect knowledge
- Normal profits

Normal profits are defined as that level of profit which just induces the participants to stay in the market. In other words companies in a _____ pay no dividends, as super-normal profits would induce other participants into the market and drive profits back to the 'normal' level.

This attribute of _____s has profound political and economic implications, as many people assume that the purpose of the market is to enable participants to make profits.

a. 7-Eleven
b. 4-4-5 Calendar
c. 529 plan
d. Perfect market

10. In economics, the _____ asserts that the objective of a firm will be the maximization of its present value, regardless of the preferences of its owners. The theorem therefore separates management's 'productive opportunities' from the entrepreneur's 'market opportunities'.

a. 7-Eleven
b. 4-4-5 Calendar
c. Fisher separation theorem
d. 529 plan

11. A _____ is a portfolio consisting of a weighted sum of every asset in the market, with weights in the proportions that they exist in the market (with the necessary assumption that these assets are infinitely divisible.)

Neha Tyagi's critique (1977) states that this is only a theoretical concept, as to create a _____ for investment purposes in practice would necessarily include every single possible available asset, including real estate, precious metals, stamp collections, jewelry, and anything with any worth, as the theoretical market being referred to would be the world market. As a result, proxies for the market are used in practice by investors.

a. Market price
b. Central Securities Depository
c. Market portfolio
d. Delta neutral

Chapter 10. The Capital Asset Pricing Model

12. _____ in finance is a risk management technique, related to hedging, that mixes a wide variety of investments within a portfolio. Because the fluctuations of a single security have less impact on a diverse portfolio, _____ minimizes the risk from any one investment.

A simple example of _____ is the following: On a particular island the entire economy consists of two companies: one that sells umbrellas and another that sells sunscreen.

a. 529 plan
b. 7-Eleven
c. 4-4-5 Calendar
d. Diversification

13. _____ refers to the stock of skills and knowledge embodied in the ability to perform labor so as to produce economic value. Many early economic theories refer to it simply as labor, one of three factors of production, and consider it to be a fungible resource -- homogeneous and easily interchangeable. Other conceptions of labor dispense with these assumptions.

a. Behavioral finance
b. Human capital
c. Market structure
d. Mercantilism

14. A _____ is a fungible, negotiable instrument representing financial value. They are broadly categorized into debt securities (such as banknotes, bonds and debentures), and equity securities; e.g., common stocks. The company or other entity issuing the _____ is called the issuer.

a. Security
b. Securities lending
c. Book entry
d. Tracking stock

15. In Modern Portfolio Theory, the _____ is the graphical representation of the Capital Asset Pricing Model. It displays the expected rate of return for an overall market as a function of systematic (non-diversifiable) risk (beta.)

The Y-Intercept (beta=0) of the _____ is equal to the risk-free interest rate.

a. Rebalancing
b. Security market line
c. Certificate in Investment Performance Measurement
d. Divestment

16. _____ is a technique to adjust income payments by means of a price index, in order to maintain the purchasing power of the public after inflation.

Applying a cost-of-living escalation COLA clause to a stream of periodic payments protects the real value of those payments and effectively transfers the risk of inflation from the payee to the payor, who must pay more each year to reflect the increases in prices. Thus, inflation _____ is often applied to pension payments, rents and other situations which are not subject to regular re-pricing in the market.

a. AAB
b. A Random Walk Down Wall Street
c. ABN Amro
d. Indexation

17. A _____ is a firm that quotes both a buy and a sell price in a financial instrument or commodity, hoping to make a profit on the bid/offer spread, or turn.

In foreign exchange trading, where most deals are conducted over-the-counter and are, therefore, completely virtual, the _____ sells to and buys from its clients. Hence, the client's loss and the spread is the _____ firm's profit, which gets thus compensated for the effort of providing liquidity in a competitive market.

a. 4-4-5 Calendar
c. 529 plan
b. 7-Eleven
d. Market maker

18. The _____ is one of several stock market indices, created by nineteenth-century Wall Street Journal editor and Dow Jones ' Company co-founder Charles Dow. Dow compiled the index to gauge the performance of the industrial sector of the American stock market. It is the second-oldest U.S. market index, after the Dow Jones Transportation Average, which Dow also created.

a. 529 plan
c. 7-Eleven
b. 4-4-5 Calendar
d. Dow Jones Industrial Average

19. _____ is the risk that the value of an investment will decrease due to moves in market factors. The five standard _____ factors are:

- Equity risk, the risk that stock prices will change.
- Interest rate risk, the risk that interest rates will change.
- Currency risk, the risk that foreign exchange rates will change.
- Commodity risk, the risk that commodity prices (e.g. grains, metals) will change.

As with other forms of risk, _____ may be measured in a number of ways. Traditionally, this is done using a Value at Risk methodology. Value at risk is well established as a risk management technique, but it contains a number of limiting assumptions that constrain its accuracy.

a. Market risk
c. Currency risk
b. Transaction risk
d. Tracking error

20. In the United States, the Financial Industry Regulatory Authority (FINRA) is a self-regulatory organization (SRO) under the Securities Exchange Act of 1934, successor to the _____, Inc.

FINRA is responsible for regulatory oversight of all securities firms that do business with the public; professional training, testing and licensing of registered persons; arbitration and mediation; market regulation by contract for The NASDAQ Stock Market, Inc., the American Stock Exchange LLC, and the International Securities Exchange, LLC; and industry utilities, such as Trade Reporting Facilities and other over-the-counter operations.

a. 7-Eleven
c. 4-4-5 Calendar
b. National Association of Securities Dealers
d. 529 plan

21. A _____ is a normalized average (typically a weighted average) of prices for a given class of goods or services in a given region, during a given interval of time. It is a statistic designed to help to compare how these prices, taken as a whole, differ between time periods or geographical locations.

a. Price Index
b. Price discrimination
c. Discounts and allowances
d. Transfer pricing

22. A _____ is the price of a single share of a no. of saleable stocks of the company. Once the stock is purchased, the owner becomes a shareholder of the company that issued the share.
a. Share price
b. Stock split
c. Whisper numbers
d. Trading curb

Chapter 11. Factor Models

1. The _____ is one of the measures of national income and input for a given country's economy. _____ is defined as the total cost of all finished goods and services produced within the country in a stipulated period of time (usually a 365-day year.) It is sometimes regarded as the sum of profits added at every level of production (the intermediate stages) of all final goods and services produced within a country in a stipulated timeframe, and it is rarely given a monetary value.

   a. Behavioral finance
   b. Macroeconomics
   c. Gross domestic product
   d. Recession

2. In probability theory and statistics, _____ is a measure of how much two variables change together (variance is a special case of the _____ when the two variables are identical.)

   If two variables tend to vary together (that is, when one of them is above its expected value, then the other variable tends to be above its expected value too), then the _____ between the two variables will be positive. On the other hand, when one of them is above its expected value the other variable tends to be below its expected value, then the _____ between the two variables will be negative.

   a. Probability distribution
   b. Covariance
   c. Frequency distribution
   d. Stratified sampling

3. The _____ is the weighted-average most likely outcome in gambling, probability theory, economics or finance.

   In gambling and probability theory, there is usually a discrete set of possible outcomes. In this case, _____ is a measure of the relative balance of win or loss weighted by their chances of occurring.

   a. AAB
   b. A Random Walk Down Wall Street
   c. ABN Amro
   d. Expected return

4. In probability and statistics, the _____ of a collection of numbers is a measure of the dispersion of the numbers from their expected (mean) value. It can apply to a probability distribution, a random variable, a population or a data set. The _____ is usually denoted with the letter σ (lowercase sigma.)

   a. Kurtosis
   b. Mean
   c. Sample size
   d. Standard deviation

5. In probability theory and statistics, the _____ of a random variable, probability distribution averaging the squared distance of its possible values from the expected value (mean.) Whereas the mean is a way to describe the location of a distribution, the _____ is a way to capture its scale or degree of being spread out. The unit of _____ is the square of the unit of the original variable.

   a. Semivariance
   b. Harmonic mean
   c. Variance
   d. Monte Carlo methods

6. _____ is a technique to adjust income payments by means of a price index, in order to maintain the purchasing power of the public after inflation.

   Applying a cost-of-living escalation COLA clause to a stream of periodic payments protects the real value of those payments and effectively transfers the risk of inflation from the payee to the payor, who must pay more each year to reflect the increases in prices. Thus, inflation _____ is often applied to pension payments, rents and other situations which are not subject to regular re-pricing in the market.

Chapter 11. Factor Models

a. Indexation
b. ABN Amro
c. A Random Walk Down Wall Street
d. AAB

7. A _____ is a firm that quotes both a buy and a sell price in a financial instrument or commodity, hoping to make a profit on the bid/offer spread, or turn.

In foreign exchange trading, where most deals are conducted over-the-counter and are, therefore, completely virtual, the _____ sells to and buys from its clients. Hence, the client's loss and the spread is the _____ firm's profit, which gets thus compensated for the effort of providing liquidity in a competitive market.

a. Market maker
b. 4-4-5 Calendar
c. 529 plan
d. 7-Eleven

8. _____ in finance is a risk management technique, related to hedging, that mixes a wide variety of investments within a portfolio. Because the fluctuations of a single security have less impact on a diverse portfolio, _____ minimizes the risk from any one investment.

A simple example of _____ is the following: On a particular island the entire economy consists of two companies: one that sells umbrellas and another that sells sunscreen.

a. 7-Eleven
b. 529 plan
c. 4-4-5 Calendar
d. Diversification

9. In economics, _____ is a rise in the general level of prices of goods and services in an economy over a period of time. The term '_____' once referred to increases in the money supply (monetary _____); however, economic debates about the relationship between money supply and price levels have led to its primary use today in describing price _____. _____ can also be described as a decline in the real value of money--a loss of purchasing power in the medium of exchange which is also the monetary unit of account.

a. ABN Amro
b. A Random Walk Down Wall Street
c. AAB
d. Inflation

10. A _____ is a payment made by a corporation to its shareholder members. When a corporation earns a profit or surplus, that money can be put to two uses: it can either be re-invested in the business (called retained earnings), or it can be paid to the shareholders as a _____. Many corporations retain a portion of their earnings and pay the remainder as a _____.

a. Dividend
b. Dividend puzzle
c. Dividend yield
d. Special dividend

11. The _____ on a company stock is the company's annual dividend payments divided by its market cap, or the dividend per share divided by the price per share. It is often expressed as a percentage.

Dividend payments on preferred shares are stipulated by the prospectus.

a. Special dividend
b. Dividend imputation
c. Dividend reinvestment plan
d. Dividend yield

Chapter 11. Factor Models

12. In finance, the term _____ describes the amount in cash that returns to the owners of a security. Normally it does not include the price variations, at the difference of the total return. _____ applies to various stated rates of return on stocks (common and preferred, and convertible), fixed income instruments (bonds, notes, bills, strips, zero coupon), and some other investment type insurance products (e.g. annuities.)

    a. Macaulay duration   b. 4-4-5 Calendar

    c. Yield to maturity   d. Yield

Chapter 12. Arbitrage Pricing Theory

1. In economics and finance, _____ is the practice of taking advantage of a price differential between two or more markets: striking a combination of matching deals that capitalize upon the imbalance, the profit being the difference between the market prices. When used by academics, an _____ is a transaction that involves no negative cash flow at any probabilistic or temporal state and a positive cash flow in at least one state; in simple terms, a risk-free profit.
   - a. Issuer
   - b. Efficient-market hypothesis
   - c. Initial margin
   - d. Arbitrage

2. _____ , in finance, is a general theory of asset pricing, that has become influential in the pricing of stocks.

   _____ holds that the expected return of a financial asset can be modeled as a linear function of various macro-economic factors or theoretical market indices, where sensitivity to changes in each factor is represented by a factor-specific beta coefficient. The model-derived rate of return will then be used to price the asset correctly - the asset price should equal the expected end of period price discounted at the rate implied by model.
   - a. AAB
   - b. ABN Amro
   - c. A Random Walk Down Wall Street
   - d. Arbitrage pricing theory

3. The _____ is the weighted-average most likely outcome in gambling, probability theory, economics or finance.

   In gambling and probability theory, there is usually a discrete set of possible outcomes. In this case, _____ is a measure of the relative balance of win or loss weighted by their chances of occurring.
   - a. ABN Amro
   - b. AAB
   - c. A Random Walk Down Wall Street
   - d. Expected return

4.
   In finance, the _____ can be the expected rate of return above the risk-free interest rate. When measuring risk, a common sense approach is to compare the risk-free return on T-bills and the very risky return on other investments. The difference between these two returns can be interpreted as a measure of the excess return on the average risky asset. This excess return is known as the _____.
   - a. Risk premium
   - b. Risk adjusted return on capital
   - c. Risk modeling
   - d. Risk aversion

5. In business and accounting, _____s are everything of value that is owned by a person or company. The balance sheet of a firm records the monetary value of the _____s owned by the firm. The two major _____ classes are tangible _____s and intangible _____s.
   - a. EBITDA
   - b. Income
   - c. Accounts payable
   - d. Asset

6. The term _____ is often used to refer to the investment management of collective investments, (not necessarily) whilst the more generic fund management may refer to all forms of institutional investment as well as investment management for private investors. Investment managers who specialize in advisory or discretionary management on behalf of (normally wealthy) private investors may often refer to their services as wealth management or portfolio management often within the context of so-called 'private banking'.

The provision of 'investment management services' includes elements of financial analysis, asset selection, stock selection, plan implementation and ongoing monitoring of investments.

a. AAB
b. A Random Walk Down Wall Street
c. ABN Amro
d. Asset Management

7. In finance, _____ is the process of estimating the potential market value of a financial asset or liability. they can be done on assets (for example, investments in marketable securities such as stocks, options, business enterprises, or intangible assets such as patents and trademarks) or on liabilities (e.g., Bonds issued by a company.) _____s are required in many contexts including investment analysis, capital budgeting, merger and acquisition transactions, financial reporting, taxable events to determine the proper tax liability, and in litigation.

a. Share
b. Margin
c. Procter ' Gamble
d. Valuation

8. The term _____ has three unrelated technical definitions, and is also used in a variety of non-technical ways.

- In financial economics, it refers to any asset used to make money, as opposed to assets used for personal enjoyment or consumption. This is an important distinction because two people can disagree sharply about the value of personal assets, one person might think a sports car is more valuable than a pickup truck, another person might have the opposite taste. But if an asset is held for the purpose of making money, taste has nothing to do with it, only differences of opinion about how much money the asset will produce. With the further assumption that people agree on the probability distribution of future cash flows, it is possible to have an objective _____ pricing model. Even without the assumption of agreement, it is possible to set rational limits on _____ value.
- In governmental accounting, it is defined as any asset used in operations with an initial useful life extending beyond one reporting period. Generally, government managers have a 'stewardship' duty to maintain _____s under their control. See International Public Sector Accounting Standards for details.
- In US tax accounting, it is defined as any property other than a list of exceptions. The main exceptions are anything held for sale, and any real estate or depreciable property used in business. Almost everything you own and use for personal purposes, pleasure or investment is a _____. If something is a _____ for tax purposes, gains or losses on sale or disposition are capital gains or capital losses. For individuals, however, capital losses on property held for personal use are generally not deductible. See the IRS publication Tax Facts about Capital Gains and Losses for details.

A well-known financial accounting textbook advises that the term be avoided except in tax accounting because it is used in so many different senses, not all of them well-defined. For example it is often used as a synonym for fixed assets or for investments in securities.

A common non-technical usage occurs when people ask that employees or the environment or something else be treated as a _____.

a. Solvency
b. Capital Asset
c. Settlement date
d. Political risk

Chapter 12. Arbitrage Pricing Theory

9. In finance, the _____ is used to determine a theoretically appropriate required rate of return of an asset, if that asset is to be added to an already well-diversified portfolio, given that asset's non-diversifiable risk. The model takes into account the asset's sensitivity to non-diversifiable risk (also known as systemic risk or market risk), often represented by the quantity beta (β) in the financial industry, as well as the expected return of the market and the expected return of a theoretical risk-free asset.

The model was introduced by Jack Treynor (1961, 1962), William Sharpe (1964), John Lintner (1965a,b) and Jan Mossin (1966) independently, building on the earlier work of Harry Markowitz on diversification and modern portfolio theory.

- a. Hull-White model
- c. Cox-Ingersoll-Ross model
- b. Random walk hypothesis
- d. Capital Asset Pricing Model

10. The institution most often referenced by the word '_____' is a public or publicly traded _____, the shares of which are traded on a public stock exchange (e.g., the New York Stock Exchange or Nasdaq in the United States) where shares of stock of _____s are bought and sold by and to the general public. Most of the largest businesses in the world are publicly traded _____s. However, the majority of _____s are said to be closely held, privately held or close _____s, meaning that no ready market exists for the trading of shares.

- a. Corporation
- c. Depository Trust Company
- b. Federal Home Loan Mortgage Corporation
- d. Protect

Chapter 13. Characteristics of Common Stocks

1. _____ is a form of corporation equity ownership represented in the securities. It is dangerous in comparison to preferred shares and some other investment options, in that in the event of bankruptcy, _____ investors receive their funds after preferred stockholders, bondholders, creditors, etc. On the other hand, common shares on average perform better than preferred shares or bonds over time.

    a. Common stock
    b. Stock market bubble
    c. Stop-limit order
    d. Stock split

2. _____ is a concept whereby a person's financial liability is limited to a fixed sum, most commonly the value of a person's investment in a company or partnership with _____. A shareholder in a limited company is not personally liable for any of the debts of the company, other than for the value of his investment in that company. The same is true for the members of a _____ partnership and the limited partners in a limited partnership.

    a. Personal property
    b. Sarbanes-Oxley Act
    c. Beneficial owner
    d. Limited liability

3. A _____ is a fungible, negotiable instrument representing financial value. They are broadly categorized into debt securities (such as banknotes, bonds and debentures), and equity securities; e.g., common stocks. The company or other entity issuing the _____ is called the issuer.

    a. Securities lending
    b. Security
    c. Book entry
    d. Tracking stock

4. The U.S. _____ is an independent agency of the United States government which holds primary responsibility for enforcing the federal securities laws and regulating the securities industry, the nation's stock and options exchanges, and other electronic securities markets. The SEC was created by section 4 of the SEC of 1934 (now codified as 15 U.S.C. § 78d and commonly referred to as the 1934 Act.)

    a. 7-Eleven
    b. 529 plan
    c. 4-4-5 Calendar
    d. Securities and Exchange Commission

5. In corporate law, a _____ is a legal document that certifies ownership of a specific number of stock shares in a corporation. In large corporations, buying shares does not always lead to a _____

Usually only shareholders with _____s can vote in a shareholders' general meeting.

    a. Stock certificate
    b. 7-Eleven
    c. 4-4-5 Calendar
    d. 529 plan

6. In the most general sense, a _____ is anything that is a hindrance, or puts individuals at a disadvantage.

Before we discuss the financial terms, we should note that a _____ can also have a much more important slang meaning.

This is best described in an example.

    a. Limited liability
    b. McFadden Act
    c. Covenant
    d. Liability

7. _____ is a multiple-winner voting system intended to promote proportional representation while also being simple to understand.

Chapter 13. Characteristics of Common Stocks

_____ is used frequently in corporate governance, where it is mandated by many U.S. states, and it was used to elect the Illinois House of Representatives from 1870 until its repeal in 1980. It was used in England in the late 19th century to elect school boards.

a. Cumulative voting
b. 529 plan
c. 7-Eleven
d. 4-4-5 Calendar

8. A _____ is an event that may occur when a corporation's stockholders develop opposition to some aspect of the corporate governance, often focusing on directorial and management positions. Corporate activists may attempt to persuade shareholders to use their proxy votes (i.e. votes by one individual or institution as the authorized representative of another) to install new management for any of a variety of reasons.

In a _____, incumbent directors and management have the odds stacked in their favor over those trying to force the corporate change.

a. Trade finance
b. Procurement
c. Forfaiting
d. Proxy fight

9. Companies that have publicly traded securities typically use _____ to keep track of the individuals and entities that own their stocks and bonds. Most _____ are banks or trust companies, but sometimes a company acts as its own transfer agent.

_____ perform three main functions:

1. Issue and cancel certificates to reflect changes in ownership. For example, when a company declares a stock dividend or stock split, the transfer agent issues new shares. _____ keep records of who owns a company's stocks and bonds and how those stocks and bonds are held--whether by the owner in certificate form, by the company in book-entry form, or by the investor's brokerage firm in street name. They also keep records of how many shares or bonds each investor owns.
2. Act as an intermediary for the company. A transfer agent may also serve as the company's paying agent to pay out interest, cash and stock dividends, or other distributions to stock- and bondholders. In addition, _____ act as proxy agent (sending out proxy materials), exchange agent (exchanging a company's stock or bonds in a merger), tender agent (tendering shares in a tender offer), and mailing agent (mailing the company's quarterly, annual, and other reports.)
3. Handle lost, destroyed, or stolen certificates. _____ help shareholders and bondholders when a stock or bond certificate has been lost, destroyed, or stolen.

In many cases, you can find out which transfer agent a company uses by visiting the investor relations section of the company's website.

a. 4-4-5 Calendar
b. Transfer agents
c. 7-Eleven
d. 529 plan

Chapter 13. Characteristics of Common Stocks

10. In business, a _____ is the purchase of one company (the target) by another (the acquirer or bidder). In the UK the term refers to the acquisition of a public company whose shares are listed on a stock exchange, in contrast to the acquisition of a private company.

Before a bidder makes an offer for another company, it usually first informs that company's board of directors.

   a. 4-4-5 Calendar
   b. 529 plan
   c. Stock swap
   d. Takeover

11. _____ is a corporate finance term denoting a type of takeover bid. The _____ is a public, open offer or invitation (usually announced in a newspaper advertisement) by a prospective acquirer to all stockholders of a publicly traded corporation (the target corporation) to tender their stock for sale at a specified price during a specified time, subject to the tendering of a minimum and maximum number of shares. In a _____, the bidder contacts shareholders directly; the directors of the company may or may not have endorsed the _____ proposal.
   a. Shareholder value
   b. Cash is king
   c. Follow-on offering
   d. Tender offer

12. _____ is the set of processes, customs, policies, laws and institutions affecting the way a corporation is directed, administered or controlled. _____ also includes the relationships among the many stakeholders involved and the goals for which the corporation is governed. The principal stakeholders are the shareholders, management and the board of directors.
   a. Patent
   b. Foreign Corrupt Practices Act
   c. Corporate governance
   d. Due diligence

13. _____ are organizations which pool large sums of money and invest those sums in companies. They include banks, insurance companies, retirement or pension funds, hedge funds and mutual funds. Their role in the economy is to act as highly specialized investors on behalf of others.
   a. ABN Amro
   b. AAB
   c. A Random Walk Down Wall Street
   d. Institutional investors

14. An _____ is a contract written by a seller that conveys to the buyer the right -- but not the obligation -- to buy (in the case of a call _____) or to sell (in the case of a put _____) a particular asset, such as a piece of property such as, among others, a futures contract. In return for granting the _____, the seller collects a payment (the premium) from the buyer.

For example, buying a call _____ provides the right to buy a specified quantity of a security at a set strike price at some time on or before expiration, while buying a put _____ provides the right to sell.

   a. Amortization
   b. Annuity
   c. AT'T Mobility LLC
   d. Option

15. In accounting, _____ or *Carrying value* is the value of an asset according to its balance sheet account balance. For assets, the value is based on the original cost of the asset less any depreciation, amortization or impairment costs made against the asset. A company's _____ is its total assets minus intangible assets and liabilities.

Chapter 13. Characteristics of Common Stocks

a. Current liabilities
b. Retained earnings
c. Pro forma
d. Book value

16. _____, in finance and accounting, means stated value or face value. From this comes the expressions at par (at the _____), over par (over _____) and under par (under _____.)

The term '_____' has several meanings depending on context and geography.

a. FIDC
b. Global Squeeze
c. Sinking fund
d. Par value

17. A _____ or reacquired stock is stock which is bought back by the issuing company, reducing the amount of outstanding stock on the open market ('open market' including insiders' holdings.)

Stock repurchases are often used as a tax-efficient method to put cash into shareholders' hands, rather than pay dividends. Sometimes, companies do this when they feel that their stock is undervalued on the open market.

a. Current asset
b. Trial balance
c. Generally Accepted Accounting Principles
d. Treasury stock

18. In business and finance, a _____ (also referred to as equity _____) of stock means a _____ of ownership in a corporation (company.) In the plural, stocks is often used as a synonym for _____s especially in the United States, but it is less commonly used that way outside of North America.

In the United Kingdom, South Africa, and Australia, stock can also refer to completely different financial instruments such as government bonds or, less commonly, to all kinds of marketable securities.

a. Procter ' Gamble
b. Margin
c. Bucket shop
d. Share

19. In some countries, including the United States and the United Kingdom, corporations can buy back their own stock in a share repurchase, also known as a _____ or share buyback. There has been a meteoric rise in the use of share repurchases in the U.S. in the past twenty years, from $5b in 1980 to $349b in 2005. A share repurchase distributes cash to existing shareholders in exchange for a fraction of the firm's outstanding equity.

a. Stockholder
b. Trading curb
c. Stock repurchase
d. Common stock

20. A _____ is a payment made by a corporation to its shareholder members. When a corporation earns a profit or surplus, that money can be put to two uses: it can either be re-invested in the business (called retained earnings), or it can be paid to the shareholders as a _____. Many corporations retain a portion of their earnings and pay the remainder as a _____.

a. Dividend
b. Special dividend
c. Dividend yield
d. Dividend puzzle

Chapter 13. Characteristics of Common Stocks

21. _____, refers to consumption opportunity gained by an entity within a specified time frame, which is generally expressed in monetary terms. However, for households and individuals, '_____ is the sum of all the wages, salaries, profits, interests payments, rents and other forms of earnings received... in a given period of time.' For firms, _____ generally refers to net-profit: what remains of revenue after expenses have been subtracted.

   a. OIBDA
   b. Accrual
   c. Annual report
   d. Income

22. An _____ is a tax levied on the financial income of people, corporations, or other legal entities. Various _____ systems exist, with varying degrees of tax incidence. Income taxation can be progressive, proportional, or regressive.

   a. ABN Amro
   b. Income Tax
   c. A Random Walk Down Wall Street
   d. AAB

23. _____ refers to stock of a company that is not fully transferable until certain conditions have been met. Upon satisfaction of those conditions, the stock becomes transferable by the person holding the award.

   Another type of _____ is a form of compensation granted by a company. Typically, the conditions that allow the shares to be transferred are a period of time, when they vest.

   a. Market for corporate control
   b. Shareholder value
   c. Cash flow
   d. Restricted stock

24. In the United States, a _____ is an offering of securities that are not registered with the Securities and Exchange Commission (SEC.) Such offerings exploit an exemption offered by the Securities Act of 1933 that comes with several restrictions, including a prohibition against general solicitation. This exemption allows companies to avoid quarterly reporting requirements and many of the legal liabilities associated with the Sarbanes-Oxley Act.

   a. 4-4-5 Calendar
   b. 529 plan
   c. 7-Eleven
   d. Private placement

25. _____ are those dividends paid out in form of additional stock shares of the issuing corporation or other corporation They are usually issued in proportion to shares owned (for example for every 100 shares of stock owned, 5% stock dividend will yield 5 extra shares). If this payment involves the issue of new shares, this is very similar to a stock split in that it increases the total number of shares while lowering the price of each share and does not change the market capitalization or the total value of the shares held

   a. The Hong Kong Securities Institute
   b. Database auditing
   c. Time-based currency
   d. Stock or scrip dividends

26. On a stock exchange, a _____ is the opposite of a stock split, i.e. a stock merge - a reduction in the number of shares and an accompanying increase in the share price. The ratio is also reversed: 1-for-2, 1-for-3 and so on.

   There is a stigma attached to doing this so it is not initiated without very good reason.

   a. Correlation trading
   b. Trade date
   c. Conglomerate merger
   d. Reverse stock split

Chapter 13. Characteristics of Common Stocks

27. A _____ or stock divide increases or decreases the number of shares in a public company. The price is adjusted such that the before and after market capitalization of the company remains the same and dilution does not occur. Options and warrants are included.
    a. Stop price
    b. Contract for difference
    c. Stock split
    d. Stop order

28. A _____ is a right to acquire certain property in preference to any other person. It usually refers to property newly coming into existence. A right to acquire existing property in preference to any other person is usually referred to as a right of first refusal.

    In practice, the most common form of _____ is the right of existing shareholders to acquire newly issued shares issued by a company in a rights issue, a usually but not always public offering.

    a. Pre-emption right
    b. Fraud deterrence
    c. Court of Audit of Belgium
    d. Down payment

29. In probability and statistics, the _____ of a collection of numbers is a measure of the dispersion of the numbers from their expected (mean) value. It can apply to a probability distribution, a random variable, a population or a data set. The _____ is usually denoted with the letter σ (lowercase sigma.)
    a. Kurtosis
    b. Mean
    c. Standard deviation
    d. Sample size

30. _____ is a risk-adjusted measure of the so-called active return on an investment. It is the return in excess of the compensation for the risk borne, and thus commonly used to assess active managers' performances. Often, the return of a benchmark is subtracted in order to consider relative performance, which yields Jensen's _____.
    a. Amortization
    b. Option
    c. Alpha
    d. Annuity

31. In statistics, the _____, R^2 is used in the context of statistical models whose main purpose is the prediction of future outcomes on the basis of other related information. It is the proportion of variability in a data set that is accounted for by the statistical model. It provides a measure of how well future outcomes are likely to be predicted by the model.
    a. 7-Eleven
    b. 4-4-5 Calendar
    c. 529 plan
    d. Coefficient of determination

32. In probability theory and statistics, _____ indicates the strength and direction of a linear relationship between two random variables. That is in contrast with the usage of the term in colloquial speech, which denotes any relationship, not necessarily linear. In general statistical usage, _____ or co-relation refers to the departure of two random variables from independence.
    a. Geometric mean
    b. Variance
    c. Probability distribution
    d. Correlation

33. In statistics, _____ or explained randomness measures the proportion to which a mathematical model accounts for the variation (= apparent randomness) of a given data set. Often, variation is quantified as variance; then, the more specific term explained variance can be used.

    The complementary part of the total variation/randomness/variance is called unexplained or residual.

Chapter 13. Characteristics of Common Stocks

a. ABN Amro
c. AAB
b. A Random Walk Down Wall Street
d. Explained variation

34. An _____ is a company whose main business is holding securities of other companies purely for investment purposes. The _____ invests money on behalf of its shareholders who in turn share in the profits and losses.
   a. Unit investment trust
   c. Investment company
   b. A Random Walk Down Wall Street
   d. AAB

35. In finance, _____ are stocks that appreciate in value and yield a high return on equity (ROE.) Analysts compute ROE by taking the company's net income and dividing it by the company's equity. To be classified as a growth stock, analysts expect to see at least 15 percent return on equity.
   a. Security Analysis
   c. Growth stocks
   b. Stock valuation
   d. 4-4-5 Calendar

36. _____ is the quotient of earnings per share divided by the share price. It is the reciprocal of the P/E ratio--the E/P or the EPS.

The _____ is quoted as a percentage, allowing an easy comparison to going bond rates.

   a. Average accounting return
   c. Assets turnover
   b. Asset turnover
   d. Earnings yield

37. In finance, the term _____ describes the amount in cash that returns to the owners of a security. Normally it does not include the price variations, at the difference of the total return. _____ applies to various stated rates of return on stocks (common and preferred, and convertible), fixed income instruments (bonds, notes, bills, strips, zero coupon), and some other investment type insurance products (e.g. annuities.)
   a. Yield to maturity
   c. Yield
   b. 4-4-5 Calendar
   d. Macaulay duration

38. A _____ is a private or public market for the trading of company stock and derivatives of company stock at an agreed price; these are securities listed on a stock exchange as well as those only traded privately.

The size of the world _____ is estimated at about $36.6 trillion US at the beginning of October 2008 . The world derivatives market has been estimated at about $480 trillion face or nominal value, 12 times the size of the entire world economy.

   a. Andrew Tobias
   c. Stock market
   b. Anton Gelonkin
   d. Adolph Coors

39. The _____ is that part of the capital markets that deals with the issuance of new securities. Companies, governments or public sector institutions can obtain funding through the sale of a new stock or bond issue. This is typically done through a syndicate of securities dealers.
   a. Sector rotation
   c. Volatility clustering
   b. Peer group analysis
   d. Primary market

Chapter 13. Characteristics of Common Stocks

40. A _____ or bank is a financial institution whose primary activity is to act as a payment agent for customers and to borrow and lend money.

The first modern bank was founded in Italy in Genoa in 1406, its name was Banco di San Giorgio (Bank of St. George.)

Many other financial activities were added over time.

a. 4-4-5 Calendar
b. Bought deal
c. Black Sea Trade and Development Bank
d. Banker

41. _____ is the acquisition of goods and/or services at the best possible total cost of ownership, in the right quantity and quality, at the right time, in the right place and from the right source for the direct benefit or use of corporations or individuals, generally via a contract. Simple _____ may involve nothing more than repeat purchasing. Complex _____ could involve finding long term partners - or even 'co-destiny' suppliers that might fundamentally commit one organization to another.

a. Synthetic CDO
b. Pac-Man defense
c. Market capitalization
d. Procurement

42. In the _____ contract the underwriter guarantees the sale of the issued stock at the agreed-upon price. For the issuer, it is the safest but the most expensive type of the contracts, since the underwriter takes the risk of sale.

In the best efforts contract the underwriter agrees to sell as many shares as possible at the agreed-upon price.

a. Firm commitment
b. Special purpose entity
c. Participating preferred stock
d. Rights issue

43. _____, is when a company issues common stock or shares to the public for the first time. They are often issued by smaller, younger companies seeking capital to expand, but can also be done by large privately-owned companies looking to become publicly traded.

In an _____ the issuer may obtain the assistance of an underwriting firm, which helps it determine what type of security to issue (common or preferred), best offering price and time to bring it to market.

a. Interest
b. Asian Financial Crisis
c. Insolvency
d. Initial public offering

44. Unemployment occurs when a person is available to work and currently seeking work, but the person is without work. The prevalence of unemployment is usually measured using the _____, which is defined as the percentage of those in the labor force who are unemployed. The _____ is also used in economic studies and economic indexes such as the United States' Conference Board's Index of Leading Indicators as a measure of the state of the macroeconomics.

a. Unemployment rate
b. A Random Walk Down Wall Street
c. AAB
d. ABN Amro

45. In finance, a _____ is a security that entitles the holder to buy stock of the company that issued it at a specified price, which is usually higher than the stock price at time of issue.

_____s are frequently attached to bonds or preferred stock as a sweetener, allowing the issuer to pay lower interest rates or dividends. They can be used to enhance the yield of the bond, and make them more attractive to potential buyers.

a. Clearing
b. Clearing house
c. Warrant
d. Credit

46. _____ is an arrangement with the U.S. Securities and Exchange Commission that allows a single registration document to be filed that permits the issuance of multiple securities.

_____ is a registration of a new issue which can be prepared up to two years in advance, so that the issue can be offered quickly as soon as funds are needed or market conditions are favorable.

For example, current market conditions in the housing market are not favorable for a specific firm to issue a public offering.

a. 4-4-5 Calendar
b. Shelf registration
c. Bought deal
d. Black Sea Trade and Development Bank

47. _____ is defined by The Wall Street Journal, as a form of barter that involves a company selling 'an unused asset to another company while at the same time agreeing to buy back the same or similar assets at about the same price.' Round trips are characteristic of the New Economy companies. They played a crucial part in temporarily inflating the market capitalization of energy traders such as Enron, CMS Energy, Reliant Energy, and Dynegy.

Other companies making unconventional _____ deals include AOL with Sun Microsystems and Global Crossing with Qwest Communications.

a. Net pay
b. Round-tripping
c. Days Sales Outstanding
d. Residual value

48. A _____ or secondary offering is an issuance of stock subsequent to the company's initial public offering. A _____ can be either of two types (or a mixture of both): dilutive and non-dilutive. A secondary offering is an offering of securities by a shareholder of the company (as opposed to the company itself, which is a primary offering).

a. Second lien loan
b. Shareholder value
c. Follow-on offering
d. Capital structure

49. The _____ is the tendency of the stock market to rise between December 31 and the end of the first week in January. There are many theories for why this happens, the main one being that it occurs because many investors choose to sell some of their stock right before the end of the year in order to claim a capital loss for tax purposes. Once the tax calendar rolls over to a new year on January 1st these same investors quickly reinvest their money in the market, causing stock prices to rise.

a. Revaluation
b. Sector rotation
c. Death spiral financing
d. January effect

Chapter 13. Characteristics of Common Stocks

50. A _____ is any actual or hypothesized stock market trend based on the calendar, such as rises and falls associated with particular days of the week or months of the year.

Examples include:

- Halloween indicator (or the 'Sell in May' principle)
- January effect
- Mark Twain effect
- Monday effect
- Weekend effect
- Turn-of-the-Month effect
- Holiday effect

a. 4-4-5 Calendar
c. 7-Eleven
b. 529 plan
d. Calendar effect

51. A _____ occurs when a financial sponsor acquires a controlling interest in a company's equity and where a significant percentage of the purchase price is financed through leverage (borrowing.) The assets of the acquired company are used as collateral for the borrowed capital, sometimes with assets of the acquiring company. The bonds or other paper issued for _____s are commonly considered not to be investment grade because of the significant risks involved.

a. Limited partnership
c. Leveraged buyout
b. Pension fund
d. Leverage

52. The phrase _____ refers to the aspect of corporate strategy, corporate finance and management dealing with the buying, selling and combining of different companies that can aid, finance, or help a growing company in a given industry grow rapidly without having to create another business entity.

An acquisition, also known as a takeover, is the buying of one company (the 'target') by another. An acquisition may be friendly or hostile.

a. 7-Eleven
c. 4-4-5 Calendar
b. 529 plan
d. Mergers and acquisitions

Chapter 14. Financial Analysis of Common Stocks

1. _____ is an international professional designation offered by the _____ Institute (formerly known as AIMR) to financial analysts who complete a series of three examinations. In order to become a '_____ Charterholder' candidates must pass all three six-hour exams, possess a bachelor's degree (or equivalent, as assessed by the _____ institute) and have 48 months of work experience in an investment decision-making position. _____ charterholders are also obligated to adhere to a strict Code of Ethics and Standards governing their professional conduct.
   a. Chartered Financial Analyst
   b. 529 plan
   c. 7-Eleven
   d. 4-4-5 Calendar

2. A _____, securities analyst, research analyst, equity analyst, or investment analyst is a person who performs financial analysis for external or internal clients as a core part of the job.

An analyst studies companies and other entities to arrive at the estimate of their financial value. It is normally done by analyzing financial reports, aided by follow-up interviews with company representatives and industry experts.

   a. Portfolio manager
   b. Stockbroker
   c. Purchasing manager
   d. Financial Analyst

3. _____ refers to an assessment of the viability, stability and profitability of a business, sub-business or project.

It is performed by professionals who prepare reports using ratios that make use of information taken from financial statements and other reports. These reports are usually presented to top management as one of their bases in making business decisions.

   a. 4-4-5 Calendar
   b. Value investing
   c. 529 plan
   d. Financial analysis

4. A _____ is a person who makes investment decisions using money other people have placed under his or her control. In other words, it is a financial career involved in investment management. They work with a team of analysts and researchers, and are ultimately responsible for establishing an investment strategy, selecting appropriate investments and allocating each investment properly for a fund- or asset-management vehicle.
   a. Day trader
   b. Purchasing manager
   c. Financial analyst
   d. Portfolio manager

5. A _____ is a fungible, negotiable instrument representing financial value. They are broadly categorized into debt securities (such as banknotes, bonds and debentures), and equity securities; e.g., common stocks. The company or other entity issuing the _____ is called the issuer.
   a. Tracking stock
   b. Book entry
   c. Securities lending
   d. Security

6. _____ of a business involves analyzing its financial statements and health, its management and competitive advantages, and its competitors and markets. The term is used to distinguish such analysis from other types of investment analysis, such as quantitative analysis and technical analysis.

_____ is performed on historical and present data, but with the goal of making financial forecasts.

Chapter 14. Financial Analysis of Common Stocks

a. Fundamental analysis
c. Stock valuation
b. 4-4-5 Calendar
d. Growth stocks

7. In finance, _____ refers to the value of a security which is intrinsic to or contained in the security itself. It is also frequently called fundamental value. It is ordinarily calculated by summing the future income generated by the asset, and discounting it to the present value.
   a. Accretion
   c. Amortization
   b. Alpha
   d. Intrinsic value

8. Modern portfolio theory (MPT) proposes how rational investors will use diversification to optimize their portfolios, and how a risky asset should be priced. The basic concepts of the theory are Markowitz diversification, the _____, capital asset pricing model, the alpha and beta coefficients, the Capital Market Line and the Securities Market Line.

MPT models an asset's return as a random variable, and models a portfolio as a weighted combination of assets so that the return of a portfolio is the weighted combination of the assets' returns.

   a. ABN Amro
   c. A Random Walk Down Wall Street
   b. AAB
   d. Efficient frontier

9. _____ is a security analysis discipline for forecasting the future direction of prices through the study of past market data, primarily price and volume. In its purest form, _____ considers only the actual price and volume behavior of the market or instrument. Technical analysts may employ models and trading rules based on price and volume transformations, such as the relative strength index, moving averages, regressions, inter-market and intra-market price correlations, cycles or, classically, through recognition of chart patterns.
   a. Technical analysis
   c. Support and resistance
   b. Point and figure
   d. Dow theory

10. In finance, a _____ is one who attempts to profit by investing in a manner that differs from the conventional wisdom, when the consensus opinion appears to be wrong.

A _____ believes that certain crowd behavior among investors can lead to exploitable mispricings in securities markets. For example, widespread pessimism about a stock can drive a price so low that it overstates the company's risks, and understates its prospects for returning to profitability.

   a. Direct access trading
   c. Secured debt
   b. Day trading
   d. Contrarian

11. The _____ is one of several stock market indices, created by nineteenth-century Wall Street Journal editor and Dow Jones ' Company co-founder Charles Dow. Dow compiled the index to gauge the performance of the industrial sector of the American stock market. It is the second-oldest U.S. market index, after the Dow Jones Transportation Average, which Dow also created.
   a. 529 plan
   c. 4-4-5 Calendar
   b. 7-Eleven
   d. Dow Jones Industrial Average

Chapter 14. Financial Analysis of Common Stocks

12. In statistics, a _____, is a type of finite impulse response filter used to analyze a set of data points by creating a series of averages of different subsets of the full data set. A _____ is not a single number, but it is a set of numbers, each of which is the average of the corresponding subset of a larger set of data points. A _____ may also use unequal weights for each data value in the subset to emphasize particular values in the subset.

   a. Gordon growth model
   b. Loans and interest, in Judaism
   c. Moving average
   d. Voluntary Emissions Reductions

13. _____ is concerned with the tasks of developing and applying quantitative or statistical methods to the study and elucidation of economic principles. _____ combines economic theory with statistics to analyze and test economic relationships. Theoretical _____ considers questions about the statistical properties of estimators and tests, while applied _____ is concerned with the application of econometric methods to assess economic theories.

   a. ABN Amro
   b. AAB
   c. A Random Walk Down Wall Street
   d. Econometrics

14. _____ s are statistical models used in econometrics. An _____ specifies the statistical relationship that is believed to hold between the various economic quantities pertaining a particular economic phenomena under study. An _____ can be derived from a deterministic economic model by allowing for uncertainty or from an economic model which itself is stochastic.

   a. ABN Amro
   b. Econometric model
   c. A Random Walk Down Wall Street
   d. AAB

15. In economics, a _____ is a mechanism that allows people to easily buy and sell (trade) financial securities (such as stocks and bonds), commodities (such as precious metals or agricultural goods), and other fungible items of value at low transaction costs and at prices that reflect the efficient-market hypothesis.

   _____ s have evolved significantly over several hundred years and are undergoing constant innovation to improve liquidity.

   Both general markets (where many commodities are traded) and specialized markets (where only one commodity is traded) exist.

   a. Cost of carry
   b. Financial market
   c. Delta hedging
   d. Secondary market

16. In finance, the Acid-test or _____ or liquid ratio measures the ability of a company to use its near cash or quick assets to immediately extinguish or retire its current liabilities. Quick assets include those current assets that presumably can be quickly converted to cash at close to their book values.

Generally, the acid test ratio should be 1:1 or better, however this varies widely by industry.

   a. Net assets
   b. P/E ratio
   c. Financial ratio
   d. Quick ratio

17. _____ or interest coverage ratio is a measure of a company's ability to honor its debt payments. It may be calculated as either EBIT or EBITDA divided by the total interest payable.

$$\text{Times-Interest-Earned} = \frac{\text{EBIT or EBITDA}}{\text{Interest Charges}}$$

- Financial ratio
- Financial leverage
- EBIT
- EBITDA
- Debt service coverage ratio

Interest Charges = Traditionally 'charges' refers to interest expense found on the income statement.

_____ or Interest Coverage is a great tool when measuring a company's ability to meet its debt obligations.

a. Times interest earned
b. Return of capital
c. Net assets
d. Cash conversion cycle

18. _____ is a fee paid on borrowed assets. It is the price paid for the use of borrowed money, or, money earned by deposited funds. Assets that are sometimes lent with _____ include money, shares, consumer goods through hire purchase, major assets such as aircraft, and even entire factories in finance lease arrangements.

a. Insolvency
b. A Random Walk Down Wall Street
c. AAB
d. Interest

19. The institution most often referenced by the word '_____' is a public or publicly traded _____, the shares of which are traded on a public stock exchange (e.g., the New York Stock Exchange or Nasdaq in the United States) where shares of stock of _____s are bought and sold by and to the general public. Most of the largest businesses in the world are publicly traded _____s. However, the majority of _____s are said to be closely held, privately held or close _____s, meaning that no ready market exists for the trading of shares.

a. Protect
b. Federal Home Loan Mortgage Corporation
c. Corporation
d. Depository Trust Company

20. _____ measures the rate of return on the ownership interest (shareholders' equity) of the common stock owners. _____ is viewed as one of the most important financial ratios. It measures a firm's efficiency at generating profits from every dollar of shareholders' equity (also known as net assets or assets minus liabilities.)

a. Return on equity
b. Return on sales
c. Return of capital
d. Diluted Earnings Per Share

21. In financial accounting, a _____ or statement of financial position is a summary of a person's or organization's balances. Assets, liabilities and ownership equity are listed as of a specific date, such as the end of its financial year. A _____ is often described as a snapshot of a company's financial condition.

a. Balance sheet
b. Financial statements
c. Statement on Auditing Standards No. 70: Service Organizations
d. Statement of retained earnings

22. In business and accounting, _____s are everything of value that is owned by a person or company. The balance sheet of a firm records the monetary value of the _____s owned by the firm. The two major _____ classes are tangible _____s and intangible _____s.
   a. EBITDA
   b. Income
   c. Asset
   d. Accounts payable

23. In accounting, a _____ is an asset on the balance sheet which is expected to be sold or otherwise used up in the near future, usually within one year, or one business cycle - whichever is longer. Typical _____s include cash, cash equivalents, accounts receivable, inventory, the portion of prepaid accounts which will be used within a year, and short-term investments.

On the balance sheet, assets will typically be classified into _____s and long-term assets.

   a. Current asset
   b. Historical cost
   c. Long-term liabilities
   d. Write-off

24. _____, refers to consumption opportunity gained by an entity within a specified time frame, which is generally expressed in monetary terms. However, for households and individuals, '_____ is the sum of all the wages, salaries, profits, interests payments, rents and other forms of earnings received... in a given period of time.' For firms, _____ generally refers to net-profit: what remains of revenue after expenses have been subtracted.
   a. Accrual
   b. Annual report
   c. OIBDA
   d. Income

25. An _____ is a financial statement for companies that indicates how Revenue is transformed into net income The purpose of the _____ is to show managers and investors whether the company made or lost money during the period being reported.

The important thing to remember about an _____ is that it represents a period of time.

   a. AAB
   b. A Random Walk Down Wall Street
   c. ABN Amro
   d. Income statement

26. An _____, operating expenditure, operational expense, operational expenditure or OPEX is an on-going cost for running a product, business, or system. Its counterpart, a capital expenditure (CAPEX), is the cost of developing or providing non-consumable parts for the product or system. For example, the purchase of a photocopier is the CAPEX, and the annual paper and toner cost is the OPEX.
   a. AAB
   b. A Random Walk Down Wall Street
   c. Operating expense
   d. ABN Amro

27. _____ are the earnings returned on the initial investment amount.

Chapter 14. Financial Analysis of Common Stocks

In the US, the Financial Accounting Standards Board (FASB) requires companies' income statements to report _____ for each of the major categories of the income statement: continuing operations, discontinued operations, extraordinary items, and net income.

The _____ formula does not include preferred dividends for categories outside of continued operations and net income.

a. Inventory turnover
c. Assets turnover
b. Average accounting return
d. Earnings per share

28. In business and finance, a _____ (also referred to as equity _____) of stock means a _____ of ownership in a corporation (company.) In the plural, stocks is often used as a synonym for _____s especially in the United States, but it is less commonly used that way outside of North America.

In the United Kingdom, South Africa, and Australia, stock can also refer to completely different financial instruments such as government bonds or, less commonly, to all kinds of marketable securities.

a. Procter ' Gamble
c. Share
b. Bucket shop
d. Margin

29. In corporate finance, _____ is a cash flow available for distribution among all the security holders of a company. They include equity holders, debt holders, preferred stock holders, convertible security holders, and so on.

Note that the first three lines above are calculated for you on the standard Statement of Cash Flows.

a. Forfaiting
c. Free cash flow
b. Safety stock
d. Funding

30. In financial accounting, a _____ or statement of cash flows is a financial statement that shows a company's flow of cash. The money coming into the business is called cash inflow, and money going out from the business is called cash outflow. The statement shows how changes in balance sheet and income accounts affect cash and cash equivalents, and breaks the analysis down to operating, investing, and financing activities.

a. Cash flow statement
c. 7-Eleven
b. 4-4-5 Calendar
d. 529 plan

Chapter 14. Financial Analysis of Common Stocks

31. _____ is the balance of the amounts of cash being received and paid by a business during a defined period of time, sometimes tied to a specific project. Measurement of _____ can be used

- to evaluate the state or performance of a business or project.
- to determine problems with liquidity. Being profitable does not necessarily mean being liquid. A company can fail because of a shortage of cash, even while profitable.
- to generate project rate of returns. The time of _____s into and out of projects are used as inputs to financial models such as internal rate of return, and net present value.
- to examine income or growth of a business when it is believed that accrual accounting concepts do not represent economic realities. Alternately, _____ can be used to 'validate' the net income generated by accrual accounting.

_____ as a generic term may be used differently depending on context, and certain _____ definitions may be adapted by analysts and users for their own uses. Common terms include operating _____ and free _____.

_____s can be classified into:

1. Operational _____s: Cash received or expended as a result of the company's core business activities.
2. Investment _____s: Cash received or expended through capital expenditure, investments or acquisitions.
3. Financing _____s: Cash received or expended as a result of financial activities, such as interests and dividends.

All three together - the net _____ - are necessary to reconcile the beginning cash balance to the ending cash balance. Loan draw downs or equity injections, that is just shifting of capital but no expenditure as such, are not considered in the net _____.

a. Cash flow
b. Corporate finance
c. Real option
d. Shareholder value

32. _____ are formal records of a business' financial activities.

_____ provide an overview of a business' financial condition in both short and long term. There are four basic _____:

1. **Balance sheet**: also referred to as statement of financial position or condition, reports on a company's assets, liabilities, and net equity as of a given point in time.
2. **Income statement**: also referred to as Profit and Loss statement (or a 'P'L'), reports on a company's income, expenses, and profits over a period of time.
3. **Statement of retained earnings**: explains the changes in a company's retained earnings over the reporting period.
4. **Statement of cash flows**: reports on a company's cash flow activities, particularly its operating, investing and financing activities.

Chapter 14. Financial Analysis of Common Stocks

a. Statement of retained earnings
b. Notes to the Financial Statements
c. Statement on Auditing Standards No. 70: Service Organizations
d. Financial statements

33. _____ is the standard framework of guidelines for financial accounting used in the United States of America. It includes the standards, conventions, and rules accountants follow in recording and summarizing transactions, and in the preparation of financial statements. _____ are now issued by the Financial Accounting Standards Board (FASB).
   a. Revenue
   b. Depreciation
   c. Net income
   d. Generally accepted accounting principles

34. _____ is a financial ratio that measures the efficiency of a company's use of its assets in generating sales revenue or sales income to the company.

$$Asset\ Turnover = \frac{Sales}{Average Total Assets}$$

- 'Sales' is the value of 'Net Sales' or 'Sales' from the company's income statement
- 'Average Total Assets' is the value of 'Total assets' from the company's balance sheet in the beginning and the end of the fiscal period divided by 2.

- Assets turnover

   a. Asset turnover
   b. Earnings yield
   c. Average accounting return
   d. Inventory turnover

35. In business, operating margin, operating income margin, _____ or return on sales (ROS) is the ratio of operating income (operating profit in the UK) divided by net sales, usually presented in percent.

(Relevant figures in italics)

It is a measurement of what proportion of a company's revenue is left over, before taxes and other indirect costs (such as rent, bonus, interest, etc.), after paying for variable costs of production as wages, raw materials, etc. A good operating margin is needed for a company to be able to pay for its fixed costs, such as interest on debt.

   a. Interest coverage ratio
   b. Average rate of return
   c. Operating leverage
   d. Operating profit margin

36. The _____ percentage shows how profitable a company's assets are in generating revenue.

Chapter 14. Financial Analysis of Common Stocks

_____ can be computed as:

$$ROA = \frac{\text{Net Income}}{\text{Total Assets}}$$

This number tells you 'what the company can do with what it's got', i.e. how many dollars of earnings they derive from each dollar of assets they control. It's a useful number for comparing competing companies in the same industry.

a. P/E ratio
b. Return on assets
c. Receivables turnover ratio
d. Return on sales

37. In finance, a _____ is collateral that the holder of a position in securities, options, or futures contracts has to deposit to cover the credit risk of his counterparty (most often his broker.) This risk can arise if the holder has done any of the following:

- borrowed cash from the counterparty to buy securities or options,
- sold securities or options short, or
- entered into a futures contract.

The collateral can be in the form of cash or securities, and it is deposited in a _____ account. On U.S. futures exchanges, '_____' was formally called performance bond.

_____ buying is buying securities with cash borrowed from a broker, using other securities as collateral.

a. Procter ' Gamble
b. Share
c. Credit
d. Margin

38. In finance, _____ (or gearing) is borrowing money to supplement existing funds for investment in such a way that the potential positive or negative outcome is magnified and/or enhanced. It generally refers to using borrowed funds, or debt, so as to attempt to increase the returns to equity. Deleveraging is the action of reducing borrowings.

a. Financial endowment
b. Pension fund
c. Limited partnership
d. Leverage

39. In finance, a _____ is a debt security, in which the authorized issuer owes the holders a debt and, depending on the terms of the _____, is obliged to pay interest (the coupon) and/or to repay the principal at a later date, termed maturity.

Thus a _____ is a loan: the issuer is the borrower, the _____ holder is the lender, and the coupon is the interest. _____s provide the borrower with external funds to finance long-term investments, or, in the case of government _____s, to finance current expenditure.

Chapter 14. Financial Analysis of Common Stocks

a. Puttable bond
b. Convertible bond
c. Catastrophe bonds
d. Bond

40. _____ is the difference between price and the costs of bringing to market whatever it is that is accounted as an enterprise (whether by harvest, extraction, manufacture, or purchase) in terms of the component costs of delivered goods and/or services and any operating or other expenses.

A key difficulty in measuring profit is in defining costs. Pure economic monetary profits can be zero or negative even in competitive equilibrium when accounted monetized costs exceed monetized price.

a. AAB
b. A Random Walk Down Wall Street
c. Economic profit
d. Accounting profit

41. _____, Net Margin, Net _____ or Net Profit Ratio all refer to a measure of profitability. It is calculated using a formula and written as a percentage or a number.

$$\text{Net profit margin} = \frac{\text{Net profit after taxes}}{\text{Net Sales}}$$

The _____ is mostly used for internal comparison.

a. 4-4-5 Calendar
b. Profit maximization
c. Profit margin
d. Net profit margin

42. _____ refers to any type of investment that yields a regular (or fixed) return.

For example, if you lend money to a borrower and the borrower has to pay interest once a month, you have been issued a fixed-income security. When a company does this, it is often called a bond or corporate bank debt (although preferred stock is also sometimes considered to be _____).

a. Fixed income
b. 4-4-5 Calendar
c. Bond market
d. 529 plan

43. _____ is a form of corporation equity ownership represented in the securities. It is dangerous in comparison to preferred shares and some other investment options, in that in the event of bankruptcy, _____ investors receive their funds after preferred stockholders, bondholders, creditors, etc. On the other hand, common shares on average perform better than preferred shares or bonds over time.

a. Common stock
b. Stock market bubble
c. Stop-limit order
d. Stock split

44. The _____ is a financial ratio that measures whether or not a firm has enough resources to pay its debts over the next 12 months. It compares a firm's current assets to its current liabilities. It is expressed as follows:

$$\text{Current ratio} = \frac{\text{Current Assets}}{\text{Current Liabilities}}$$

For example, if WXY Company's current assets are $50,000,000 and its current liabilities are $40,000,000, then its _____ would be $50,000,000 divided by $40,000,000, which equals 1.25.

a. Sustainable growth rate
b. Debt service coverage ratio
c. PEG ratio
d. Current ratio

45. _____ is a measure of the ability of a debtor to pay their debts as and when they fall due. It is usually expressed as a ratio or a percentage of current liabilities.

For a corporation with a published balance sheet there are various ratios used to calculate a measure of liquidity.

a. Accounting liquidity
b. Operating leverage
c. Invested capital
d. Operating profit margin

46. A _____ is the price of a single share of a no. of saleable stocks of the company. Once the stock is purchased, the owner becomes a shareholder of the company that issued the share.
a. Stock split
b. Whisper numbers
c. Share price
d. Trading curb

47. In finance, _____ is the process of estimating the potential market value of a financial asset or liability. they can be done on assets (for example, investments in marketable securities such as stocks, options, business enterprises, or intangible assets such as patents and trademarks) or on liabilities (e.g., Bonds issued by a company.) _____s are required in many contexts including investment analysis, capital budgeting, merger and acquisition transactions, financial reporting, taxable events to determine the proper tax liability, and in litigation.
a. Margin
b. Procter ' Gamble
c. Share
d. Valuation

48. _____ is the trading of a corporation's stock or other securities (e.g. bonds or stock options) by individuals with potential access to non-public information about the company. In most countries, trading by corporate insiders such as officers, key employees, directors, and large shareholders may be legal, if this trading is done in a way that does not take advantage of non-public information. However, the term is frequently used to refer to a practice in which an insider or a related party trades based on material non-public information obtained during the performance of the insider's duties at the corporation, or otherwise in breach of a fiduciary duty or other relationship of trust and confidence or where the non-public information was misappropriated from the company.
a. Insider trading
b. Open outcry
c. Equity investment
d. Intellidex

49. _____ are organizations which pool large sums of money and invest those sums in companies. They include banks, insurance companies, retirement or pension funds, hedge funds and mutual funds. Their role in the economy is to act as highly specialized investors on behalf of others.
a. ABN Amro
b. AAB
c. Institutional investors
d. A Random Walk Down Wall Street

Chapter 14. Financial Analysis of Common Stocks

50. The U.S. _____ is an independent agency of the United States government which holds primary responsibility for enforcing the federal securities laws and regulating the securities industry, the nation's stock and options exchanges, and other electronic securities markets. The SEC was created by section 4 of the SEC of 1934 (now codified as 15 U.S.C. Â§ 78d and commonly referred to as the 1934 Act.)
    a. Securities and Exchange Commission
    b. 529 plan
    c. 7-Eleven
    d. 4-4-5 Calendar

51. In economics and contract theory, _____ deals with the study of decisions in transactions where one party has more or better information than the other. This creates an imbalance of power in transactions which can sometimes cause the transactions to go awry. Examples of this problem are adverse selection and moral hazard.
    a. A Random Walk Down Wall Street
    b. AAB
    c. ABN Amro
    d. Information asymmetry

52. The _____ of 1934 is a law governing the secondary trading of securities (stocks, bonds, and debentures) in the United States of America. The Act, 48 Stat. 881 (enacted June 6, 1934), codified at 15 U.S.C. Â§ 78a et seq., was a sweeping piece of legislation. The Act and related statutes form the basis of regulation of the financial markets and their participants in the United States.
    a. 529 plan
    b. Securities Exchange Act
    c. 4-4-5 Calendar
    d. 7-Eleven

53. In finance, _____ or 'shorting' is the practice of selling a financial instrument that the seller does not own at the time of the sale. _____ is done with intent of later purchasing the financial instrument at a lower price. Short-sellers attempt to profit from an expected decline in the price of a financial instrument.
    a. Short selling
    b. Short ratio
    c. 529 plan
    d. 4-4-5 Calendar

54. An _____ is a contract written by a seller that conveys to the buyer the right -- but not the obligation -- to buy (in the case of a call _____) or to sell (in the case of a put _____) a particular asset, such as a piece of property such as, among others, a futures contract. In return for granting the _____, the seller collects a payment (the premium) from the buyer.

For example, buying a call _____ provides the right to buy a specified quantity of a security at a set strike price at some time on or before expiration, while buying a put _____ provides the right to sell.

    a. Amortization
    b. AT'T Mobility LLC
    c. Annuity
    d. Option

Chapter 14. Financial Analysis of Common Stocks

55. An _____ is a document a company presents at an annual general meeting for approval by its shareholders, or a charitable organization presents its trustees. The report is made up of reports, which may include the following:

- Chairman's report
- CEO's report
- Auditor's report on corporate governance
- Mission statement
- Corporate governance statement of compliance
- Statement of directors' responsibilities
- Invitation to the company's AGM

as well as financial statements including:

- Auditor's report on the financial statements
- Balance sheet
- Statement of retained earnings
- Income statement
- Cash flow statement
- Notes to the financial statements
- Accounting policies

Other information deemed relevant to stakeholders may be included, such as a report on operations for manufacturing firms. In the case of larger companies, it is usually a sleek, colorful, high gloss publication.

The details provided in the report are of use to investors to understand the company's financial position and future direction.

a. Outstanding balance
c. Accrued liabilities
b. Amortization schedule
d. Annual report

56. _____ is a charting technique used in technical analysis, a form of heterodox economics used to attempt to predict financial market prices. _____ charting is unique in that it does not plot price against time as all other techniques do. Instead in plots price against changes in direction by plotting a column of Xs as the price rises and a column of Os as the price falls.

a. Dow theory
c. Money flow
b. Technical analysis
d. Point and figure

57. _____ is a heterodox theory on stock price movements that is used as the basis for technical analysis. The theory was derived from 255 Wall Street Journal editorials written by Charles H. Dow (1851-1902), journalist, founder and first editor of the Wall Street Journal and co-founder of Dow Jones and Company. Following Dow's death, William P. Hamilton, Robert Rhea and E. George Schaefer organized and collectively represented '_____,' based on Dow's editorials.

a. Point and figure
c. Technical analysis
b. Money flow
d. Dow Theory

58. The _____ is a financial technical analysis momentum oscillator measuring the velocity and magnitude of directional price movement by comparing upward and downward close-to-close movements.

Chapter 14. Financial Analysis of Common Stocks

The _____ was developed by J. Welles Wilder and published in Commodities magazine (now called Futures magazine) in June 1978, and in his New Concepts in Technical Trading Systems the same year.

a. Stock or scrip dividends
c. Global depository receipt

b. Database auditing
d. Relative strength Index

Chapter 15. Dividend Discount Models

1. A '_____' is a 'Charge' that is paid to obtain the right to delay a payment. Essentially, the payer purchases the right to make a given payment in the future instead of in the Present. The '_____', or 'Charge' that must be paid to delay the payment, is simply the difference between what the payment amount would be if it were paid in the present and what the payment amount would be paid if it were paid in the future.
   a. Value at risk
   b. Risk modeling
   c. Discount
   d. Risk aversion

2. The _____ is an interest rate a central bank charges depository institutions that borrow reserves from it.

   The term _____ has two meanings:

   - the same as interest rate; the term 'discount' does not refer to the meaning of the word, but to the purpose of using the quantity, such as computations of present value, e.g. net present value / discounted cash flow

   - the annual effective _____, which is the annual interest divided by the capital including that interest; this rate is lower than the interest rate; it corresponds to using the value after a year as the nominal value, and seeing the initial value as the nominal value minus a discount; it is used for Treasury Bills and similar financial instruments

   The annual effective _____ is the annual interest divided by the capital including that interest, which is the interest rate divided by 100% plus the interest rate. It is the annual discount factor to be applied to the future cash flow, to find the discount, subtracted from a future value to find the value one year earlier.

   For example, suppose there is a government bond that sells for $95 and pays $100 in a year's time.

   a. Fisher equation
   b. Stochastic volatility
   c. Black-Scholes
   d. Discount rate

3. A _____ is a payment made by a corporation to its shareholder members. When a corporation earns a profit or surplus, that money can be put to two uses: it can either be re-invested in the business (called retained earnings), or it can be paid to the shareholders as a _____. Many corporations retain a portion of their earnings and pay the remainder as a _____.
   a. Special dividend
   b. Dividend puzzle
   c. Dividend
   d. Dividend yield

4. _____, refers to consumption opportunity gained by an entity within a specified time frame, which is generally expressed in monetary terms. However, for households and individuals, '_____ is the sum of all the wages, salaries, profits, interests payments, rents and other forms of earnings received... in a given period of time.' For firms, _____ generally refers to net-profit: what remains of revenue after expenses have been subtracted.
   a. Annual report
   b. OIBDA
   c. Accrual
   d. Income

5. In finance, _____ is the process of estimating the potential market value of a financial asset or liability. they can be done on assets (for example, investments in marketable securities such as stocks, options, business enterprises, or intangible assets such as patents and trademarks) or on liabilities (e.g., Bonds issued by a company.) _____s are required in many contexts including investment analysis, capital budgeting, merger and acquisition transactions, financial reporting, taxable events to determine the proper tax liability, and in litigation.

Chapter 15. Dividend Discount Models

a. Margin
b. Valuation
c. Share
d. Procter ' Gamble

6. The _____ is a capital budgeting metric used by firms to decide whether they should make investments. It is an indicator of the efficiency or quality of an investment, as opposed to net present value (NPV), which indicates value or magnitude.

The IRR is the annualized effective compounded return rate which can be earned on the invested capital, i.e., the yield on the investment.

a. AAB
b. A Random Walk Down Wall Street
c. ABN Amro
d. Internal rate of return

7. _____ or net present worth (NPW) is defined as the total present value (PV) of a time series of cash flows. It is a standard method for using the time value of money to appraise long-term projects. Used for capital budgeting, and widely throughout economics, it measures the excess or shortfall of cash flows, in present value terms, once financing charges are met.

a. Net present value
b. Present value of costs
c. Tax shield
d. Negative gearing

8. _____ is the value on a given date of a future payment or series of future payments, discounted to reflect the time value of money and other factors such as investment risk. _____ calculations are widely used in business and economics to provide a means to compare cash flows at different times on a meaningful 'like to like' basis.

The most commonly applied model of the time value of money is compound interest.

a. Present value of benefits
b. Present value
c. Negative gearing
d. Net present value

9. In finance, _____, also known as return on investment is the ratio of money gained or lost on an investment relative to the amount of money invested. The amount of money gained or lost may be referred to as interest, profit/loss, gain/loss, or net income/loss. The money invested may be referred to as the asset, capital, principal, or the cost basis of the investment.

a. Doctrine of the Proper Law
b. Stock or scrip dividends
c. Composiition of Creditors
d. Rate of return

10. In finance, _____ is a measurement of return on an asset or portfolio. It is one of the simplest measures of investment performance.

_____ is the percentage by which the value of a portfolio (or asset) has grown for a particular period.

a. Stock market index option
b. Market integration
c. Creditor
d. Holding period return

11. The _____ of a stock is a measure of the price paid for a share relative to the annual income or profit earned by the firm per share. It is a financial ratio used for valuation: a higher _____ means that investors are paying more for each unit of income, so the stock is more expensive compared to one with lower _____.

Chapter 15. Dividend Discount Models

The _____ has units of years, which can be interpreted as 'number of years of earnings to pay back purchase price'.

   a. P/E ratio
   b. Return of capital
   c. Sustainable growth rate
   d. Quick ratio

12. _____ is the fraction of net income a firm pays to its stockholders in dividends:

The part of the earnings not paid to investors is left for investment to provide for future earnings growth. Investors seeking high current income and limited capital growth prefer companies with high _____. However investors seeking capital growth may prefer lower payout ratio because capital gains are taxed at a lower rate.

   a. Dividend payout ratio
   b. Dividend puzzle
   c. Dividend yield
   d. Dividend imputation

13. In finance, _____ refers to the value of a security which is intrinsic to or contained in the security itself. It is also frequently called fundamental value. It is ordinarily calculated by summing the future income generated by the asset, and discounting it to the present value.

   a. Alpha
   b. Amortization
   c. Accretion
   d. Intrinsic value

14. _____ indicates the percentage of a company's earnings that are not paid out in dividends but credited to retained earnings. It is the opposite of the dividend payout ratio, so that also called the retention rate.

_____ = 1 - Dividend Payout Ratio

   a. Dow Jones Indexes
   b. Bankassurer
   c. Retention ratio
   d. Fair market value

15. In investments, _____ refers to the annual rate of growth of earnings. When the dividend payout ratio is the same, the dividend growth rate is equal to the _____ rate.

_____ rate is a key value that is needed when the DCF model, or the Gordon's model is used for stock valuation.

   a. Annuity
   b. Alternative display facility
   c. Alternative asset
   d. Earnings growth

16. _____ is a risk-adjusted measure of the so-called active return on an investment. It is the return in excess of the compensation for the risk borne, and thus commonly used to assess active managers' performances. Often, the return of a benchmark is subtracted in order to consider relative performance, which yields Jensen's _____.

Chapter 15. Dividend Discount Models

a. Amortization
b. Annuity
c. Option
d. Alpha

17. A _____ is a fungible, negotiable instrument representing financial value. They are broadly categorized into debt securities (such as banknotes, bonds and debentures), and equity securities; e.g., common stocks. The company or other entity issuing the _____ is called the issuer.

a. Security
b. Tracking stock
c. Book entry
d. Securities lending

18. In Modern Portfolio Theory, the _____ is the graphical representation of the Capital Asset Pricing Model. It displays the expected rate of return for an overall market as a function of systematic (non-diversifiable) risk (beta.)

The Y-Intercept (beta=0) of the _____ is equal to the risk-free interest rate.

a. Certificate in Investment Performance Measurement
b. Security market line
c. Rebalancing
d. Divestment

19. The _____ is the weighted-average most likely outcome in gambling, probability theory, economics or finance.

In gambling and probability theory, there is usually a discrete set of possible outcomes. In this case, _____ is a measure of the relative balance of win or loss weighted by their chances of occurring.

a. ABN Amro
b. Expected return
c. A Random Walk Down Wall Street
d. AAB

20. _____ is a technique to adjust income payments by means of a price index, in order to maintain the purchasing power of the public after inflation.

Applying a cost-of-living escalation COLA clause to a stream of periodic payments protects the real value of those payments and effectively transfers the risk of inflation from the payee to the payor, who must pay more each year to reflect the increases in prices. Thus, inflation _____ is often applied to pension payments, rents and other situations which are not subject to regular re-pricing in the market.

a. Indexation
b. A Random Walk Down Wall Street
c. ABN Amro
d. AAB

21. A _____ is a firm that quotes both a buy and a sell price in a financial instrument or commodity, hoping to make a profit on the bid/offer spread, or turn.

In foreign exchange trading, where most deals are conducted over-the-counter and are, therefore, completely virtual, the _____ sells to and buys from its clients. Hence, the client's loss and the spread is the _____ firm's profit, which gets thus compensated for the effort of providing liquidity in a competitive market.

a. 7-Eleven
c. 529 plan
b. 4-4-5 Calendar
d. Market maker

22. _____, is when a company issues common stock or shares to the public for the first time. They are often issued by smaller, younger companies seeking capital to expand, but can also be done by large privately-owned companies looking to become publicly traded.

In an _____ the issuer may obtain the assistance of an underwriting firm, which helps it determine what type of security to issue (common or preferred), best offering price and time to bring it to market.

a. Initial public offering
c. Asian Financial Crisis
b. Insolvency
d. Interest

23. _____ is a form of corporation equity ownership represented in the securities. It is dangerous in comparison to preferred shares and some other investment options, in that in the event of bankruptcy, _____ investors receive their funds after preferred stockholders, bondholders, creditors, etc. On the other hand, common shares on average perform better than preferred shares or bonds over time.

a. Stock market bubble
c. Common stock
b. Stop-limit order
d. Stock split

Chapter 16. Dividends and Earnings

1. A _____ is a payment made by a corporation to its shareholder members. When a corporation earns a profit or surplus, that money can be put to two uses: it can either be re-invested in the business (called retained earnings), or it can be paid to the shareholders as a _____. Many corporations retain a portion of their earnings and pay the remainder as a _____.

    a. Dividend yield
    b. Special dividend
    c. Dividend puzzle
    d. Dividend

2. The _____, in Corporate finance, is a decision made by the directors of a company. It relates to the amount and timing of any cash payments made to the company's stockholders. The decision is an important one for the firm as it may influence its capital structure and stock price.

    a. Dividend puzzle
    b. Dividend yield
    c. Dividend decision
    d. Dividend payout ratio

3. _____ is an estimate of the fair value of corporations and their stocks, by using fundamental economic criteria. This theoretical valuation has to be perfected with market criteria, as the final purpose is to determine potential market prices.

    a. Growth stocks
    b. 4-4-5 Calendar
    c. Stock valuation
    d. Security Analysis

4. In finance, _____ is the process of estimating the potential market value of a financial asset or liability. they can be done on assets (for example, investments in marketable securities such as stocks, options, business enterprises, or intangible assets such as patents and trademarks) or on liabilities (e.g., Bonds issued by a company.) _____s are required in many contexts including investment analysis, capital budgeting, merger and acquisition transactions, financial reporting, taxable events to determine the proper tax liability, and in litigation.

    a. Margin
    b. Procter ' Gamble
    c. Share
    d. Valuation

5. _____, is when a company issues common stock or shares to the public for the first time. They are often issued by smaller, younger companies seeking capital to expand, but can also be done by large privately-owned companies looking to become publicly traded.

    In an _____ the issuer may obtain the assistance of an underwriting firm, which helps it determine what type of security to issue (common or preferred), best offering price and time to bring it to market.

    a. Insolvency
    b. Interest
    c. Initial public offering
    d. Asian Financial Crisis

6. _____ or net present worth (NPW) is defined as the total present value (PV) of a time series of cash flows. It is a standard method for using the time value of money to appraise long-term projects. Used for capital budgeting, and widely throughout economics, it measures the excess or shortfall of cash flows, in present value terms, once financing charges are met.

    a. Present value of costs
    b. Negative gearing
    c. Tax shield
    d. Net present value

Chapter 16. Dividends and Earnings

7. In economics, business, and accounting, a _____ is the value of money that has been used up to produce something, and hence is not available for use anymore. In business, the _____ may be one of acquisition, in which case the amount of money expended to acquire it is counted as _____. In this case, money is the input that is gone in order to acquire the thing.

   a. Marginal cost
   b. Cost
   c. Sliding scale fees
   d. Fixed costs

8. _____ is the value on a given date of a future payment or series of future payments, discounted to reflect the time value of money and other factors such as investment risk. _____ calculations are widely used in business and economics to provide a means to compare cash flows at different times on a meaningful 'like to like' basis.

The most commonly applied model of the time value of money is compound interest.

   a. Negative gearing
   b. Net present value
   c. Present value of benefits
   d. Present value

9. _____ is a form of corporation equity ownership represented in the securities. It is dangerous in comparison to preferred shares and some other investment options, in that in the event of bankruptcy, _____ investors receive their funds after preferred stockholders, bondholders, creditors, etc. On the other hand, common shares on average perform better than preferred shares or bonds over time.

   a. Common stock
   b. Stock market bubble
   c. Stock split
   d. Stop-limit order

10. In some countries, including the United States and the United Kingdom, corporations can buy back their own stock in a share repurchase, also known as a _____ or share buyback. There has been a meteoric rise in the use of share repurchases in the U.S. in the past twenty years, from $5b in 1980 to $349b in 2005. A share repurchase distributes cash to existing shareholders in exchange for a fraction of the firm's outstanding equity.

   a. Common stock
   b. Trading curb
   c. Stock repurchase
   d. Stockholder

11. A '_____' is a 'Charge' that is paid to obtain the right to delay a payment. Essentially, the payer purchases the right to make a given payment in the future instead of in the Present. The '_____', or 'Charge' that must be paid to delay the payment, is simply the difference between what the payment amount would be if it were paid in the present and what the payment amount would be paid if it were paid in the future.

   a. Risk aversion
   b. Risk modeling
   c. Discount
   d. Value at risk

12. _____ is the price at which an asset would trade in a competitive Walrasian auction setting. _____ is often used interchangeably with open _____, fair value or fair _____, although these terms have distinct definitions in different standards, and may differ in some circumstances.

International Valuation Standards defines _____ as 'the estimated amount for which a property should exchange on the date of valuation between a willing buyer and a willing seller in an arm'e;s-length transaction after proper marketing wherein the parties had each acted knowledgeably, prudently, and without compulsion.'

_____ is a concept distinct from market price, which is 'e;the price at which one can transact'e;, while _____ is 'e;the true underlying value'e; according to theoretical standards.

a. Wrap account
b. Market value
c. T-Model
d. Debt restructuring

13. _____ is the fraction of net income a firm pays to its stockholders in dividends:

The part of the earnings not paid to investors is left for investment to provide for future earnings growth. Investors seeking high current income and limited capital growth prefer companies with high _____. However investors seeking capital growth may prefer lower payout ratio because capital gains are taxed at a lower rate.

a. Dividend payout ratio
b. Dividend puzzle
c. Dividend imputation
d. Dividend yield

14. In economics and contract theory, _____ deals with the study of decisions in transactions where one party has more or better information than the other. This creates an imbalance of power in transactions which can sometimes cause the transactions to go awry. Examples of this problem are adverse selection and moral hazard.

a. ABN Amro
b. A Random Walk Down Wall Street
c. Information asymmetry
d. AAB

15. _____ are the earnings returned on the initial investment amount.

In the US, the Financial Accounting Standards Board (FASB) requires companies' income statements to report _____ for each of the major categories of the income statement: continuing operations, discontinued operations, extraordinary items, and net income.

The _____ formula does not include preferred dividends for categories outside of continued operations and net income.

a. Average accounting return
b. Inventory turnover
c. Earnings per share
d. Assets turnover

16. _____ measures the rate of return on the ownership interest (shareholders' equity) of the common stock owners. _____ is viewed as one of the most important financial ratios. It measures a firm's efficiency at generating profits from every dollar of shareholders' equity (also known as net assets or assets minus liabilities.)

a. Return of capital
b. Diluted Earnings Per Share
c. Return on sales
d. Return on equity

17. In business and finance, a _____ (also referred to as equity _____) of stock means a _____ of ownership in a corporation (company.) In the plural, stocks is often used as a synonym for _____s especially in the United States, but it is less commonly used that way outside of North America.

Chapter 16. Dividends and Earnings

In the United Kingdom, South Africa, and Australia, stock can also refer to completely different financial instruments such as government bonds or, less commonly, to all kinds of marketable securities.

a. Bucket shop
c. Procter ' Gamble
b. Share
d. Margin

18. _____ is the standard framework of guidelines for financial accounting used in the United States of America. It includes the standards, conventions, and rules accountants follow in recording and summarizing transactions, and in the preparation of financial statements. _____ are now issued by the Financial Accounting Standards Board (FASB).

a. Net income
c. Revenue
b. Depreciation
d. Generally accepted accounting principles

19. An _____ is a document a company presents at an annual general meeting for approval by its shareholders, or a charitable organization presents its trustees. The report is made up of reports, which may include the following:

- Chairman's report
- CEO's report
- Auditor's report on corporate governance
- Mission statement
- Corporate governance statement of compliance
- Statement of directors' responsibilities
- Invitation to the company's AGM

as well as financial statements including:

- Auditor's report on the financial statements
- Balance sheet
- Statement of retained earnings
- Income statement
- Cash flow statement
- Notes to the financial statements
- Accounting policies

Other information deemed relevant to stakeholders may be included, such as a report on operations for manufacturing firms. In the case of larger companies, it is usually a sleek, colorful, high gloss publication.

The details provided in the report are of use to investors to understand the company's financial position and future direction.

a. Accrued liabilities
c. Annual report
b. Amortization schedule
d. Outstanding balance

Chapter 16. Dividends and Earnings

20. Modern portfolio theory (MPT) proposes how rational investors will use diversification to optimize their portfolios, and how a risky asset should be priced. The basic concepts of the theory are Markowitz diversification, the _____, capital asset pricing model, the alpha and beta coefficients, the Capital Market Line and the Securities Market Line.

MPT models an asset's return as a random variable, and models a portfolio as a weighted combination of assets so that the return of a portfolio is the weighted combination of the assets' returns.

 a. Efficient frontier
 b. AAB
 c. A Random Walk Down Wall Street
 d. ABN Amro

21. A _____, is a mathematical formalization of a trajectory that consists of taking successive random steps. The results of _____ analysis have been applied to computer science, physics, ecology, economics and a number of other fields as a fundamental model for random processes in time. For example, the path traced by a molecule as it travels in a liquid or a gas, the search path of a foraging animal, the price of a fluctuating stock and the financial status of a gambler can all be modeled as _____s.
 a. 7-Eleven
 b. 4-4-5 Calendar
 c. 529 plan
 d. Random walk

22. The _____ is a random-based mobility model used in mobility management schemes for mobile communication systems. The mobility model is designed to describe the movement pattern of mobile users, and how their location, velocity and acceleration change over time. Mobility models are used for simulation purposes when new network protocols are evaluated.
 a. 529 plan
 b. 7-Eleven
 c. Random waypoint model
 d. 4-4-5 Calendar

23. The institution most often referenced by the word '_____' is a public or publicly traded _____, the shares of which are traded on a public stock exchange (e.g., the New York Stock Exchange or Nasdaq in the United States) where shares of stock of _____s are bought and sold by and to the general public. Most of the largest businesses in the world are publicly traded _____s. However, the majority of _____s are said to be closely held, privately held or close _____s, meaning that no ready market exists for the trading of shares.
 a. Protect
 b. Federal Home Loan Mortgage Corporation
 c. Depository Trust Company
 d. Corporation

24. In finance, an _____ is the difference between the expected return of a security and the actual return. _____s are sometimes triggered by 'events.' Events can include mergers, dividend announcements, company earning announcements, interest rate increases, lawsuits, etc. all which can contribute to an _____.
 a. ABN Amro
 b. AAB
 c. A Random Walk Down Wall Street
 d. Abnormal return

25. _____ refers to an assessment of the viability, stability and profitability of a business, sub-business or project.

It is performed by professionals who prepare reports using ratios that make use of information taken from financial statements and other reports. These reports are usually presented to top management as one of their bases in making business decisions.

a. Value investing
c. 529 plan

b. 4-4-5 Calendar
d. Financial analysis

Chapter 17. Investment Management

1. _____ is a form of corporation equity ownership represented in the securities. It is dangerous in comparison to preferred shares and some other investment options, in that in the event of bankruptcy, _____ investors receive their funds after preferred stockholders, bondholders, creditors, etc. On the other hand, common shares on average perform better than preferred shares or bonds over time.
   a. Stock split
   b. Stock market bubble
   c. Common stock
   d. Stop-limit order

2. _____ refers to an assessment of the viability, stability and profitability of a business, sub-business or project.

It is performed by professionals who prepare reports using ratios that make use of information taken from financial statements and other reports. These reports are usually presented to top management as one of their bases in making business decisions.

   a. 529 plan
   b. Value investing
   c. 4-4-5 Calendar
   d. Financial analysis

3. A _____ is a person who makes investment decisions using money other people have placed under his or her control. In other words, it is a financial career involved in investment management. They work with a team of analysts and researchers, and are ultimately responsible for establishing an investment strategy, selecting appropriate investments and allocating each investment properly for a fund- or asset-management vehicle.
   a. Purchasing manager
   b. Day trader
   c. Portfolio manager
   d. Financial analyst

4. In finance, a _____ is a debt security, in which the authorized issuer owes the holders a debt and, depending on the terms of the _____, is obliged to pay interest (the coupon) and/or to repay the principal at a later date, termed maturity.

Thus a _____ is a loan: the issuer is the borrower, the _____ holder is the lender, and the coupon is the interest. _____s provide the borrower with external funds to finance long-term investments, or, in the case of government _____s, to finance current expenditure.

   a. Puttable bond
   b. Catastrophe bonds
   c. Convertible bond
   d. Bond

5. A _____ is a fungible, negotiable instrument representing financial value. They are broadly categorized into debt securities (such as banknotes, bonds and debentures), and equity securities; e.g., common stocks. The company or other entity issuing the _____ is called the issuer.
   a. Tracking stock
   b. Book entry
   c. Securities lending
   d. Security

6. _____, authored by professors Benjamin Graham and David Dodd of Columbia Business School, laid the intellectual foundation for what would later be called value investing. The work was first published in 1934, following unprecedented losses on Wall Street. In summing up lessons learned, Graham and Dodd chided Wall Street for its myopic focus on a company's reported earnings per share, and were particularly harsh on the favored 'earnings trends.' They encouraged investors to take an entirely different approach by gauging the rough value of the operating business that lay behind the security.

Chapter 17. Investment Management

a. Growth stocks
b. Stock valuation
c. Security analysis
d. 4-4-5 Calendar

7. An _____ is any government regulation or law that encourages or discourages foreign investment in the local economy, e.g. currency exchange limits.

As globalization integrates the economies of neighboring and of trading states, they are typically forced to trade off such rules as part of a common tax, tariff and trade regime, e.g. as defined by a free trade pact. _____ favoring local investors over global ones is typically discouraged in such pacts, and the idea of a separate _____ rapidly becomes a fiction or fantasy, as real decisions reflect the real need for nations to compete for investment, even from their own local investors.

a. ABN Amro
b. Investment policy
c. A Random Walk Down Wall Street
d. AAB

8. The _____ is the guaranteed payoff at which a person is 'indifferent' between accepting the guaranteed payoff and a higher but uncertain payoff. (It is the amount of the higher payout minus the risk premium).

a. 529 plan
b. 7-Eleven
c. 4-4-5 Calendar
d. Certainty equivalent

9. _____ refers to a portfolio management strategy where the manager makes specific investments with the goal of outperforming an investment benchmark index. Investors or mutual funds that do not aspire to create a return in excess of a benchmark index will often invest in an index fund that replicates as closely as possible the investment weighting and returns of that index; this is called passive management. _____ is the opposite of passive management, because in passive management the manager does not seek to outperform the benchmark index.

a. A Random Walk Down Wall Street
b. AAB
c. ABN Amro
d. Active management

10. An _____ or index tracker is a collective investment scheme (usually a mutual fund or exchange-traded fund) that aims to replicate the movements of an index of a specific financial market regardless of market conditions.

Tracking can be achieved by trying to hold all of the securities in the index, in the same proportions as the index. Other methods include statistically sampling the market and holding 'representative' securities.

a. Investment company
b. AAB
c. Index fund
d. A Random Walk Down Wall Street

11. _____ is a financial strategy in which a fund manager makes as few portfolio decisions as possible, in order to minimize transaction costs, including the incidence of capital gains tax. One popular method is to mimic the performance of an externally specified index--called 'index funds'. The ethos of an index fund is aptly summed up in the injunction to an index fund manager: 'Don't just do something, sit there!'

_____ is most common on the equity market, where index funds track a stock market index, but it is becoming more common in other investment types, including bonds, commodities and hedge funds.

Chapter 17. Investment Management

a. Net asset value
b. Trust company
c. Savings and loan association
d. Passive management

12. In business and accounting, _____s are everything of value that is owned by a person or company. The balance sheet of a firm records the monetary value of the _____s owned by the firm. The two major _____ classes are tangible _____s and intangible _____s.
 a. Income
 b. Accounts payable
 c. EBITDA
 d. Asset

13. _____ is a term used to refer to how an investor distributes his or her investments among various classes of investment vehicles (e.g., stocks and bonds.)

A large part of financial planning is finding an _____ that is appropriate for a given person in terms of their appetite for and ability to shoulder risk. This can depend on various factors; see investor profile.

 a. Alternative investment
 b. Investing online
 c. Asset allocation
 d. Investment performance

14. In finance, _____ is that risk which is common to an entire market and not to any individual entity or component thereof. It should be distinguished from systemic risk which is the risk that the entire financial system will collapse as a result of some catastrophic event.

Risks can be reduced in four main ways: Avoidance, Reduction, Retention and Transfer.

 a. Primary market
 b. Conglomerate merger
 c. Capital surplus
 d. Systematic risk

15. _____ is the strategy of making buy or sell decisions of financial assets (often stocks) by attempting to predict future market price movements. The prediction may be based on an outlook of market or economic conditions resulting from technical or fundamental analysis. This is an investment strategy based on the outlook for an aggregate market, rather than for a particular financial asset.
 a. Market timing
 b. Divestment
 c. Portable alpha
 d. Late trading

16. _____ refers to different style characteristics of equities, bonds or financial derivatives within a given investment philosophy.

Theory would favor a combination of big capitalization, passive and value. Of course one could almost get that when investing in an important Index like S'P 500, Euro-Stoxx or the like.

 a. ABN Amro
 b. A Random Walk Down Wall Street
 c. AAB
 d. Investment style

Chapter 17. Investment Management

17. An _____ is a contract written by a seller that conveys to the buyer the right -- but not the obligation -- to buy (in the case of a call _____) or to sell (in the case of a put _____) a particular asset, such as a piece of property such as, among others, a futures contract. In return for granting the _____, the seller collects a payment (the premium) from the buyer.

For example, buying a call _____ provides the right to buy a specified quantity of a security at a set strike price at some time on or before expiration, while buying a put _____ provides the right to sell.

   a. Annuity
   c. Amortization
   b. AT'T Mobility LLC
   d. Option

18. A _____ is a payment made by a corporation to its shareholder members. When a corporation earns a profit or surplus, that money can be put to two uses: it can either be re-invested in the business (called retained earnings), or it can be paid to the shareholders as a _____. Many corporations retain a portion of their earnings and pay the remainder as a _____.

   a. Dividend yield
   c. Dividend puzzle
   b. Dividend
   d. Special dividend

19. _____ are organizations which pool large sums of money and invest those sums in companies. They include banks, insurance companies, retirement or pension funds, hedge funds and mutual funds. Their role in the economy is to act as highly specialized investors on behalf of others.

   a. AAB
   c. ABN Amro
   b. A Random Walk Down Wall Street
   d. Institutional investors

20. In economics and related disciplines, a _____ is a cost incurred in making an economic exchange. For example, most people, when buying or selling a stock, must pay a commission to their broker; that commission is a _____ of doing the stock deal. Or consider buying a banana from a store; to purchase the banana, your costs will be not only the price of the banana itself, but also the energy and effort it requires to find out which of the various banana products you prefer, where to get them and at what price, the cost of traveling from your house to the store and back, the time waiting in line, and the effort of the paying itself; the costs above and beyond the cost of the banana are the _____s.

   a. Transaction cost
   c. Variable costs
   b. Fixed costs
   d. Marginal cost

21. In economics, business, and accounting, a _____ is the value of money that has been used up to produce something, and hence is not available for use anymore. In business, the _____ may be one of acquisition, in which case the amount of money expended to acquire it is counted as _____. In this case, money is the input that is gone in order to acquire the thing.

   a. Cost
   c. Fixed costs
   b. Marginal cost
   d. Sliding scale fees

22. _____ is a term that refers both to:

- a formal discipline used to help appraise, or assess, the case for a project or proposal, which itself is a process known as project appraisal; and
- an informal approach to making decisions of any kind.

Chapter 17. Investment Management

Under both definitions the process involves, whether explicitly or implicitly, weighing the total expected costs against the total expected benefits of one or more actions in order to choose the best or most profitable option.

A hallmark of _____ is that all benefits and all costs are expressed in money terms, and are adjusted for the time value of money, so that all flows of benefits and flows of project costs over time (which tend to occur at different points in time) are expressed on a common basis in terms of their present value.

   a. 4-4-5 Calendar
   b. 7-Eleven
   c. Cost-benefit analysis
   d. 529 plan

23. _____ is a distortion of evidence or data that arises from the way that the data are collected. It is sometimes referred to as the selection effect. The term _____ most often refers to the distortion of a statistical analysis, due to the method of collecting samples.
   a. 7-Eleven
   b. Selection bias
   c. 529 plan
   d. 4-4-5 Calendar

24. An _____ is a swap where a set of future cash flows are exchanged between two counterparties. The two cash flows are usually referred to as 'legs'. One of these cash flow streams can be pegged to floating rate of interest or pay a fixed rate
   a. Interest rate derivative
   b. Interest rate swap
   c. Interest rate future
   d. Equity swap

25. In finance, a _____ is a derivative in which two counterparties agree to exchange one stream of cash flows against another stream. These streams are called the legs of the _____.

The cash flows are calculated over a notional principal amount, which is usually not exchanged between counterparties.

   a. Volatility swap
   b. Local volatility
   c. Volatility arbitrage
   d. Swap

26. _____ is a fee paid on borrowed assets. It is the price paid for the use of borrowed money , or, money earned by deposited funds . Assets that are sometimes lent with _____ include money, shares, consumer goods through hire purchase, major assets such as aircraft, and even entire factories in finance lease arrangements.
   a. AAB
   b. Insolvency
   c. A Random Walk Down Wall Street
   d. Interest

27. An _____ is the price a borrower pays for the use of money they do not own, and the return a lender receives for deferring the use of funds, by lending it to the borrower. _____s are normally expressed as a percentage rate over the period of one year.

_____s targets are also a vital tool of monetary policy and are used to control variables like investment, inflation, and unemployment.

a. AAB
b. A Random Walk Down Wall Street
c. Interest rate
d. ABN Amro

28. An _____ is a derivative in which one party exchanges a stream of interest payments for another party's stream of cash flows. _____s can be used by hedgers to manage their fixed or floating assets and liabilities. They can also be used by speculators to replicate unfunded bond exposures to profit from changes in interest rates.

a. Equity swap
b. International Swaps and Derivatives Association
c. Implied volatility
d. Interest rate swap

29. The _____ is a daily reference rate based on the interest rates at which banks borrow unsecured funds from banks in the London wholesale money market (or interbank market.) It is roughly comparable to the U.S. Federal funds rate.

During 1984 it became apparent that an increasing number of banks were trading actively in a variety of relatively new market instruments, notably interest rate swaps, foreign currency options and forward rate agreements.

a. Risk-free interest rate
b. Shanghai Interbank Offered Rate
c. Fixed interest
d. London Interbank Offered Rate

Chapter 18. Portfolio Performance Evaluation

1. In finance, a _____ is a debt security, in which the authorized issuer owes the holders a debt and, depending on the terms of the _____, is obliged to pay interest (the coupon) and/or to repay the principal at a later date, termed maturity.

Thus a _____ is a loan: the issuer is the borrower, the _____ holder is the lender, and the coupon is the interest. _____s provide the borrower with external funds to finance long-term investments, or, in the case of government _____s, to finance current expenditure.

   a. Convertible bond
   c. Catastrophe bonds
   b. Bond
   d. Puttable bond

2. _____ is a form of corporation equity ownership represented in the securities. It is dangerous in comparison to preferred shares and some other investment options, in that in the event of bankruptcy, _____ investors receive their funds after preferred stockholders, bondholders, creditors, etc. On the other hand, common shares on average perform better than preferred shares or bonds over time.
   a. Stop-limit order
   c. Stock market bubble
   b. Common stock
   d. Stock split

3. _____ is a technique to adjust income payments by means of a price index, in order to maintain the purchasing power of the public after inflation.

Applying a cost-of-living escalation COLA clause to a stream of periodic payments protects the real value of those payments and effectively transfers the risk of inflation from the payee to the payor, who must pay more each year to reflect the increases in prices. Thus, inflation _____ is often applied to pension payments, rents and other situations which are not subject to regular re-pricing in the market.

   a. A Random Walk Down Wall Street
   c. AAB
   b. ABN Amro
   d. Indexation

4. A _____ is a firm that quotes both a buy and a sell price in a financial instrument or commodity, hoping to make a profit on the bid/offer spread, or turn.

In foreign exchange trading, where most deals are conducted over-the-counter and are, therefore, completely virtual, the _____ sells to and buys from its clients. Hence, the client's loss and the spread is the _____ firm's profit, which gets thus compensated for the effort of providing liquidity in a competitive market.

   a. 529 plan
   c. 4-4-5 Calendar
   b. 7-Eleven
   d. Market maker

5. A _____ or stock divide increases or decreases the number of shares in a public company. The price is adjusted such that the before and after market capitalization of the company remains the same and dilution does not occur. Options and warrants are included.
   a. Stop order
   c. Contract for difference
   b. Stock split
   d. Stop price

Chapter 18. Portfolio Performance Evaluation

6. The _____ is one of several stock market indices, created by nineteenth-century Wall Street Journal editor and Dow Jones ' Company co-founder Charles Dow. Dow compiled the index to gauge the performance of the industrial sector of the American stock market. It is the second-oldest U.S. market index, after the Dow Jones Transportation Average, which Dow also created.
   a. 529 plan
   b. 7-Eleven
   c. Dow Jones Industrial Average
   d. 4-4-5 Calendar

7. In the United States, the Financial Industry Regulatory Authority (FINRA) is a self-regulatory organization (SRO) under the Securities Exchange Act of 1934, successor to the _____, Inc.

FINRA is responsible for regulatory oversight of all securities firms that do business with the public; professional training, testing and licensing of registered persons; arbitration and mediation; market regulation by contract for The NASDAQ Stock Market, Inc., the American Stock Exchange LLC, and the International Securities Exchange, LLC; and industry utilities, such as Trade Reporting Facilities and other over-the-counter operations.

   a. 529 plan
   b. National Association of Securities Dealers
   c. 4-4-5 Calendar
   d. 7-Eleven

8. A _____ is a normalized average (typically a weighted average) of prices for a given class of goods or services in a given region, during a given interval of time. It is a statistic designed to help to compare how these prices, taken as a whole, differ between time periods or geographical locations.
   a. Price discrimination
   b. Transfer pricing
   c. Discounts and allowances
   d. Price Index

9. A _____ is a fungible, negotiable instrument representing financial value. They are broadly categorized into debt securities (such as banknotes, bonds and debentures), and equity securities; e.g., common stocks. The company or other entity issuing the _____ is called the issuer.
   a. Book entry
   b. Tracking stock
   c. Securities lending
   d. Security

10. A _____, securities exchange or (in Europe) bourse is a corporation or mutual organization which provides 'trading' facilities for stock brokers and traders, to trade stocks and other securities. _____s also provide facilities for the issue and redemption of securities as well as other financial instruments and capital events including the payment of income and dividends. The securities traded on a _____ include: shares issued by companies, unit trusts and other pooled investment products and bonds.
   a. 4-4-5 Calendar
   b. 529 plan
   c. Stock Exchange
   d. 7-Eleven

11. A _____ is the price of a single share of a no. of saleable stocks of the company. Once the stock is purchased, the owner becomes a shareholder of the company that issued the share.
   a. Whisper numbers
   b. Trading curb
   c. Share price
   d. Stock split

Chapter 18. Portfolio Performance Evaluation

12. The _____, in mathematics, is a type of mean or average, which indicates the central tendency or typical value of a set of numbers. It is similar to the arithmetic mean, which is what most people think of with the word 'average,' except that instead of adding the set of numbers and then dividing the sum by the count of numbers in the set, n, the numbers are multiplied and then the nth root of the resulting product is taken.

For instance, the _____ of two numbers, say 2 and 8, is just the square root (i.e., the second root) of their product, 16, which is 4.

a. Standard deviation
b. Geometric mean
c. Kurtosis
d. Statistics

13. In statistics, _____ has two related meanings:

- the arithmetic _____
- the expected value of a random variable, which is also called the population _____.

It is sometimes stated that the '_____' is average. This is incorrect if '_____' is taken in the specific sense of 'arithmetic _____' as there are different types of averages: the _____, median, and mode. Other simple statistical analyses use measures of spread, such as range, interquartile range, or standard deviation. For a real-valued random variable X, the _____ is the expectation of X. Note that not every probability distribution has a defined _____; see the Cauchy distribution for an example.

a. Harmonic mean
b. Probability distribution
c. Sample size
d. Mean

14. _____ is a risk-adjusted measure of the so-called active return on an investment. It is the return in excess of the compensation for the risk borne, and thus commonly used to assess active managers' performances. Often, the return of a benchmark is subtracted in order to consider relative performance, which yields Jensen's _____.

a. Alpha
b. Amortization
c. Option
d. Annuity

15. In Modern Portfolio Theory, the _____ is the graphical representation of the Capital Asset Pricing Model. It displays the expected rate of return for an overall market as a function of systematic (non-diversifiable) risk (beta.)

The Y-Intercept (beta=0) of the _____ is equal to the risk-free interest rate.

a. Rebalancing
b. Certificate in Investment Performance Measurement
c. Divestment
d. Security market line

16. In statistics, the _____, R^2 is used in the context of statistical models whose main purpose is the prediction of future outcomes on the basis of other related information. It is the proportion of variability in a data set that is accounted for by the statistical model. It provides a measure of how well future outcomes are likely to be predicted by the model.

a. 7-Eleven
b. 529 plan
c. Coefficient of determination
d. 4-4-5 Calendar

17. In probability theory and statistics, _____ indicates the strength and direction of a linear relationship between two random variables. That is in contrast with the usage of the term in colloquial speech, which denotes any relationship, not necessarily linear. In general statistical usage, _____ or co-relation refers to the departure of two random variables from independence.

    a. Geometric mean   b. Probability distribution
    c. Variance   d. Correlation

18. The _____ is a measure of the excess return (or Risk Premium) per unit of risk in an investment asset or a trading strategy it is defined as:

$$S = \frac{R - R_f}{\sigma} = \frac{E[R - R_f]}{\sqrt{\text{var}[R - R_f]}},$$

where R is the asset return, R_f is the return on a benchmark asset, such as the risk free rate of return, $E[R - R_f]$ is the expected value of the excess of the asset return over the benchmark return, and σ is the standard deviation of the asset excess return.

Note, if R_f is a constant risk free return throughout the period,

$$\sqrt{\text{var}[R - R_f]} = \sqrt{\text{var}[R]}.$$

The _____ is used to characterize how well the return of an asset compensates the investor for the risk taken. When comparing two assets each with the expected return E[R] against the same benchmark with return R_f, the asset with the higher _____ gives more return for the same risk.

    a. Current ratio   b. P/E ratio
    c. Receivables turnover ratio   d. Sharpe ratio

19. _____ is the risk that the value of an investment will decrease due to moves in market factors. The five standard _____ factors are:

- Equity risk, the risk that stock prices will change.
- Interest rate risk, the risk that interest rates will change.
- Currency risk, the risk that foreign exchange rates will change.
- Commodity risk, the risk that commodity prices (e.g. grains, metals) will change.

As with other forms of risk, _____ may be measured in a number of ways. Traditionally, this is done using a Value at Risk methodology. Value at risk is well established as a risk management technique, but it contains a number of limiting assumptions that constrain its accuracy.

    a. Tracking error   b. Currency risk
    c. Transaction risk   d. Market risk

20. _____ is the strategy of making buy or sell decisions of financial assets (often stocks) by attempting to predict future market price movements. The prediction may be based on an outlook of market or economic conditions resulting from technical or fundamental analysis. This is an investment strategy based on the outlook for an aggregate market, rather than for a particular financial asset.
   a. Late trading
   b. Divestment
   c. Portable alpha
   d. Market timing

21. A _____ is a person who makes investment decisions using money other people have placed under his or her control. In other words, it is a financial career involved in investment management. They work with a team of analysts and researchers, and are ultimately responsible for establishing an investment strategy, selecting appropriate investments and allocating each investment properly for a fund- or asset-management vehicle.
   a. Portfolio manager
   b. Purchasing manager
   c. Financial analyst
   d. Day trader

22. _____ is a fee paid on borrowed assets. It is the price paid for the use of borrowed money, or, money earned by deposited funds. Assets that are sometimes lent with _____ include money, shares, consumer goods through hire purchase, major assets such as aircraft, and even entire factories in finance lease arrangements.
   a. A Random Walk Down Wall Street
   b. Insolvency
   c. AAB
   d. Interest

23. An _____ is the price a borrower pays for the use of money they do not own, and the return a lender receives for deferring the use of funds, by lending it to the borrower. _____s are normally expressed as a percentage rate over the period of one year.

   _____s targets are also a vital tool of monetary policy and are used to control variables like investment, inflation, and unemployment.

   a. Interest rate
   b. ABN Amro
   c. A Random Walk Down Wall Street
   d. AAB

24. In economics and finance, _____ is the practice of taking advantage of a price differential between two or more markets: striking a combination of matching deals that capitalize upon the imbalance, the profit being the difference between the market prices. When used by academics, an _____ is a transaction that involves no negative cash flow at any probabilistic or temporal state and a positive cash flow in at least one state; in simple terms, a risk-free profit.
   a. Issuer
   b. Initial margin
   c. Efficient-market hypothesis
   d. Arbitrage

25. _____, in finance, is a general theory of asset pricing, that has become influential in the pricing of stocks.

   _____ holds that the expected return of a financial asset can be modeled as a linear function of various macro-economic factors or theoretical market indices, where sensitivity to changes in each factor is represented by a factor-specific beta coefficient. The model-derived rate of return will then be used to price the asset correctly - the asset price should equal the expected end of period price discounted at the rate implied by model.

a. A Random Walk Down Wall Street
b. ABN Amro
c. AAB
d. Arbitrage pricing theory

26. In business and accounting, _____s are everything of value that is owned by a person or company. The balance sheet of a firm records the monetary value of the _____s owned by the firm. The two major _____ classes are tangible _____s and intangible _____s.
   a. Accounts payable
   b. Asset
   c. Income
   d. EBITDA

27. In finance, _____ is the process of estimating the potential market value of a financial asset or liability. they can be done on assets (for example, investments in marketable securities such as stocks, options, business enterprises, or intangible assets such as patents and trademarks) or on liabilities (e.g., Bonds issued by a company.) _____s are required in many contexts including investment analysis, capital budgeting, merger and acquisition transactions, financial reporting, taxable events to determine the proper tax liability, and in litigation.
   a. Share
   b. Procter ' Gamble
   c. Margin
   d. Valuation

28. The term _____ has three unrelated technical definitions, and is also used in a variety of non-technical ways.

   - In financial economics, it refers to any asset used to make money, as opposed to assets used for personal enjoyment or consumption. This is an important distinction because two people can disagree sharply about the value of personal assets, one person might think a sports car is more valuable than a pickup truck, another person might have the opposite taste. But if an asset is held for the purpose of making money, taste has nothing to do with it, only differences of opinion about how much money the asset will produce. With the further assumption that people agree on the probability distribution of future cash flows, it is possible to have an objective _____ pricing model. Even without the assumption of agreement, it is possible to set rational limits on _____ value.
   - In governmental accounting, it is defined as any asset used in operations with an initial useful life extending beyond one reporting period. Generally, government managers have a 'stewardship' duty to maintain _____s under their control. See International Public Sector Accounting Standards for details.
   - In US tax accounting, it is defined as any property other than a list of exceptions. The main exceptions are anything held for sale, and any real estate or depreciable property used in business. Almost everything you own and use for personal purposes, pleasure or investment is a _____. If something is a _____ for tax purposes, gains or losses on sale or disposition are capital gains or capital losses. For individuals, however, capital losses on property held for personal use are generally not deductible. See the IRS publication Tax Facts about Capital Gains and Losses for details.

A well-known financial accounting textbook advises that the term be avoided except in tax accounting because it is used in so many different senses, not all of them well-defined. For example it is often used as a synonym for fixed assets or for investments in securities.

A common non-technical usage occurs when people ask that employees or the environment or something else be treated as a _____.

   a. Political risk
   b. Solvency
   c. Settlement date
   d. Capital Asset

29. In finance, the _____ is used to determine a theoretically appropriate required rate of return of an asset, if that asset is to be added to an already well-diversified portfolio, given that asset's non-diversifiable risk. The model takes into account the asset's sensitivity to non-diversifiable risk (also known as systemic risk or market risk), often represented by the quantity beta (β) in the financial industry, as well as the expected return of the market and the expected return of a theoretical risk-free asset.

The model was introduced by Jack Treynor (1961, 1962), William Sharpe (1964), John Lintner (1965a,b) and Jan Mossin (1966) independently, building on the earlier work of Harry Markowitz on diversification and modern portfolio theory.

a. Cox-Ingersoll-Ross model
b. Random walk hypothesis
c. Hull-White model
d. Capital Asset Pricing Model

Chapter 19. Types of Fixed-Income Securities

1. The coupon or _____ of a bond is the amount of interest paid per year expressed as a percentage of the face value of the bond.

For example if you hold $10,000 nominal of a bond described as a 4.5% loan stock, you will receive $450 in interest each year (probably in two installments of $225 each.)

Not all bonds have coupons.

   a. Revenue bonds
   b. Puttable bond
   c. Zero-coupon bond
   d. Coupon rate

2. A _____ is an international bond that is denominated in a currency not native to the country where it is issued. It can be categorised according to the currency in which it is issued. London is one of the centers of the _____ market, but _____s may be traded throughout the world - for example in Singapore or Tokyo.

   a. Education production function
   b. Eurobond
   c. Interest rate option
   d. Economic entity

3. _____ refers to any type of investment that yields a regular (or fixed) return.

For example, if you lend money to a borrower and the borrower has to pay interest once a month, you have been issued a fixed-income security. When a company does this, it is often called a bond or corporate bank debt (although preferred stock is also sometimes considered to be _____).

   a. 529 plan
   b. 4-4-5 Calendar
   c. Bond market
   d. Fixed income

4. _____ is a life of security. It may also refer to the final payment date of a loan or other financial instrument, at which point all remaining interest and principal is due to be paid.

1, 3, 6 months _____ band can be calculated by using 30-day per month periods.

   a. Replacement cost
   b. Primary market
   c. Maturity
   d. False billing

5. A '_____' is a 'Charge' that is paid to obtain the right to delay a payment. Essentially, the payer purchases the right to make a given payment in the future instead of in the Present. The '_____', or 'Charge' that must be paid to delay the payment, is simply the difference between what the payment amount would be if it were paid in the present and what the payment amount would be paid if it were paid in the future.

   a. Risk modeling
   b. Risk aversion
   c. Value at risk
   d. Discount

6. In finance, the _____ is the global financial market for short-term borrowing and lending. It provides short-term liquidity funding for the global financial system. The _____ is where short-term obligations such as Treasury bills, commercial paper and bankers' acceptances are bought and sold.

   a. Consumer debt
   b. Cramdown
   c. Debt-for-equity swap
   d. Money market

Chapter 19. Types of Fixed-Income Securities

7. A _____ is a fungible, negotiable instrument representing financial value. They are broadly categorized into debt securities (such as banknotes, bonds and debentures), and equity securities; e.g., common stocks. The company or other entity issuing the _____ is called the issuer.
   - a. Tracking stock
   - b. Securities lending
   - c. Book entry
   - d. Security

8. In the global money market, _____ is an unsecured promissory note with a fixed maturity of one to 270 days. _____ is a money-market security issued (sold) by large banks and corporations to get money to meet short term debt obligations (for example, payroll), and is only backed by an issuing bank or corporation's promise to pay the face amount on the maturity date specified on the note. Since it is not backed by collateral, only firms with excellent credit ratings from a recognized rating agency will be able to sell their _____ at a reasonable price.
   - a. Book building
   - b. Commercial paper
   - c. Trade-off theory
   - d. Financial distress

9. A _____ or bank is a financial institution whose primary activity is to act as a payment agent for customers and to borrow and lend money.

   The first modern bank was founded in Italy in Genoa in 1406, its name was Banco di San Giorgio (Bank of St. George.)

   Many other financial activities were added over time.

   - a. Black Sea Trade and Development Bank
   - b. Bought deal
   - c. 4-4-5 Calendar
   - d. Banker

10. A _____ s a time deposit, a financial product commonly offered to consumers by banks, thrift institutions, and credit unions.

    They are similar to savings accounts in that they are insured and thus virtually risk-free; they are 'money in the bank'. They are different from savings accounts in that they have a specific, fixed term (often three months, six months, or one to five years), and, usually, a fixed interest rate.

    - a. Time deposit
    - b. Reserve requirement
    - c. Variable rate mortgage
    - d. Certificate of deposit

11. _____s are deposits denominated in United States dollars at banks outside the United States, and thus are not under the jurisdiction of the Federal Reserve. Consequently, such deposits are subject to much less regulation than similar deposits within the United States, allowing for higher margins. There is nothing 'European' about _____ deposits; a US dollar-denominated deposit in Tokyo or Caracas would likewise be deemed _____ deposits.
    - a. AAB
    - b. A Random Walk Down Wall Street
    - c. ABN Amro
    - d. Eurodollar

12. _____ is the term used to describe deposits residing in banks that are located outside the borders of the country that issues the currency the deposit is denominated in. For example a deposit denominated in US dollars residing in a Japanese bank is a _____ deposit, or more specifically a Eurodollar deposit.

Chapter 19. Types of Fixed-Income Securities

Key points are the location of the bank and the denomination of the currency, not the nationality of the bank or the owner of the deposit/loan.

a. ABN Amro
b. Eurocurrency
c. A Random Walk Down Wall Street
d. AAB

13. _____ is that which is owed; usually referencing assets owed, but the term can cover other obligations. In the case of assets, _____ is a means of using future purchasing power in the present before a summation has been earned. Some companies and corporations use _____ as a part of their overall corporate finance strategy.
a. Partial Payment
b. Credit cycle
c. Cross-collateralization
d. Debt

14. The official bank rate has existing in various forms since 1694 and has ranged from 0.5% to 17%. The name of this key interest rate has changed over the years. The current name 'Official Bank Rate' was introduced in 2006 and replaced the previous title '_____' (repo is short for repurchase agreement) in 1997.
a. London Interbank Offered Rate
b. London Interbank Bid Rate
c. Cash accumulation equation
d. Repo rate

15. A _____ allows a borrower to use a financial security as collateral for a cash loan at a fixed rate of interest. In a repo, the borrower agrees to immediately sell a security to a lender and also agrees to buy the same security from the lender at a fixed price at some later date. A repo is equivalent to a cash transaction combined with a forward contract.
a. Contango
b. Volatility arbitrage
c. Total return swap
d. Repurchase agreement

16. _____ occurs when an entity that has issued callable bonds calls those debt securities from the debt holders with the express purpose of reissuing new debt at a lower coupon rate. In essence, the issue of new, lower-interest debt allows the company to prematurely refund the older, higher-interest debt.

On the contrary, NonRefundable Bonds may be callable but they cannot be re-issued with a lower coupon rate.

a. No-arbitrage bounds
b. Market neutral
c. Systematic risk
d. Refunding

17. _____ mature in one year or less. Like zero-coupon bonds, they do not pay interest prior to maturity; instead they are sold at a discount of the par value to create a positive yield to maturity. Many regard _____ as the least risky investment available to U.S. investors.
a. Treasury Inflation Protected Securities
b. Treasury securities
c. 4-4-5 Calendar
d. Treasury bills

18. In finance, the term _____ describes the amount in cash that returns to the owners of a security. Normally it does not include the price variations, at the difference of the total return. _____ applies to various stated rates of return on stocks (common and preferred, and convertible), fixed income instruments (bonds, notes, bills, strips, zero coupon), and some other investment type insurance products (e.g. annuities).

Chapter 19. Types of Fixed-Income Securities

a. Yield to maturity
b. 4-4-5 Calendar
c. Yield
d. Macaulay duration

19. In finance, _____ is the interest that has accumulated since the principal investment, or since the previous interest payment if there has been one already. For a financial instrument such as a bond, interest is calculated and paid in set intervals.

The primary formula for calculating the interest accrued in a given period is:

$$I_A = T \times P \times R$$

where I_A is the _____, T is the fraction of the year, P is the principal, and R is the annualized interest rate.

a. AAB
b. ABN Amro
c. A Random Walk Down Wall Street
d. Accrued interest

20. A _____ is a document that indicates that the bearer of the document has title to property, such as shares or bonds. They differ from normal registered instruments, in that no records are kept of who owns the underlying property, or of the transactions involving transfer of ownership. Whoever physically holds the bearer bond papers owns the property.

a. Securities lending
b. Marketable
c. Book entry
d. Bearer instrument

21. _____ are government bonds issued by the United States Department of the Treasury through the Bureau of the Public Debt. They are the debt financing instruments of the U.S. Federal government, and they are often referred to simply as Treasuries or Treasurys. There are four types of marketable _____: Treasury bills, Treasury notes, Treasury bonds, and Treasury Inflation Protected Securities (TIPS.)

a. Treasury securities
b. 4-4-5 Calendar
c. Treasury Inflation Protected Securities
d. Treasury Inflation-Protected Securities

22. _____ is a fee paid on borrowed assets. It is the price paid for the use of borrowed money, or, money earned by deposited funds. Assets that are sometimes lent with _____ include money, shares, consumer goods through hire purchase, major assets such as aircraft, and even entire factories in finance lease arrangements.

a. Interest
b. A Random Walk Down Wall Street
c. Insolvency
d. AAB

23. In economic models, the _____ time frame assumes no fixed factors of production. Firms can enter or leave the marketplace, and the cost (and availability) of land, labor, raw materials, and capital goods can be assumed to vary. In contrast, in the short-run time frame, certain factors are assumed to be fixed, because there is not sufficient time for them to change.

a. 4-4-5 Calendar
b. Short-run
c. Long-run
d. 529 plan

24. In finance, a _____ is a debt security, in which the authorized issuer owes the holders a debt and, depending on the terms of the _____, is obliged to pay interest (the coupon) and/or to repay the principal at a later date, termed maturity.

Chapter 19. Types of Fixed-Income Securities

Thus a _____ is a loan: the issuer is the borrower, the _____ holder is the lender, and the coupon is the interest. _____s provide the borrower with external funds to finance long-term investments, or, in the case of government _____s, to finance current expenditure.

a. Puttable bond
b. Convertible bond
c. Bond
d. Catastrophe bonds

25. A _____ is a bond issued by a corporation. The term is usually applied to longer-term debt instruments, generally with a maturity date falling at least a year after their issue date. (The term 'commercial paper' is sometimes used for instruments with a shorter maturity.)

a. Government bond
b. Corporate bond
c. Brady bonds
d. Serial bond

26. In financial accounting, _____s are precautions for which the amount or probability of occurrence are not known. Typical examples are _____s for warranty costs and _____ for taxes the term reserve is used instead of term _____; such a use, however, is inconsistent with the terminology suggested by International Accounting Standards Board.

a. Petty cash
b. Momentum Accounting and Triple-Entry Bookkeeping
c. Money measurement concept
d. Provision

27. A _____ is a bond bought at a price lower than its face value, with the face value repaid at the time of maturity. It does not make periodic interest payments, or have so-called 'coupons,' hence the term _____. Investors earn return from the compounded interest all paid at maturity plus the difference between the discounted price of the bond and its par value.

a. Zero-coupon bond
b. Bond fund
c. Corporate bond
d. Clean price

28. In finance, 'participation' is an ownership interest in a mortgage or other loan. In particular, _____ is a cooperation of multiple lenders to issue a loan (known as participation loan) to one borrower. This is usually done in order to reduce individual risks of the lenders.

a. Securitization
b. Short positions
c. Doctrine of the Proper Law
d. Loan participation

29. _____ is a structured finance process that involves pooling and repackaging of cash-flow-producing financial assets into securities, which are then sold to investors. The term '_____' is derived from the fact that the form of financial instruments used to obtain funds from the investors are securities. As a portfolio risk backed by amortizing cash flows - and unlike general corporate debt - the credit quality of securitized debt is non-stationary due to changes in volatility that are time- and structure-dependent.

a. Special journals
b. Reputational risk
c. The Glass-Steagall Act of 1933
d. Securitization

30. _____ is early repayment of a loan by a borrower.

Chapter 19. Types of Fixed-Income Securities

In the case of a mortgage-backed security (MBS), _____ is perceived as a risk, because mortgage debts are often paid off early in order to incur lower total interest payments through cheaper refinancing. The new financing may be cheaper because the borrower's credit rating has improved or because interest rates are lower, but in either case, the payments that would have been made to the MBS investor would be above market rates.

a. Retention ratio
b. Disposal tax effect
c. Bankruptcy remote
d. Prepayment

31. In lending agreements, _____ is a borrower's pledge of specific property to a lender, to secure repayment of a loan. The _____ serves as protection for a lender against a borrower's risk of default - that is, a borrower failing to pay the principal and interest under the terms of a loan obligation. If a borrower does default on a loan (due to insolvency or other event), that borrower forfeits (gives up) the property pledged as _____ ollateral - and the lender then becomes the owner of the _____.

a. Collateral
b. Nominal value
c. Future-oriented
d. Refinancing risk

32. In structured finance, a _____ is one of a number of related securities offered as part of the same transaction. The word _____ is French for slice, section, series, or portion. In the financial sense of the word, each bond is a different slice of the deal's risk.

a. Yield curve spread
b. Credit enhancement
c. Tranche
d. 4-4-5 Calendar

33. A _____ is a payment made by a corporation to its shareholder members. When a corporation earns a profit or surplus, that money can be put to two uses: it can either be re-invested in the business (called retained earnings), or it can be paid to the shareholders as a _____. Many corporations retain a portion of their earnings and pay the remainder as a _____.

a. Dividend puzzle
b. Dividend yield
c. Dividend
d. Special dividend

34. _____ are bonds that have a variable coupon, equal to a money market reference rate, like LIBOR or federal funds rate, plus a spread. The spread is a rate that remains constant. Almost all _____ have quarterly coupons, i.e. they pay out interest every three months, though counter examples do exist.

a. CVECAs
b. Loan participation
c. Floating rate notes
d. Gordon growth model

35. An _____ is a type of bond or other type of debt instrument used in finance whose coupon rate has an inverse relationship to short-term interest rates (or its reference rate.) With an _____, as interest rates rise the coupon rate falls. The basic structure is the same as an ordinary floating rate note except for the direction in which the coupon rate is adjusted.

a. ABN Amro
b. AAB
c. A Random Walk Down Wall Street
d. Inverse floater

Chapter 19. Types of Fixed-Income Securities

36. _____ is the process of decreasing an amount over a period of time. The word comes from Middle English amortisen to kill, alienate in mortmain, from Anglo-French amorteser, alteration of amortir, from Vulgar Latin admortire to kill, from Latin ad- + mort-, mors death. Particular instances of the term include:

- _____ (business), the allocation of a lump sum amount to different time periods, particularly for loans and other forms of finance, including related interest or other finance charges.
  - _____ schedule, a table detailing each periodic payment on a loan (typically a mortgage), as generated by an _____ calculator.
  - Negative _____, an _____ schedule where the loan amount actually increases through not paying the full interest
- Amortized analysis, analyzing the execution cost of algorithms over a sequence of operations.
- _____ of capital expenditures of certain assets under accounting rules, particularly intangible assets, in a manner analogous to depreciation.
- _____ (tax law)

_____ is also used in the context of zoning regulations and describes the time in which a property owner has to relocate when the property's use constitutes a preexisting nonconforming use under zoning regulations.

- Depreciation

a. Intrinsic value
b. Option
c. AT'T Inc.
d. Amortization

37. In the United States, a _____ is a bond issued by a city or other local government, or their agencies. Potential issuers of these bonds include cities, counties, redevelopment agencies, school districts, publicly owned airports and seaports, and any other governmental entity (or group of governments) below the state level. They may be general obligations of the issuer or secured by specified revenues.

a. Puttable bond
b. Premium bond
c. Municipal bond
d. Senior debt

38. A _____ is a legal pledge in United States municipal finance, in which an entity pledges its full faith and credit to repay its debt, typically a _____ bond.

a. General obligation
b. Covenant
c. Financial Institutions Reform Recovery and Enforcement Act
d. Letter of credit

39. In business, _____ is income that a company receives from its normal business activities, usually from the sale of goods and services to customers. Some companies also receive _____ from interest, dividends or royalties paid to them by other companies. _____ may refer to business income in general, or it may refer to the amount, in a monetary unit, received during a period of time, as in 'Last year, Company X had _____ of $32 million.'

In many countries, including the UK, _____ is referred to as turnover.

Chapter 19. Types of Fixed-Income Securities 115

a. Furniture, Fixtures and Equipment
b. Bottom line
c. Revenue
d. Matching principle

40. _____ are bonds issued by governments, authorities, or public benefit corporations that are guaranteed by the revenue flow of the issuing agency.

The Supreme Court decision of Pollock versus Farmer's Loan and Trust Company of 1895 initiated a wave or series of innovations for the financial services community in both tax-treatment and regulation from government. This specific case, according to a leading investment bank's research, resulted in the 'intergovernmental tax immunity doctrine,' ultimately leading to 'tax-free status.' Municipal bonds are generally exempt from federal tax on their interest payments (not capital gains.)

a. Private activity bond
b. Gilts
c. Callable bond
d. Revenue bonds

41. In economics, the concept of the _____ refers to the decision-making time frame of a firm in which at least one factor of production is fixed. Costs which are fixed in the _____ have no impact on a firms decisions. For example a firm can raise output by increasing the amount of labour through overtime.

a. 4-4-5 Calendar
b. Long-run
c. 529 plan
d. Short-run

42. A _____ is a bond bought at a price lower than its face value, with the face value repaid at the time of maturity. It does not make periodic interest payments, or so-called 'coupons,' hence the term zero-coupon bond. Investors earn return from the compounded interest all paid at maturity plus the difference between the discounted price of the bond and its par value.

a. Callable bond
b. Bowie bonds
c. Municipal bond
d. Zero coupon bond

43. The institution most often referenced by the word '_____' is a public or publicly traded _____, the shares of which are traded on a public stock exchange (e.g., the New York Stock Exchange or Nasdaq in the United States) where shares of stock of _____s are bought and sold by and to the general public. Most of the largest businesses in the world are publicly traded _____s. However, the majority of _____s are said to be closely held, privately held or close _____s, meaning that no ready market exists for the trading of shares.

a. Protect
b. Corporation
c. Depository Trust Company
d. Federal Home Loan Mortgage Corporation

44. _____s are financial bonds that mature in installments over a period of time. In effect, a $100,000, 5-year _____ would mature in a $20,000 annuity over a 5-year interval. Bond issues consisting of a series of blocks of securities maturing in sequence, the coupon rate can be different.

a. Bond fund
b. Callable bond
c. Brady bonds
d. Serial bond

45. A _____ is a fund established by a government agency or business for the purpose of reducing debt.

The _____ was first used in Great Britain in the 18th century to reduce national debt. While used by Robert Walpole in 1716 and effectively in the 1720s and early 1730s, it originated in the commercial tax syndicates of the Italian peninsula of the 14th century to retire redeemable public debt of those cities.

   a. Modern portfolio theory
   c. Debtor
   b. Security interest
   d. Sinking fund

46. A _____ is defined as a certificate of agreement of loans which is given under the company's stamp and carries an undertaking that the _____ holder will get a fixed return (fixed on the basis of interest rates) and the principal amount whenever the _____ matures.

In finance, a _____ is a long-term debt instrument used by governments and large companies to obtain funds. It is defined as 'a debt secured only by the debtor's earning power, not by a lien on any specific asset.' It is similar to a bond except the securitization conditions are different.

   a. Collection agency
   c. Partial Payment
   b. Collateral Management
   d. Debenture

47. An _____ is a security whose value and income payments are derived from and collateralized (or 'backed') by a specified pool of underlying assets. The pool of assets is typically a group of small and illiquid assets that are unable to be sold individually. Pooling the assets allows them to be sold to general investors, a process called securitization, and allows the risk of investing in the underlying assets to be diversified because each security will represent a fraction of the total value of the diverse pool of underlying assets.
   a. Asset-backed security
   c. ABN Amro
   b. A Random Walk Down Wall Street
   d. AAB

48. An _____ can be defined as a contract which provides an income stream in return for an initial payment.

An immediate _____ is an _____ for which the time between the contract date and the date of the first payment is not longer than the time interval between payments. A common use for an immediate _____ is to provide a pension to a retired person or persons.

   a. AT'T Inc.
   c. Intrinsic value
   b. Amortization
   d. Annuity

49. _____ is a combination of straight bond and embedded put option. The holder of the _____ has the right, but not the obligation, to demand early repayment of the principal. The put option is usually exercisable on specified dates.
   a. Brady bonds
   c. Convertible bond
   b. Callable bond
   d. Puttable bond

50. _____ is a legally declared inability or impairment of ability of an individual or organization to pay their creditors. Creditors may file a _____ petition against a debtor ('involuntary _____') in an effort to recoup a portion of what they are owed or initiate a restructuring. In the majority of cases, however, _____ is initiated by the debtor (a 'voluntary _____' that is filed by the bankrupt individual or organization.)

Chapter 19. Types of Fixed-Income Securities 117

a. 4-4-5 Calendar
b. Debt settlement
c. 529 plan
d. Bankruptcy

51. _____ are organizations which pool large sums of money and invest those sums in companies. They include banks, insurance companies, retirement or pension funds, hedge funds and mutual funds. Their role in the economy is to act as highly specialized investors on behalf of others.
   a. AAB
   b. Institutional investors
   c. A Random Walk Down Wall Street
   d. ABN Amro

52. In law, _____ refers to the process by which a company (or part of a company) is brought to an end, and the assets and property of the company redistributed. _____ can also be referred to as winding-up or dissolution, although dissolution technically refers to the last stage of _____. The process of _____ also arises when customs, an authority or agency in a country responsible for collecting and safeguarding customs duties, determines the final computation or ascertainment of the duties or drawback accruing on an entry.
   a. 4-4-5 Calendar
   b. 529 plan
   c. Debt settlement
   d. Liquidation

53. In the United States, a _____ is an offering of securities that are not registered with the Securities and Exchange Commission (SEC.) Such offerings exploit an exemption offered by the Securities Act of 1933 that comes with several restrictions, including a prohibition against general solicitation. This exemption allows companies to avoid quarterly reporting requirements and many of the legal liabilities associated with the Sarbanes-Oxley Act.
   a. 4-4-5 Calendar
   b. 529 plan
   c. 7-Eleven
   d. Private placement

54. _____ is defined by The Wall Street Journal, as a form of barter that involves a company selling 'an unused asset to another company while at the same time agreeing to buy back the same or similar assets at about the same price.' Round trips are characteristic of the New Economy companies. They played a crucial part in temporarily inflating the market capitalization of energy traders such as Enron, CMS Energy, Reliant Energy, and Dynegy.

Other companies making unconventional _____ deals include AOL with Sun Microsystems and Global Crossing with Qwest Communications.

   a. Days Sales Outstanding
   b. Round-tripping
   c. Net pay
   d. Residual value

55. The U.S. _____ is an independent agency of the United States government which holds primary responsibility for enforcing the federal securities laws and regulating the securities industry, the nation's stock and options exchanges, and other electronic securities markets. The SEC was created by section 4 of the SEC of 1934 (now codified as 15 U.S.C. Â§ 78d and commonly referred to as the 1934 Act.)
   a. Securities and Exchange Commission
   b. 7-Eleven
   c. 4-4-5 Calendar
   d. 529 plan

56. A _____ or market-based mechanism is any of a wide variety of ways to match up buyers and sellers.

Chapter 19. Types of Fixed-Income Securities

An example of a _____ uses announced bid and ask prices. Generally speaking, when two parties wish to engage in a trade, the purchaser will announce a price he is willing to pay (the bid price) and seller will announce a price he is willing to accept (the ask price).

a. 529 plan
b. 7-Eleven
c. 4-4-5 Calendar
d. Price mechanism

57. The _____ for securities is the difference between the price quoted by a market maker for an immediate sale and an immediate purchase The size of the bid-offer spread in a given commodity is a measure of the liquidity of the market.

The trader initiating the transaction is said to demand liquidity, and the other party to the transaction supplies liquidity.

a. Capital outflow
b. Defined contribution plan
c. Trade-off
d. Bid/offer spread

58. In finance, _____ occurs when a debtor has not met its legal obligations according to the debt contract, e.g. it has not made a scheduled payment, or has violated a loan covenant (condition) of the debt contract. _____ may occur if the debtor is either unwilling or unable to pay their debt. This can occur with all debt obligations including bonds, mortgages, loans, and promissory notes.

a. Vendor finance
b. Debt validation
c. Credit crunch
d. Default

59. _____ are securities of companies or government entities that are either already in default, under bankruptcy protection, or in distress and heading toward such a condition. The most common _____ are bonds and bank debt. While there is no precise definition, fixed income instruments with a yield to maturity in excess of 1000 basis points over the risk-free rate of return (e.g. Treasuries) are commonly thought of as being distressed.

a. 4-4-5 Calendar
b. 7-Eleven
c. Distressed securities
d. 529 plan

60. In economics and related disciplines, a _____ is a cost incurred in making an economic exchange. For example, most people, when buying or selling a stock, must pay a commission to their broker; that commission is a _____ of doing the stock deal. Or consider buying a banana from a store; to purchase the banana, your costs will be not only the price of the banana itself, but also the energy and effort it requires to find out which of the various banana products you prefer, where to get them and at what price, the cost of traveling from your house to the store and back, the time waiting in line, and the effort of the paying itself; the costs above and beyond the cost of the banana are the _____s.

a. Variable costs
b. Transaction cost
c. Marginal cost
d. Fixed costs

61. In economics, business, and accounting, a _____ is the value of money that has been used up to produce something, and hence is not available for use anymore. In business, the _____ may be one of acquisition, in which case the amount of money expended to acquire it is counted as _____. In this case, money is the input that is gone in order to acquire the thing.

Chapter 19. Types of Fixed-Income Securities 119

a. Sliding scale fees
b. Cost
c. Marginal cost
d. Fixed costs

62. The _____, interest yield, income yield, flat yield or running yield is a financial term used in reference to bonds and other fixed-interest securities such as gilts. It is the ratio of the annual interest payment and the bond's current price.

The _____ only therefore refers to the yield of the bond at the current moment. It does not reflect the total return over the life of the bond. In particular, it takes no account of reinvestment risk (the uncertainty about the rate at which future cashflows can be reinvested) or the fact that bonds usually mature at par value, which can be an important component of a bond's return.

a. Perpetuity
b. Modified Internal Rate of Return
c. Stochastic volatility
d. Current yield

63. _____, refers to consumption opportunity gained by an entity within a specified time frame, which is generally expressed in monetary terms. However, for households and individuals, '_____ is the sum of all the wages, salaries, profits, interests payments, rents and other forms of earnings received... in a given period of time.' For firms, _____ generally refers to net-profit: what remains of revenue after expenses have been subtracted.

a. Annual report
b. Income
c. OIBDA
d. Accrual

64. The _____ is an American stock exchange. It is the largest electronic screen-based equity securities trading market in the United States. With approximately 3,200 companies, it has more trading volume per day than any other stock exchange in the world.

a. 529 plan
b. 7-Eleven
c. 4-4-5 Calendar
d. Nasdaq

65. In finance, a _____ is a type of bond that can be converted into shares of stock in the issuing company, usually at some pre-announced ratio. It is a hybrid security with debt- and equity-like features. Although it typically has a low coupon rate, the holder is compensated with the ability to convert the bond to common stock, usually at a substantial discount to the stock's market value.

a. Corporate bond
b. Bond fund
c. Gilts
d. Convertible bond

66. In business and finance, a _____ (also referred to as equity _____) of stock means a _____ of ownership in a corporation (company.) In the plural, stocks is often used as a synonym for _____s especially in the United States, but it is less commonly used that way outside of North America.

In the United Kingdom, South Africa, and Australia, stock can also refer to completely different financial instruments such as government bonds or, less commonly, to all kinds of marketable securities.

a. Bucket shop
b. Share
c. Procter ' Gamble
d. Margin

Chapter 19. Types of Fixed-Income Securities

67. A _____ is a type of auction where the auctioneer begins with a high asking price which is lowered until some participant is willing to accept the auctioneer's price, or a predetermined reserve price (the seller's minimum acceptable price) is reached. The winning participant pays the last announced price. This is also known as a 'clock auction' or an open-outcry descending-price auction.

   a. Dutch auction   b. 7-Eleven
   c. 4-4-5 Calendar   d. 529 plan

68. _____ is capital stock which provides a specific dividend that is paid before any dividends are paid to common stock holders, and which takes precedence over common stock in the event of a liquidation. This form of financing is used by private equity investors and venture capital firms. Holders of _____ get both their money back (with interest) and the money that is distributable with respect to the percentage of common shares into which their preferred stock can convert.

   a. Cash is king   b. Shareholder value
   c. Participating preferred stock   d. Preferred stock

69. _____ is typically a higher ranking stock than voting shares, and its terms are negotiated between the corporation and the investor.

_____ usually carry no voting rights, but may carry superior priority over common stock in the payment of dividends and upon liquidation. _____ may carry a dividend that is paid out prior to any dividends to common stock holders.

   a. Second lien loan   b. Trade-off theory
   c. Follow-on offering   d. Preferred stock

Chapter 20. Fundamentals of Bond Valuation

1. In finance, a _____ is a debt security, in which the authorized issuer owes the holders a debt and, depending on the terms of the _____, is obliged to pay interest (the coupon) and/or to repay the principal at a later date, termed maturity.

Thus a _____ is a loan: the issuer is the borrower, the _____ holder is the lender, and the coupon is the interest. _____s provide the borrower with external funds to finance long-term investments, or, in the case of government _____s, to finance current expenditure.

   a. Convertible bond
   b. Catastrophe bonds
   c. Puttable bond
   d. Bond

2. _____ is the process of determining the fair price of a bond. As with any security or capital investment, the fair value of a bond is the present value of the stream of cash flows it is expected to generate. Hence, the price or value of a bond is determined by discounting the bond's expected cash flows to the present using the appropriate discount rate.
   a. Bond fund
   b. Collateralized debt obligations
   c. Catastrophe bonds
   d. Bond valuation

3. The _____ or redemption yield is the yield promised to the bondholder on the assumption that the bond or other fixed-interest security such as gilts will be held to maturity, that all coupon and principal payments will be made and coupon payments are reinvested at the bond's promised yield at the same rate as invested. It is a measure of the return of the bond. This technique in theory allows investors to calculate the fair value of different financial instruments.
   a. Macaulay duration
   b. 4-4-5 Calendar
   c. Yield
   d. Yield to maturity

4. A _____ is a bond bought at a price lower than its face value, with the face value repaid at the time of maturity. It does not make periodic interest payments, or have so-called 'coupons,' hence the term _____. Investors earn return from the compounded interest all paid at maturity plus the difference between the discounted price of the bond and its par value.
   a. Clean price
   b. Bond fund
   c. Corporate bond
   d. Zero-coupon bond

5. In finance, the _____ of a financial asset measures the sensitivity of the asset's price to interest rate movements, expressed as a number of years. The reason for expressing this sensitivity in years is that the time that will elapse until a cash flow is received allows more interest to accumulate. Therefore the price of an asset with long term cashflows has more interest rate sensitivity than an asset with cashflows in the near future.
   a. Macaulay duration
   b. 4-4-5 Calendar
   c. Yield to maturity
   d. Duration

6. In finance, _____ is the process of estimating the potential market value of a financial asset or liability. they can be done on assets (for example, investments in marketable securities such as stocks, options, business enterprises, or intangible assets such as patents and trademarks) or on liabilities (e.g., Bonds issued by a company.) _____s are required in many contexts including investment analysis, capital budgeting, merger and acquisition transactions, financial reporting, taxable events to determine the proper tax liability, and in litigation.
   a. Valuation
   b. Share
   c. Margin
   d. Procter ' Gamble

Chapter 20. Fundamentals of Bond Valuation

7. _____ is a fee paid on borrowed assets. It is the price paid for the use of borrowed money, or, money earned by deposited funds. Assets that are sometimes lent with _____ include money, shares, consumer goods through hire purchase, major assets such as aircraft, and even entire factories in finance lease arrangements.
   a. Insolvency
   b. A Random Walk Down Wall Street
   c. AAB
   d. Interest

8. A _____ is a fungible, negotiable instrument representing financial value. They are broadly categorized into debt securities (such as banknotes, bonds and debentures), and equity securities; e.g., common stocks. The company or other entity issuing the _____ is called the issuer.
   a. Securities lending
   b. Book entry
   c. Tracking stock
   d. Security

9. _____ are government bonds issued by the United States Department of the Treasury through the Bureau of the Public Debt. They are the debt financing instruments of the U.S. Federal government, and they are often referred to simply as Treasuries or Treasurys. There are four types of marketable _____: Treasury bills, Treasury notes, Treasury bonds, and Treasury Inflation Protected Securities (TIPS.)
   a. Treasury securities
   b. Treasury Inflation-Protected Securities
   c. Treasury Inflation Protected Securities
   d. 4-4-5 Calendar

10. An _____ is the price a borrower pays for the use of money they do not own, and the return a lender receives for deferring the use of funds, by lending it to the borrower. _____s are normally expressed as a percentage rate over the period of one year.

    _____s targets are also a vital tool of monetary policy and are used to control variables like investment, inflation, and unemployment.

    a. AAB
    b. ABN Amro
    c. Interest rate
    d. A Random Walk Down Wall Street

11. _____ is the risk (variability in value) borne by an interest-bearing asset, such as a loan or a bond, due to variability of interest rates. In general, as rates rise, the price of a fixed rate bond will fall, and vice versa. _____ is commonly measured by the bond's duration.
    a. A Random Walk Down Wall Street
    b. Official bank rate
    c. International Fisher effect
    d. Interest rate Risk

12. _____ is a system of tracking ownership of securities where no certificate is given to investors. In the case of _____ only issues, while investors do not receive certificates, a custodian holds one or more global certificates. Dematerialized securities, in contrast are ones in which no certificates exist (instead, the security issuer or its agent keeps records, usually electronically, of who holds outstanding securities.)
    a. Marketable
    b. Securities lending
    c. Book entry
    d. Tracking stock

13. _____ is a method for constructing a (zero-coupon) fixed-income yield curve from the prices of a set of coupon-bearing products by forward substitution.

Using these zero-coupon products it becomes possible to derive par swap rates (forward and spot) for all maturities by making a few assumptions (including linear interpolation.) The term structure of spot returns is recovered from the bond yields by solving for them recursively, this iterative process is called the BootStrap Method.

a. Reserve requirement
b. Bullet loan
c. Probability of default
d. Bootstrapping

14. The _____ of a commodity, a security or a currency is the price that is quoted for immediate (spot) settlement (payment and delivery.) Spot settlement is normally one or two business days from trade date. This is in contrast with the forward price established in a forward contract or futures contract, where contract terms (price) are set now, but delivery and payment will occur at a future date.

a. Long position
b. Spot rate
c. Limits to arbitrage
d. Market anomaly

15. In finance, the _____ approach describes a method of valuing a project, company, or asset using the concepts of the time value of money. All future cash flows are estimated and discounted to give their present values. The discount rate used is generally the appropriate cost of capital and may incorporate judgments of the uncertainty (riskiness) of the future cash flows.

a. Net present value
b. Present value of benefits
c. Future-oriented
d. Discounted cash flow

16. A '_____' is a 'Charge' that is paid to obtain the right to delay a payment. Essentially, the payer purchases the right to make a given payment in the future instead of in the Present. The '_____', or 'Charge' that must be paid to delay the payment, is simply the difference between what the payment amount would be if it were paid in the present and what the payment amount would be paid if it were paid in the future.

a. Risk modeling
b. Risk aversion
c. Value at risk
d. Discount

17. _____ is the balance of the amounts of cash being received and paid by a business during a defined period of time, sometimes tied to a specific project. Measurement of _____ can be used

- to evaluate the state or performance of a business or project.
- to determine problems with liquidity. Being profitable does not necessarily mean being liquid. A company can fail because of a shortage of cash, even while profitable.
- to generate project rate of returns. The time of _____s into and out of projects are used as inputs to financial models such as internal rate of return, and net present value.
- to examine income or growth of a business when it is believed that accrual accounting concepts do not represent economic realities. Alternately, _____ can be used to 'validate' the net income generated by accrual accounting.

_____ as a generic term may be used differently depending on context, and certain _____ definitions may be adapted by analysts and users for their own uses. Common terms include operating _____ and free _____.

124 *Chapter 20. Fundamentals of Bond Valuation*

_____s can be classified into:

1. Operational _____s: Cash received or expended as a result of the company's core business activities.
2. Investment _____s: Cash received or expended through capital expenditure, investments or acquisitions.
3. Financing _____s: Cash received or expended as a result of financial activities, such as interests and dividends.

All three together - the net _____ - are necessary to reconcile the beginning cash balance to the ending cash balance. Loan draw downs or equity injections, that is just shifting of capital but no expenditure as such, are not considered in the net _____.

a. Corporate finance
c. Shareholder value
b. Cash flow
d. Real option

18. The _____, P(T), is the number which a future cash flow, to be received at time T, must be multiplied by in order to obtain the current present value. Thus, a fixed annually compounded discount rate is

$$P(T) = \frac{1}{(1+r)^T}$$

For fixed continuously compounded discount rate we have

$$P(T) = e^{-rT}$$

For discounts in marketing, see discounts and allowances, sales promotion, and pricing.

a. Discount factor
c. Discount
b. Risk modeling
d. Risk premium

19. A _____ is used in economic models to describe the weights placed on rewards received at different points in time. For example, if time is discrete and utility is time-separable, with the _____

f(t)

total utility is given by

Chapter 20. Fundamentals of Bond Valuation

Total utility in the continuous-time case is given by

$$$$

provided that this integral exists.

a. 7-Eleven
b. 4-4-5 Calendar
c. Discount function
d. 529 plan

20. The _____ or forward rate is the agreed upon price of an asset in a forward contract. Using the rational pricing assumption, we can express the _____ in terms of the spot price and any dividends etc., so that there is no possibility for arbitrage.

The _____ is given by:

$$$$

where

F is the _____ to be paid at time T
e^x is the exponential function
r is the risk-free interest rate
q is the cost-of-carry
S_0 is the spot price of the asset (i.e. what it would sell for at time 0)
D_i is a dividend which is guaranteed to be paid at time t_i where $0 < t_i < T$.

The two questions here are what price the short position (the seller of the asset) should offer to maximize his gain, and what price the long position (the buyer of the asset) should accept to maximize his gain?

At the very least we know that both do not want to lose any money in the deal.

a. Financial Gerontology
b. Biweekly Mortgage
c. Security interest
d. Forward price

21. A _____ is an agreement between two parties to buy or sell an asset at a specified point of time in the future. The price of the underlying instrument, in whatever form, is paid before control of the instrument changes. This is one of the many forms of buy/sell orders where the time of trade is not the time where the securities themselves are exchanged.

a. Loan Credit Default Swap Index
b. Constant maturity credit default swap
c. Forward contract
d. Derivatives markets

Chapter 20. Fundamentals of Bond Valuation

22. A _____ is an exchange of promises between two or more parties to do an act which is enforceable in a court of law. It is where an unqualified offer meets a qualified acceptance and the parties reach Consensus ad Idem. The parties must have the necessary capacity to _____ and the _____ must not be either trifling, indeterminate, impossible or illegal.
    a. 7-Eleven
    b. 529 plan
    c. 4-4-5 Calendar
    d. Contract

23. _____ is the concept of adding accumulated interest back to the principal, so that interest is earned on interest from that moment on. The act of declaring interest to be principal is called compounding (i.e., interest is compounded.) A loan, for example, may have its interest compounded every month: in this case, a loan with $100 principal and 1% interest per month would have a balance of $101 at the end of the first month.
    a. 4-4-5 Calendar
    b. Risk management
    c. Penny stock
    d. Compound interest

24. In finance, the term _____ describes the amount in cash that returns to the owners of a security. Normally it does not include the price variations, at the difference of the total return. _____ applies to various stated rates of return on stocks (common and preferred, and convertible), fixed income instruments (bonds, notes, bills, strips, zero coupon), and some other investment type insurance products (e.g. annuities.)
    a. 4-4-5 Calendar
    b. Yield to maturity
    c. Macaulay duration
    d. Yield

25. In finance, the _____ is the relation between the interest rate (or cost of borrowing) and the time to maturity of the debt for a given borrower in a given currency. For example, the current U.S. dollar interest rates paid on U.S. Treasury securities for various maturities are closely watched by many traders, and are commonly plotted on a graph such as the one on the right which is informally called 'the _____.' More formal mathematical descriptions of this relation are often called the term structure of interest rates.

The yield of a debt instrument is the annualized percentage increase in the value of the investment.

    a. 7-Eleven
    b. 529 plan
    c. 4-4-5 Calendar
    d. Yield curve

26. In finance, the yield curve is the relation between the interest rate (or cost of borrowing) and the time to maturity of the debt for a given borrower in a given currency. For example, the current U.S. dollar interest rates paid on U.S. Treasury securities for various maturities are closely watched by many traders, and are commonly plotted on a graph such as the one on the right which is informally called 'the yield curve.' More formal mathematical descriptions of this relation are often called the _____.

The yield of a debt instrument is the annualized percentage increase in the value of the investment.

    a. 4-4-5 Calendar
    b. 7-Eleven
    c. 529 plan
    d. Term structure of Interest rates

Chapter 20. Fundamentals of Bond Valuation

27. In economics, _____ is a rise in the general level of prices of goods and services in an economy over a period of time. The term '_____' once referred to increases in the money supply (monetary _____); however, economic debates about the relationship between money supply and price levels have led to its primary use today in describing price _____.
_____ can also be described as a decline in the real value of money--a loss of purchasing power in the medium of exchange which is also the monetary unit of account.

   a. ABN Amro
   c. AAB
   b. Inflation
   d. A Random Walk Down Wall Street

28. _____ is a measure of the ability of a debtor to pay their debts as and when they fall due. It is usually expressed as a ratio or a percentage of current liabilities.

For a corporation with a published balance sheet there are various ratios used to calculate a measure of liquidity.

   a. Operating leverage
   c. Invested capital
   b. Operating profit margin
   d. Accounting liquidity

29. John Maynard Keynes developed the _____ of Interest in the General Theory of Employment Interest and Money. The primary consideration of the _____ is the demand for money as an asset, as a means for holding wealth. Interest rates, he argues, cannot be a reward for savings as such because, if a person hoards his savings in cash, keeping it under his mattress say, he will receive no interest, although he has nevertheless, refrained from consuming all his current income.

   a. 7-Eleven
   c. Liquidity preference
   b. 529 plan
   d. 4-4-5 Calendar

30. _____ is a term used to explain a difference between two types of financial securities (e.g. stocks), that have all the same qualities except liquidity. For example:

_____ is a segment of a three-part theory that works to explain the behavior of yield curves for interest rates. The upwards-curving component of the interest yield can be explained by the _____.

   a. 4-4-5 Calendar
   c. 7-Eleven
   b. 529 plan
   d. Liquidity premium

31. An _____ can be defined as a contract which provides an income stream in return for an initial payment.

An immediate _____ is an _____ for which the time between the contract date and the date of the first payment is not longer than the time interval between payments. A common use for an immediate _____ is to provide a pension to a retired person or persons.

   a. Intrinsic value
   c. AT'T Inc.
   b. Annuity
   d. Amortization

32. The _____, interest yield, income yield, flat yield or running yield is a financial term used in reference to bonds and other fixed-interest securities such as gilts. It is the ratio of the annual interest payment and the bond's current price.

The _____ only therefore refers to the yield of the bond at the current moment. It does not reflect the total return over the life of the bond. In particular, it takes no account of reinvestment risk (the uncertainty about the rate at which future cashflows can be reinvested) or the fact that bonds usually mature at par value, which can be an important component of a bond's return.

a. Stochastic volatility
b. Perpetuity
c. Modified Internal Rate of Return
d. Current yield

Chapter 21. Bond Analysis

1. In finance, a _____ is a debt security, in which the authorized issuer owes the holders a debt and, depending on the terms of the _____, is obliged to pay interest (the coupon) and/or to repay the principal at a later date, termed maturity.

Thus a _____ is a loan: the issuer is the borrower, the _____ holder is the lender, and the coupon is the interest. _____s provide the borrower with external funds to finance long-term investments, or, in the case of government _____s, to finance current expenditure.

 a. Convertible bond
 b. Catastrophe bonds
 c. Puttable bond
 d. Bond

2. _____ is the process of determining the fair price of a bond. As with any security or capital investment, the fair value of a bond is the present value of the stream of cash flows it is expected to generate. Hence, the price or value of a bond is determined by discounting the bond's expected cash flows to the present using the appropriate discount rate.
 a. Bond fund
 b. Catastrophe bonds
 c. Collateralized debt obligations
 d. Bond valuation

3. In finance, _____ refers to the value of a security which is intrinsic to or contained in the security itself. It is also frequently called fundamental value. It is ordinarily calculated by summing the future income generated by the asset, and discounting it to the present value.
 a. Accretion
 b. Alpha
 c. Amortization
 d. Intrinsic value

4. The _____ or redemption yield is the yield promised to the bondholder on the assumption that the bond or other fixed-interest security such as gilts will be held to maturity, that all coupon and principal payments will be made and coupon payments are reinvested at the bond's promised yield at the same rate as invested. It is a measure of the return of the bond. This technique in theory allows investors to calculate the fair value of different financial instruments.
 a. Yield to maturity
 b. Macaulay duration
 c. Yield
 d. 4-4-5 Calendar

5. _____, refers to consumption opportunity gained by an entity within a specified time frame, which is generally expressed in monetary terms. However, for households and individuals, '_____ is the sum of all the wages, salaries, profits, interests payments, rents and other forms of earnings received... in a given period of time.' For firms, _____ generally refers to net-profit: what remains of revenue after expenses have been subtracted.
 a. Accrual
 b. Annual report
 c. OIBDA
 d. Income

6. In finance, _____ is the process of estimating the potential market value of a financial asset or liability. they can be done on assets (for example, investments in marketable securities such as stocks, options, business enterprises, or intangible assets such as patents and trademarks) or on liabilities (e.g., Bonds issued by a company.) _____s are required in many contexts including investment analysis, capital budgeting, merger and acquisition transactions, financial reporting, taxable events to determine the proper tax liability, and in litigation.
 a. Procter ' Gamble
 b. Margin
 c. Share
 d. Valuation

Chapter 21. Bond Analysis

7. _____ or net present worth (NPW) is defined as the total present value (PV) of a time series of cash flows. It is a standard method for using the time value of money to appraise long-term projects. Used for capital budgeting, and widely throughout economics, it measures the excess or shortfall of cash flows, in present value terms, once financing charges are met.

   a. Net present value
   b. Tax shield
   c. Negative gearing
   d. Present value of costs

8. _____ is the value on a given date of a future payment or series of future payments, discounted to reflect the time value of money and other factors such as investment risk. _____ calculations are widely used in business and economics to provide a means to compare cash flows at different times on a meaningful 'like to like' basis.

The most commonly applied model of the time value of money is compound interest.

   a. Present value
   b. Present value of benefits
   c. Negative gearing
   d. Net present value

9. A _____ is a unit that is equal to 1/100th of a percentage point. It is frequently used to express percentage point changes of less than 1%. It avoids the ambiguity between relative and absolute discussions about rates.

   a. 4-4-5 Calendar
   b. 529 plan
   c. Basis point
   d. Bond market

10. The coupon or _____ of a bond is the amount of interest paid per year expressed as a percentage of the face value of the bond.

For example if you hold $10,000 nominal of a bond described as a 4.5% loan stock, you will receive $450 in interest each year (probably in two installments of $225 each.)

Not all bonds have coupons.

   a. Coupon rate
   b. Zero-coupon bond
   c. Revenue bonds
   d. Puttable bond

11. _____ is a fee paid on borrowed assets. It is the price paid for the use of borrowed money , or, money earned by deposited funds . Assets that are sometimes lent with _____ include money, shares, consumer goods through hire purchase, major assets such as aircraft, and even entire factories in finance lease arrangements.

   a. AAB
   b. A Random Walk Down Wall Street
   c. Interest
   d. Insolvency

12. An _____ is the price a borrower pays for the use of money they do not own, and the return a lender receives for deferring the use of funds, by lending it to the borrower. _____s are normally expressed as a percentage rate over the period of one year.

_____s targets are also a vital tool of monetary policy and are used to control variables like investment, inflation, and unemployment.

Chapter 21. Bond Analysis

a. ABN Amro
b. AAB
c. A Random Walk Down Wall Street
d. Interest rate

13. _____ is a life of security. It may also refer to the final payment date of a loan or other financial instrument, at which point all remaining interest and principal is due to be paid.

1, 3, 6 months _____ band can be calculated by using 30-day per month periods.

a. Replacement cost
b. False billing
c. Primary market
d. Maturity

14. In finance, the term _____ describes the amount in cash that returns to the owners of a security. Normally it does not include the price variations, at the difference of the total return. _____ applies to various stated rates of return on stocks (common and preferred, and convertible), fixed income instruments (bonds, notes, bills, strips, zero coupon), and some other investment type insurance products (e.g. annuities.)

a. Yield to maturity
b. Macaulay duration
c. 4-4-5 Calendar
d. Yield

15. In finance, the yield curve is the relation between the interest rate (or cost of borrowing) and the time to maturity of the debt for a given borrower in a given currency. For example, the current U.S. dollar interest rates paid on U.S. Treasury securities for various maturities are closely watched by many traders, and are commonly plotted on a graph such as the one on the right which is informally called 'the yield curve.' More formal mathematical descriptions of this relation are often called the _____.

The yield of a debt instrument is the annualized percentage increase in the value of the investment.

a. 4-4-5 Calendar
b. 529 plan
c. 7-Eleven
d. Term structure of Interest rates

16. In financial accounting, _____s are precautions for which the amount or probability of occurrence are not known. Typical examples are _____s for warranty costs and _____ for taxes the term reserve is used instead of term _____; such a use, however, is inconsistent with the terminology suggested by International Accounting Standards Board.

a. Money measurement concept
b. Momentum Accounting and Triple-Entry Bookkeeping
c. Provision
d. Petty cash

17. _____ is a measure of the ability of a debtor to pay their debts as and when they fall due. It is usually expressed as a ratio or a percentage of current liabilities.

For a corporation with a published balance sheet there are various ratios used to calculate a measure of liquidity.

a. Invested capital
b. Accounting liquidity
c. Operating leverage
d. Operating profit margin

18. In the United States, a _____ is a bond issued by a city or other local government, or their agencies. Potential issuers of these bonds include cities, counties, redevelopment agencies, school districts, publicly owned airports and seaports, and any other governmental entity (or group of governments) below the state level. They may be general obligations of the issuer or secured by specified revenues.
   a. Senior debt
   b. Puttable bond
   c. Premium bond
   d. Municipal bond

19. _____ is a combination of straight bond and embedded put option. The holder of the _____ has the right, but not the obligation, to demand early repayment of the principal. The put option is usually exercisable on specified dates.
   a. Brady bonds
   b. Callable bond
   c. Convertible bond
   d. Puttable bond

20. A '_____' is a 'Charge' that is paid to obtain the right to delay a payment. Essentially, the payer purchases the right to make a given payment in the future instead of in the Present. The '_____', or 'Charge' that must be paid to delay the payment, is simply the difference between what the payment amount would be if it were paid in the present and what the payment amount would be paid if it were paid in the future.
   a. Discount
   b. Value at risk
   c. Risk aversion
   d. Risk modeling

21. A _____ is a bond bought at a price lower than its face value, with the face value repaid at the time of maturity. It does not make periodic interest payments, or so-called 'coupons,' hence the term zero-coupon bond. Investors earn return from the compounded interest all paid at maturity plus the difference between the discounted price of the bond and its par value.
   a. Callable bond
   b. Municipal bond
   c. Bowie bonds
   d. Zero coupon bond

22. The institution most often referenced by the word '_____' is a public or publicly traded _____, the shares of which are traded on a public stock exchange (e.g., the New York Stock Exchange or Nasdaq in the United States) where shares of stock of _____s are bought and sold by and to the general public. Most of the largest businesses in the world are publicly traded _____s. However, the majority of _____s are said to be closely held, privately held or close _____s, meaning that no ready market exists for the trading of shares.
   a. Depository Trust Company
   b. Protect
   c. Federal Home Loan Mortgage Corporation
   d. Corporation

23. In finance, _____ occurs when a debtor has not met its legal obligations according to the debt contract, e.g. it has not made a scheduled payment, or has violated a loan covenant (condition) of the debt contract. _____ may occur if the debtor is either unwilling or unable to pay their debt. This can occur with all debt obligations including bonds, mortgages, loans, and promissory notes.
   a. Vendor finance
   b. Debt validation
   c. Credit crunch
   d. Default

24. _____ is the risk of loss due to a debtor's non-payment of a loan or other line of credit (either the principal or interest (coupon) or both)

Chapter 21. Bond Analysis

Most lenders employ their own models (credit scorecards) to rank potential and existing customers according to risk, and then apply appropriate strategies. With products such as unsecured personal loans or mortgages, lenders charge a higher price for higher risk customers and vice versa. With revolving products such as credit cards and overdrafts, risk is controlled through careful setting of credit limits.

a. Liquidity risk
b. Market risk
c. Credit risk
d. Transaction risk

25. The value of speculative bonds is affected to a higher degree than investment grade bonds by the possibility of default. For example, in a recession interest rates may drop, and the drop in interest rates tends to increase the value of investment grade bonds; however, a recession tends to increase the possibility of default in speculative-grade bonds.

The original speculative grade bonds were bonds that once had been investment grade at time of issue, but where the credit rating of the issuer had slipped and the possibility of default increased significantly. These bonds are called '_____'.

a. Fallen angels
b. Seed round
c. Sharpe ratio
d. Return on capital employed

26. In finance, a _____ (non-investment grade bond, speculative grade bond or junk bond) is a bond that is rated below investment grade at the time of purchase. These bonds have a higher risk of default or other adverse credit events, but typically pay higher yields than better quality bonds in order to make them attractive to investors.
a. Volatility
b. High yield bond
c. Private equity
d. Sharpe ratio

27. In finance, _____ (or gearing) is borrowing money to supplement existing funds for investment in such a way that the potential positive or negative outcome is magnified and/or enhanced. It generally refers to using borrowed funds, or debt, so as to attempt to increase the returns to equity. Deleveraging is the action of reducing borrowings.
a. Leverage
b. Financial endowment
c. Pension fund
d. Limited partnership

28. An _____ can be defined as a contract which provides an income stream in return for an initial payment.

An immediate _____ is an _____ for which the time between the contract date and the date of the first payment is not longer than the time interval between payments. A common use for an immediate _____ is to provide a pension to a retired person or persons.

a. Amortization
b. Annuity
c. AT'T Inc.
d. Intrinsic value

29.

In finance, the _____ can be the expected rate of return above the risk-free interest rate. When measuring risk, a common sense approach is to compare the risk-free return on T-bills and the very risky return on other investments. The difference between these two returns can be interpreted as a measure of the excess return on the average risky asset. This excess return is known as the _____.

a. Risk premium
c. Risk adjusted return on capital

b. Risk aversion
d. Risk modeling

30. In finance, the _____ is the difference between the quoted rates of return on two different investments, usually of different credit quality.

It is a compound of yield and spread.

The '_____ of X over Y' is simply the percentage return on investment (ROI) from financial instrument X minus the percentage return on investment from financial instrument Y (per annum.)

a. Portfolio insurance
c. Duty of loyalty

b. Debtor-in-possession financing
d. Yield spread

31. In economics, a _____ is a mechanism that allows people to easily buy and sell (trade) financial securities (such as stocks and bonds), commodities (such as precious metals or agricultural goods), and other fungible items of value at low transaction costs and at prices that reflect the efficient-market hypothesis.

_____s have evolved significantly over several hundred years and are undergoing constant innovation to improve liquidity.

Both general markets (where many commodities are traded) and specialized markets (where only one commodity is traded) exist.

a. Delta hedging
c. Financial market

b. Secondary market
d. Cost of carry

32. _____ of a business involves analyzing its financial statements and health, its management and competitive advantages, and its competitors and markets. The term is used to distinguish such analysis from other types of investment analysis, such as quantitative analysis and technical analysis.

_____ is performed on historical and present data, but with the goal of making financial forecasts.

a. Stock valuation
c. Growth stocks

b. 4-4-5 Calendar
d. Fundamental analysis

Chapter 21. Bond Analysis

33. _____ is the balance of the amounts of cash being received and paid by a business during a defined period of time, sometimes tied to a specific project. Measurement of _____ can be used

- to evaluate the state or performance of a business or project.
- to determine problems with liquidity. Being profitable does not necessarily mean being liquid. A company can fail because of a shortage of cash, even while profitable.
- to generate project rate of returns. The time of _____s into and out of projects are used as inputs to financial models such as internal rate of return, and net present value.
- to examine income or growth of a business when it is believed that accrual accounting concepts do not represent economic realities. Alternately, _____ can be used to 'validate' the net income generated by accrual accounting.

_____ as a generic term may be used differently depending on context, and certain _____ definitions may be adapted by analysts and users for their own uses. Common terms include operating _____ and free _____.

_____s can be classified into:

1. Operational _____s: Cash received or expended as a result of the company's core business activities.
2. Investment _____s: Cash received or expended through capital expenditure, investments or acquisitions.
3. Financing _____s: Cash received or expended as a result of financial activities, such as interests and dividends.

All three together - the net _____ - are necessary to reconcile the beginning cash balance to the ending cash balance. Loan draw downs or equity injections, that is just shifting of capital but no expenditure as such, are not considered in the net _____.

a. Cash flow
b. Real option
c. Corporate finance
d. Shareholder value

34. In finance, a _____ or accounting ratio is a ratio of two selected numerical values taken from an enterprise's financial statements. There are many standard ratios used to try to evaluate the overall financial condition of a corporation or other organization. They may be used by managers within a firm, by current and potential shareholders (owners) of a firm, and by a firm's creditors. Security analysts use these to compare the strengths and weaknesses in various companies.

a. Sustainable growth rate
b. Financial ratio
c. Return on capital employed
d. Price/cash flow ratio

35. In corporate finance, _____ is a cash flow available for distribution among all the security holders of a company. They include equity holders, debt holders, preferred stock holders, convertible security holders, and so on.

Note that the first three lines above are calculated for you on the standard Statement of Cash Flows.

a. Free cash flow
b. Forfaiting
c. Safety stock
d. Funding

Chapter 22. Bond Portfolio Management

1. _____ refers to a portfolio management strategy where the manager makes specific investments with the goal of outperforming an investment benchmark index. Investors or mutual funds that do not aspire to create a return in excess of a benchmark index will often invest in an index fund that replicates as closely as possible the investment weighting and returns of that index; this is called passive management. _____ is the opposite of passive management, because in passive management the manager does not seek to outperform the benchmark index.
    a. ABN Amro
    b. A Random Walk Down Wall Street
    c. AAB
    d. Active management

2. In finance, a _____ is a debt security, in which the authorized issuer owes the holders a debt and, depending on the terms of the _____, is obliged to pay interest (the coupon) and/or to repay the principal at a later date, termed maturity.

    Thus a _____ is a loan: the issuer is the borrower, the _____ holder is the lender, and the coupon is the interest. _____s provide the borrower with external funds to finance long-term investments, or, in the case of government _____s, to finance current expenditure.

    a. Convertible bond
    b. Catastrophe bonds
    c. Puttable bond
    d. Bond

3. Modern portfolio theory (MPT) proposes how rational investors will use diversification to optimize their portfolios, and how a risky asset should be priced. The basic concepts of the theory are Markowitz diversification, the _____, capital asset pricing model, the alpha and beta coefficients, the Capital Market Line and the Securities Market Line.

    MPT models an asset's return as a random variable, and models a portfolio as a weighted combination of assets so that the return of a portfolio is the weighted combination of the assets' returns.

    a. ABN Amro
    b. A Random Walk Down Wall Street
    c. AAB
    d. Efficient frontier

4. _____ is a financial strategy in which a fund manager makes as few portfolio decisions as possible, in order to minimize transaction costs, including the incidence of capital gains tax. One popular method is to mimic the performance of an externally specified index--called 'index funds'. The ethos of an index fund is aptly summed up in the injunction to an index fund manager: 'Don't just do something, sit there!'

    _____ is most common on the equity market, where index funds track a stock market index, but it is becoming more common in other investment types, including bonds, commodities and hedge funds.

    a. Passive management
    b. Trust company
    c. Net asset value
    d. Savings and loan association

5. _____ mature in one year or less. Like zero-coupon bonds, they do not pay interest prior to maturity; instead they are sold at a discount of the par value to create a positive yield to maturity. Many regard _____ as the least risky investment available to U.S. investors.
    a. 4-4-5 Calendar
    b. Treasury bills
    c. Treasury Inflation Protected Securities
    d. Treasury securities

Chapter 22. Bond Portfolio Management

6. The _____ is a financial market where participants buy and sell debt securities, usually in the form of bonds. As of 2006, the size of the international _____ is an estimated $45 trillion, of which the size of the outstanding U.S. _____ debt was $25.2 trillion.

Nearly all of the $923 billion average daily trading volume in the U.S. _____ takes place between broker-dealers and large institutions in a decentralized, over-the-counter market.

a. 529 plan
b. Fixed income
c. 4-4-5 Calendar
d. Bond market

7. In statistics and signal processing, an _____ is a type of random process which is often used to model and predict various types of natural phenomena.

The notation AR(p) refers to the _____ of order p. The AR(p) model is defined as

[image] >

where [image] > are the parameters of the model, c is a constant and [image] > is white noise.

a. A Random Walk Down Wall Street
b. Autoregressive model
c. ABN Amro
d. AAB

8. _____ is a fee paid on borrowed assets. It is the price paid for the use of borrowed money, or, money earned by deposited funds. Assets that are sometimes lent with _____ include money, shares, consumer goods through hire purchase, major assets such as aircraft, and even entire factories in finance lease arrangements.

a. A Random Walk Down Wall Street
b. Insolvency
c. AAB
d. Interest

9. An _____ is the price a borrower pays for the use of money they do not own, and the return a lender receives for deferring the use of funds, by lending it to the borrower. _____s are normally expressed as a percentage rate over the period of one year.

_____s targets are also a vital tool of monetary policy and are used to control variables like investment, inflation, and unemployment.

a. AAB
b. ABN Amro
c. A Random Walk Down Wall Street
d. Interest rate

10. _____ is a form of corporation equity ownership represented in the securities. It is dangerous in comparison to preferred shares and some other investment options, in that in the event of bankruptcy, _____ investors receive their funds after preferred stockholders, bondholders, creditors, etc. On the other hand, common shares on average perform better than preferred shares or bonds over time.

a. Stock market bubble
b. Stop-limit order
c. Common stock
d. Stock split

11. In economics, _____ is the total amount of money available in an economy at a particular point in time. There are several ways to define 'money', but each includes currency in circulation and demand deposits.

_____ data are recorded and published.

a. 7-Eleven
b. 529 plan
c. 4-4-5 Calendar
d. Money supply

12. In financial accounting, the term _____ is most commonly used to describe any part of shareholders' equity, except for basic share capital. Sometimes, the term is used instead of the term provision; such a use, however, is inconsistent with the terminology suggested by International Accounting Standards Board. For more information about provisions, see provision (accounting.)

a. Treasury stock
b. Reserve
c. FIFO and LIFO accounting
d. Closing entries

13. The _____ requirement is the amount required to be collateralized in order to open a position. Thereafter, the amount required to be kept in collateral until the position is closed is the maintenance requirement. The maintenance requirement is the minimum amount to be collateralized in order to keep an open position.

a. Initial margin
b. Issuer
c. Arbitrage
d. Efficient-market hypothesis

14. The _____ is the amount required to be collateralized in order to open a position. Thereafter, the amount required to be kept in collateral until the position is closed is the maintenance requirement. The maintenance requirement is the minimum amount to be collateralized in order to keep an open position.

a. AAB
b. A Random Walk Down Wall Street
c. ABN Amro
d. Initial margin requirement

15. In finance, a _____ is collateral that the holder of a position in securities, options, or futures contracts has to deposit to cover the credit risk of his counterparty (most often his broker.) This risk can arise if the holder has done any of the following:

- borrowed cash from the counterparty to buy securities or options,
- sold securities or options short, or
- entered into a futures contract.

The collateral can be in the form of cash or securities, and it is deposited in a _____ account. On U.S. futures exchanges, '_____' was formally called performance bond.

_____ buying is buying securities with cash borrowed from a broker, using other securities as collateral.

a. Procter ' Gamble
b. Credit
c. Share
d. Margin

16. The coupon or _____ of a bond is the amount of interest paid per year expressed as a percentage of the face value of the bond.

For example if you hold $10,000 nominal of a bond described as a 4.5% loan stock, you will receive $450 in interest each year (probably in two installments of $225 each.)

Not all bonds have coupons.

a. Zero-coupon bond
c. Puttable bond
b. Revenue bonds
d. Coupon rate

17. A '_____' is a 'Charge' that is paid to obtain the right to delay a payment. Essentially, the payer purchases the right to make a given payment in the future instead of in the Present. The '_____', or 'Charge' that must be paid to delay the payment, is simply the difference between what the payment amount would be if it were paid in the present and what the payment amount would be paid if it were paid in the future.

a. Risk aversion
c. Risk modeling
b. Value at risk
d. Discount

18. A _____ is a bond bought at a price lower than its face value, with the face value repaid at the time of maturity. It does not make periodic interest payments, or so-called 'coupons,' hence the term zero-coupon bond. Investors earn return from the compounded interest all paid at maturity plus the difference between the discounted price of the bond and its par value.

a. Zero coupon bond
c. Callable bond
b. Municipal bond
d. Bowie bonds

19. In finance, the _____ of a financial asset measures the sensitivity of the asset's price to interest rate movements, expressed as a number of years. The reason for expressing this sensitivity in years is that the time that will elapse until a cash flow is received allows more interest to accumulate. Therefore the price of an asset with long term cashflows has more interest rate sensitivity than an asset with cashflows in the near future.

a. 4-4-5 Calendar
c. Duration
b. Macaulay duration
d. Yield to maturity

20. _____ is the weighted average maturity of a bond where the weights are the relative discounted cash flows in each period.

,

It will be seen that this is the same formula for the duration as given above.

Macaulay showed that an unweighted average maturity is not useful in predicting interest rate risk.

a. Yield to maturity
c. Yield
b. 4-4-5 Calendar
d. Macaulay duration

Chapter 22. Bond Portfolio Management

21. In financial accounting, _____s are precautions for which the amount or probability of occurrence are not known. Typical examples are _____s for warranty costs and _____ for taxes the term reserve is used instead of term _____; such a use, however, is inconsistent with the terminology suggested by International Accounting Standards Board.
   a. Provision
   b. Money measurement concept
   c. Petty cash
   d. Momentum Accounting and Triple-Entry Bookkeeping

22. A _____ is a bond bought at a price lower than its face value, with the face value repaid at the time of maturity. It does not make periodic interest payments, or have so-called 'coupons,' hence the term _____. Investors earn return from the compounded interest all paid at maturity plus the difference between the discounted price of the bond and its par value.
   a. Corporate bond
   b. Bond fund
   c. Clean price
   d. Zero-coupon bond

23. _____ is the risk (variability in value) borne by an interest-bearing asset, such as a loan or a bond, due to variability of interest rates. In general, as rates rise, the price of a fixed rate bond will fall, and vice versa. _____ is commonly measured by the bond's duration.
   a. Official bank rate
   b. International Fisher effect
   c. A Random Walk Down Wall Street
   d. Interest rate Risk

24. In finance, the yield curve is the relation between the interest rate (or cost of borrowing) and the time to maturity of the debt for a given borrower in a given currency. For example, the current U.S. dollar interest rates paid on U.S. Treasury securities for various maturities are closely watched by many traders, and are commonly plotted on a graph such as the one on the right which is informally called 'the yield curve.' More formal mathematical descriptions of this relation are often called the _____.

The yield of a debt instrument is the annualized percentage increase in the value of the investment.

   a. 529 plan
   b. 4-4-5 Calendar
   c. 7-Eleven
   d. Term structure of Interest rates

25. In finance, _____ occurs when a debtor has not met its legal obligations according to the debt contract, e.g. it has not made a scheduled payment, or has violated a loan covenant (condition) of the debt contract. _____ may occur if the debtor is either unwilling or unable to pay their debt. This can occur with all debt obligations including bonds, mortgages, loans, and promissory notes.
   a. Debt validation
   b. Credit crunch
   c. Default
   d. Vendor finance

26. _____ is the risk of loss due to a debtor's non-payment of a loan or other line of credit (either the principal or interest (coupon) or both)

Most lenders employ their own models (credit scorecards) to rank potential and existing customers according to risk, and then apply appropriate strategies. With products such as unsecured personal loans or mortgages, lenders charge a higher price for higher risk customers and vice versa. With revolving products such as credit cards and overdrafts, risk is controlled through careful setting of credit limits.

Chapter 22. Bond Portfolio Management

a. Liquidity risk
b. Transaction risk
c. Market risk
d. Credit risk

27. An _____ is a contract written by a seller that conveys to the buyer the right -- but not the obligation -- to buy (in the case of a call _____) or to sell (in the case of a put _____) a particular asset, such as a piece of property such as, among others, a futures contract. In return for granting the _____, the seller collects a payment (the premium) from the buyer.

For example, buying a call _____ provides the right to buy a specified quantity of a security at a set strike price at some time on or before expiration, while buying a put _____ provides the right to sell.

a. Annuity
b. Amortization
c. AT'T Mobility LLC
d. Option

28. In finance, the term _____ describes the amount in cash that returns to the owners of a security. Normally it does not include the price variations, at the difference of the total return. _____ applies to various stated rates of return on stocks (common and preferred, and convertible), fixed income instruments (bonds, notes, bills, strips, zero coupon), and some other investment type insurance products (e.g. annuities.)

a. 4-4-5 Calendar
b. Yield to maturity
c. Macaulay duration
d. Yield

29. In finance, the _____ is the relation between the interest rate (or cost of borrowing) and the time to maturity of the debt for a given borrower in a given currency. For example, the current U.S. dollar interest rates paid on U.S. Treasury securities for various maturities are closely watched by many traders, and are commonly plotted on a graph such as the one on the right which is informally called 'the _____.' More formal mathematical descriptions of this relation are often called the term structure of interest rates.

The yield of a debt instrument is the annualized percentage increase in the value of the investment.

a. 4-4-5 Calendar
b. 7-Eleven
c. Yield curve
d. 529 plan

30. _____ is the action of bringing a portfolio of investments that has deviated away from one's target asset allocation back into line. Under-weighted securities can be purchased with newly saved money; alternatively, over-weighted securities can be sold to purchase under-weighted securities.

The investments in a portfolio will perform according to the market.

a. Market timing
b. Security market line
c. Divestment
d. Rebalancing

31. A _____ is the counterpart to a deterministic process (or deterministic system) in probability theory. Instead of dealing with only one possible 'reality' of how the process might evolve under time (as is the case, for example, for solutions of an ordinary differential equation), in a stochastic or random process there is some indeterminacy in its future evolution described by probability distributions. This means that even if the initial condition (or starting point) is known, there are many possibilities the process might go to, but some paths are more probable and others less.

a. 529 plan
c. 7-Eleven
b. 4-4-5 Calendar
d. Stochastic process

32. _____, refers to consumption opportunity gained by an entity within a specified time frame, which is generally expressed in monetary terms. However, for households and individuals, '_____ is the sum of all the wages, salaries, profits, interests payments, rents and other forms of earnings received... in a given period of time.' For firms, _____ generally refers to net-profit: what remains of revenue after expenses have been subtracted.

a. OIBDA
c. Annual report
b. Accrual
d. Income

33. In finance, _____ is the process of estimating the potential market value of a financial asset or liability. they can be done on assets (for example, investments in marketable securities such as stocks, options, business enterprises, or intangible assets such as patents and trademarks) or on liabilities (e.g., Bonds issued by a company.) _____s are required in many contexts including investment analysis, capital budgeting, merger and acquisition transactions, financial reporting, taxable events to determine the proper tax liability, and in litigation.

a. Share
c. Valuation
b. Procter ' Gamble
d. Margin

34. In finance, a _____ is a derivative in which two counterparties agree to exchange one stream of cash flows against another stream. These streams are called the legs of the _____.

The cash flows are calculated over a notional principal amount, which is usually not exchanged between counterparties.

a. Local volatility
c. Volatility swap
b. Swap
d. Volatility arbitrage

35. An _____ is an exchange of tangible assets for intangible assets or vice versa. Since it is a swap of assets, the procedure takes place on the active side of the balance sheet and has no impact on the latter in regards to volume. As an example, a company may sell equity and receive the value in cash thus increasing liquidity.

a. ABN Amro
c. AAB
b. A Random Walk Down Wall Street
d. Asset swap

36. _____ is a technique to adjust income payments by means of a price index, in order to maintain the purchasing power of the public after inflation.

Applying a cost-of-living escalation COLA clause to a stream of periodic payments protects the real value of those payments and effectively transfers the risk of inflation from the payee to the payor, who must pay more each year to reflect the increases in prices. Thus, inflation _____ is often applied to pension payments, rents and other situations which are not subject to regular re-pricing in the market.

a. A Random Walk Down Wall Street
c. Indexation
b. AAB
d. ABN Amro

37. The _____, interest yield, income yield, flat yield or running yield is a financial term used in reference to bonds and other fixed-interest securities such as gilts. It is the ratio of the annual interest payment and the bond's current price.

The _____ only therefore refers to the yield of the bond at the current moment. It does not reflect the total return over the life of the bond. In particular, it takes no account of reinvestment risk (the uncertainty about the rate at which future cashflows can be reinvested) or the fact that bonds usually mature at par value, which can be an important component of a bond's return.

a. Current yield
b. Perpetuity
c. Stochastic volatility
d. Modified Internal Rate of Return

38. _____ is a risk-adjusted measure of the so-called active return on an investment. It is the return in excess of the compensation for the risk borne, and thus commonly used to assess active managers' performances. Often, the return of a benchmark is subtracted in order to consider relative performance, which yields Jensen's _____.

a. Alpha
b. Amortization
c. Option
d. Annuity

39. In business and accounting, _____s are everything of value that is owned by a person or company. The balance sheet of a firm records the monetary value of the _____s owned by the firm. The two major _____ classes are tangible _____s and intangible _____s.

a. Asset
b. Accounts payable
c. EBITDA
d. Income

40. _____ is a term used to refer to how an investor distributes his or her investments among various classes of investment vehicles (e.g., stocks and bonds.)

A large part of financial planning is finding an _____ that is appropriate for a given person in terms of their appetite for and ability to shoulder risk. This can depend on various factors; see investor profile.

a. Alternative investment
b. Investment performance
c. Investing online
d. Asset allocation

41. The _____ is the tendency of the stock market to rise between December 31 and the end of the first week in January. There are many theories for why this happens, the main one being that it occurs because many investors choose to sell some of their stock right before the end of the year in order to claim a capital loss for tax purposes. Once the tax calendar rolls over to a new year on January 1st these same investors quickly reinvest their money in the market, causing stock prices to rise.

a. Revaluation
b. Death spiral financing
c. Sector rotation
d. January effect

Chapter 23. Investment Companies

1. _____ in finance is a risk management technique, related to hedging, that mixes a wide variety of investments within a portfolio. Because the fluctuations of a single security have less impact on a diverse portfolio, _____ minimizes the risk from any one investment.

   A simple example of _____ is the following: On a particular island the entire economy consists of two companies: one that sells umbrellas and another that sells sunscreen.

   a. Diversification
   b. 7-Eleven
   c. 4-4-5 Calendar
   d. 529 plan

2. _____, in microeconomics, are the cost advantages that a business obtains due to expansion. _____ may be utilized by any size firm expanding its scale of operation.
   a. Uniform Commercial Code
   b. Employee Retirement Income Security Act
   c. Articles of incorporation
   d. Economies of scale

3. An _____ is a company whose main business is holding securities of other companies purely for investment purposes. The _____ invests money on behalf of its shareholders who in turn share in the profits and losses.
   a. AAB
   b. Unit investment trust
   c. A Random Walk Down Wall Street
   d. Investment company

4. _____ is a term used to describe the value of an entity's assets less the value of its liabilities. The term is commonly used in relation to collective investment schemes. It may also be used as a synonym for the book value of a firm.
   a. Passive management
   b. Net asset value
   c. Retail broker
   d. Financial intermediary

5. In business and accounting, _____s are everything of value that is owned by a person or company. The balance sheet of a firm records the monetary value of the _____s owned by the firm. The two major _____ classes are tangible _____s and intangible _____s.
   a. Accounts payable
   b. Income
   c. EBITDA
   d. Asset

6. The _____ is the financial market where previously issued securities and financial instruments such as stock, bonds, options, and futures are bought and sold. The term '_____' is also used refer to the market for any used goods or assets, or an alternative use for an existing product or asset where the customer base is the second market

   With primary issuances of securities or financial instruments, or the primary market, investors purchase these securities directly from issuers such as corporations issuing shares in an IPO or private placement, or directly from the federal government in the case of treasuries.

   a. Performance attribution
   b. Secondary market
   c. Financial market
   d. Delta neutral

7. A _____ is a fungible, negotiable instrument representing financial value. They are broadly categorized into debt securities (such as banknotes, bonds and debentures), and equity securities; e.g., common stocks. The company or other entity issuing the _____ is called the issuer.

Chapter 23. Investment Companies

a. Book entry
b. Security
c. Securities lending
d. Tracking stock

8. A _____ is a US investment company offering a fixed (unmanaged) portfolio of securities having a definite life. _____s are assembled by a sponsor and sold through brokers to investors.

A _____ portfolio may contain one of several different types of securities.

a. Investment company
b. A Random Walk Down Wall Street
c. Unit investment trust
d. AAB

9. An _____, operating expenditure, operational expense, operational expenditure or OPEX is an on-going cost for running a product, business, or system. Its counterpart, a capital expenditure (CAPEX), is the cost of developing or providing non-consumable parts for the product or system. For example, the purchase of a photocopier is the CAPEX, and the annual paper and toner cost is the OPEX.

a. ABN Amro
b. AAB
c. A Random Walk Down Wall Street
d. Operating expense

10. A _____, is a collective investment scheme with a limited number of shares.

New shares are rarely issued after the fund is launched; shares are not normally redeemable for cash or securities until the fund liquidates. Typically an investor can acquire shares in a _____ by buying shares on a secondary market from a broker, market maker, or other investor as opposed to an open-end fund where all transactions eventually involve the fund company creating new shares on the fly (in exchange for either cash or securities) or redeeming shares (for cash or securities.)

a. Mutual fund fees and expenses
b. Stock fund
c. Money market funds
d. Closed-end fund

11. A '_____' is a 'Charge' that is paid to obtain the right to delay a payment. Essentially, the payer purchases the right to make a given payment in the future instead of in the Present. The '_____', or 'Charge' that must be paid to delay the payment, is simply the difference between what the payment amount would be if it were paid in the present and what the payment amount would be paid if it were paid in the future.

a. Risk aversion
b. Value at risk
c. Risk modeling
d. Discount

12. A _____ is a bond bought at a price lower than its face value, with the face value repaid at the time of maturity. It does not make periodic interest payments, or so-called 'coupons,' hence the term zero-coupon bond. Investors earn return from the compounded interest all paid at maturity plus the difference between the discounted price of the bond and its par value.

a. Callable bond
b. Bowie bonds
c. Municipal bond
d. Zero coupon bond

13. _____, is when a company issues common stock or shares to the public for the first time. They are often issued by smaller, younger companies seeking capital to expand, but can also be done by large privately-owned companies looking to become publicly traded.

In an _____ the issuer may obtain the assistance of an underwriting firm, which helps it determine what type of security to issue (common or preferred), best offering price and time to bring it to market.

- a. Asian Financial Crisis
- b. Initial public offering
- c. Interest
- d. Insolvency

14. An _____ can be defined as a contract which provides an income stream in return for an initial payment.

An immediate _____ is an _____ for which the time between the contract date and the date of the first payment is not longer than the time interval between payments. A common use for an immediate _____ is to provide a pension to a retired person or persons.

- a. Annuity
- b. AT'T Inc.
- c. Intrinsic value
- d. Amortization

15. In finance, a _____ is a debt security, in which the authorized issuer owes the holders a debt and, depending on the terms of the _____, is obliged to pay interest (the coupon) and/or to repay the principal at a later date, termed maturity.

Thus a _____ is a loan: the issuer is the borrower, the _____ holder is the lender, and the coupon is the interest. _____s provide the borrower with external funds to finance long-term investments, or, in the case of government _____s, to finance current expenditure.

- a. Convertible bond
- b. Catastrophe bonds
- c. Puttable bond
- d. Bond

16. _____, in accrual accounting, is any account where the asset or liability is not realized until a future date, e.g. annuities, charges, taxes, income, etc. The _____ item may be carried, dependent on type of deferral, as either an asset or liability. See also: accrual

_____ is also used in the university admissions process. It is the action by which a school rejects a student for early admission but still opts to review that student in the general admissions pool.

- a. Revenue
- b. Net profit
- c. Current asset
- d. Deferred

17. _____ also known as Deferred Sales Charge, is a fee paid when shares are sold. This fee typically goes to the brokers that sell the fund's shares. The amount of this type of load will depend on how long the investor holds his or her shares and typically decreases to zero if the investor holds his or her shares long enough.

- a. Money market funds
- b. Mutual fund fees and expenses
- c. Closed-end fund
- d. Back-end load

Chapter 23. Investment Companies

18. A _____ is a collective investment scheme that invests in bonds and other debt securities. _____s yield monthly dividends that include interest payments on the fund's underlying securities plus any capital appreciation in the prices of the portfolio's bonds. _____s tend to pay higher dividends than CDs and money market accounts, and they generally pay out dividends more frequently and regularly than individual bonds.
   a. Premium bond
   b. Bond fund
   c. Gilts
   d. Private activity bond

19. _____ is a term used to refer to how an investor distributes his or her investments among various classes of investment vehicles (e.g., stocks and bonds.)

   A large part of financial planning is finding an _____ that is appropriate for a given person in terms of their appetite for and ability to shoulder risk. This can depend on various factors; see investor profile.

   a. Investing online
   b. Alternative investment
   c. Investment performance
   d. Asset allocation

20. _____ is a form of corporation equity ownership represented in the securities. It is dangerous in comparison to preferred shares and some other investment options, in that in the event of bankruptcy, _____ investors receive their funds after preferred stockholders, bondholders, creditors, etc. On the other hand, common shares on average perform better than preferred shares or bonds over time.
   a. Stock split
   b. Stop-limit order
   c. Stock market bubble
   d. Common stock

21. _____, refers to consumption opportunity gained by an entity within a specified time frame, which is generally expressed in monetary terms. However, for households and individuals, '_____ is the sum of all the wages, salaries, profits, interests payments, rents and other forms of earnings received... in a given period of time.' For firms, _____ generally refers to net-profit: what remains of revenue after expenses have been subtracted.
   a. OIBDA
   b. Accrual
   c. Income
   d. Annual report

22. A _____ or equity fund is a fund that invests in Equities more commonly known as stocks. Such funds are typically held either in stock or cash, as opposed to Bonds, notes, or other securities. This may be a mutual fund or exchange-traded fund.
   a. Closed-end fund
   b. Stock fund
   c. Money market funds
   d. Mutual fund fees and expenses

23. An _____ or index tracker is a collective investment scheme (usually a mutual fund or exchange-traded fund) that aims to replicate the movements of an index of a specific financial market regardless of market conditions.

   Tracking can be achieved by trying to hold all of the securities in the index, in the same proportions as the index. Other methods include statistically sampling the market and holding 'representative' securities.

   a. AAB
   b. Investment company
   c. A Random Walk Down Wall Street
   d. Index fund

Chapter 23. Investment Companies

24. _____ refers to a tax levied by various jurisdictions on the profits made by companies or associations. It is a tax on the value of the corporation's profits.

The measure of taxable profits varies from country to country.

a. Proxy fight
c. Trade finance
b. Corporate tax
d. First-mover advantage

25. An _____ is a tax levied on the financial income of people, corporations, or other legal entities. Various _____ systems exist, with varying degrees of tax incidence. Income taxation can be progressive, proportional, or regressive.

a. A Random Walk Down Wall Street
c. ABN Amro
b. Income tax
d. AAB

26. A _____ is an exemption from all or certain taxes of a state or nation in which part of the taxes that would normally be collected from an individual or an organization are instead foregone.

Normally a _____ is provided to an individual or organization which falls within a class which the government wishes to promote economically, such as charitable organizations. _____s are usually meant to either reduce the tax burden on a particular segment of society in the interests of fairness or to promote some type of economic activity through reducing the tax burden on those organizations or individuals who are involved in that activity.

a. Tax incidence
c. Federal Open Market Committee
b. Tax compliance solution
d. Tax exemption

27. _____ refers to different style characteristics of equities, bonds or financial derivatives within a given investment philosophy.

Theory would favor a combination of big capitalization, passive and value. Of course one could almost get that when investing in an important Index like S'P 500, Euro-Stoxx or the like.

a. A Random Walk Down Wall Street
c. AAB
b. ABN Amro
d. Investment style

28. An _____ is a contract written by a seller that conveys to the buyer the right -- but not the obligation -- to buy (in the case of a call _____) or to sell (in the case of a put _____) a particular asset, such as a piece of property such as, among others, a futures contract. In return for granting the _____, the seller collects a payment (the premium) from the buyer.

For example, buying a call _____ provides the right to buy a specified quantity of a security at a set strike price at some time on or before expiration, while buying a put _____ provides the right to sell.

a. AT'T Mobility LLC
c. Amortization
b. Annuity
d. Option

Chapter 23. Investment Companies

29. _____ is a risk-adjusted measure of the so-called active return on an investment. It is the return in excess of the compensation for the risk borne, and thus commonly used to assess active managers' performances. Often, the return of a benchmark is subtracted in order to consider relative performance, which yields Jensen's _____.

   a. Annuity
   b. Option
   c. Alpha
   d. Amortization

30. In finance, _____ is the process of estimating the potential market value of a financial asset or liability. they can be done on assets (for example, investments in marketable securities such as stocks, options, business enterprises, or intangible assets such as patents and trademarks) or on liabilities (e.g., Bonds issued by a company.) _____s are required in many contexts including investment analysis, capital budgeting, merger and acquisition transactions, financial reporting, taxable events to determine the proper tax liability, and in litigation.

   a. Share
   b. Margin
   c. Valuation
   d. Procter ' Gamble

31. The term _____ has three unrelated technical definitions, and is also used in a variety of non-technical ways.

   - In financial economics, it refers to any asset used to make money, as opposed to assets used for personal enjoyment or consumption. This is an important distinction because two people can disagree sharply about the value of personal assets, one person might think a sports car is more valuable than a pickup truck, another person might have the opposite taste. But if an asset is held for the purpose of making money, taste has nothing to do with it, only differences of opinion about how much money the asset will produce. With the further assumption that people agree on the probability distribution of future cash flows, it is possible to have an objective _____ pricing model. Even without the assumption of agreement, it is possible to set rational limits on _____ value.
   - In governmental accounting, it is defined as any asset used in operations with an initial useful life extending beyond one reporting period. Generally, government managers have a 'stewardship' duty to maintain _____s under their control. See International Public Sector Accounting Standards for details.
   - In US tax accounting, it is defined as any property other than a list of exceptions. The main exceptions are anything held for sale, and any real estate or depreciable property used in business. Almost everything you own and use for personal purposes, pleasure or investment is a _____. If something is a _____ for tax purposes, gains or losses on sale or disposition are capital gains or capital losses. For individuals, however, capital losses on property held for personal use are generally not deductible. See the IRS publication Tax Facts about Capital Gains and Losses for details.

A well-known financial accounting textbook advises that the term be avoided except in tax accounting because it is used in so many different senses, not all of them well-defined. For example it is often used as a synonym for fixed assets or for investments in securities.

A common non-technical usage occurs when people ask that employees or the environment or something else be treated as a _____.

   a. Settlement date
   b. Political risk
   c. Solvency
   d. Capital Asset

Chapter 23. Investment Companies

32. In finance, the _____ is used to determine a theoretically appropriate required rate of return of an asset, if that asset is to be added to an already well-diversified portfolio, given that asset's non-diversifiable risk. The model takes into account the asset's sensitivity to non-diversifiable risk (also known as systemic risk or market risk), often represented by the quantity beta (β) in the financial industry, as well as the expected return of the market and the expected return of a theoretical risk-free asset.

The model was introduced by Jack Treynor (1961, 1962), William Sharpe (1964), John Lintner (1965a,b) and Jan Mossin (1966) independently, building on the earlier work of Harry Markowitz on diversification and modern portfolio theory.

 a. Hull-White model
 b. Cox-Ingersoll-Ross model
 c. Random walk hypothesis
 d. Capital Asset Pricing Model

33. In finance, _____ is the tendency for failed companies to be excluded from performance studies because they no longer exist. It often causes the results of studies to skew higher because only companies which were successful enough to survive until the end of the period are included.

For example, a mutual fund company's selection of funds today will include only those that have been successful in the past.

 a. 7-Eleven
 b. Survivorship bias
 c. 529 plan
 d. 4-4-5 Calendar

34. In business and finance, a _____ (also referred to as equity _____) of stock means a _____ of ownership in a corporation (company.) In the plural, stocks is often used as a synonym for _____s especially in the United States, but it is less commonly used that way outside of North America.

In the United Kingdom, South Africa, and Australia, stock can also refer to completely different financial instruments such as government bonds or, less commonly, to all kinds of marketable securities.

 a. Margin
 b. Bucket shop
 c. Procter ' Gamble
 d. Share

35. A _____ or _____ is a tax designation for a corporation investing in real estate that reduces or eliminates corporate income taxes. In return, _____s are required to distribute 95% of their income, which may be taxable in the hands of the investors. The _____ structure was designed to provide a similar structure for investment in real estate as mutual funds provide for investment in stocks.

 a. Real estate investing
 b. Liquidation value
 c. Real estate investment trust
 d. Tenancy

36. A _____ is one in which a brokerage manages an investor's portfolio for a flat quarterly or annual fee. This fee covers all administrative, commission, and management expenses. Sometimes this also includes funds of funds. This type of account is also known as an investment platform.

 a. Net worth
 b. Payback period
 c. Floating charge
 d. Wrap account

37. _____, in bookkeeping, refers to assets, liabilities, income, and expenses recorded on individual pages of the so called book of final entry or ledger. Changes in _____ value are made by chronologically posting debit (DR) and credit (CR) entries to its page. Examples of _____s are cash, _____s receivable, mortgages, loans, land and buildings, common stock, sales, services provided, wages, and payroll overhead.
   a. Alpha
   b. Accretion
   c. Account
   d. Option

Chapter 24. Options

1. The term _____ refers to three closely related concepts:

   - The _____ model is a mathematical model of the market for an equity, in which the equity's price is a stochastic process.
   - The _____ PDE is a partial differential equation which (in the model) must be satisfied by the price of a derivative on the equity.
   - The _____ formula is the result obtained by solving the _____ PDE for a European call option.

Fischer Black and Myron Scholes first articulated the _____ formula in their 1973 paper, 'The Pricing of Options and Corporate Liabilities.' The foundation for their research relied on work developed by scholars such as Jack L. Treynor, Paul Samuelson, A. James Boness, Sheen T. Kassouf, and Edward O. Thorp. The fundamental insight of _____ is that the option is implicitly priced if the stock is traded.

Robert C. Merton was the first to publish a paper expanding the mathematical understanding of the options pricing model and coined the term '_____' options pricing model.

   a. Black-Scholes
   b. Stochastic volatility
   c. Perpetuity
   d. Modified Internal Rate of Return

2. A _____ is a financial contract between two parties, the buyer and the seller of this type of option. Often it is simply labeled a 'call'. The buyer of the option has the right, but not the obligation to buy an agreed quantity of a particular commodity or financial instrument (the underlying instrument) from the seller of the option at a certain time (the expiration date) for a certain price (the strike price.)

   a. Bear spread
   b. Bear call spread
   c. Bull spread
   d. Call option

3. In options, the _____ is a key variable in a derivatives contract between two parties. Where the contract requires delivery of the underlying instrument, the trade will be at the _____, regardless of the spot price (market price) of the underlying instrument at that time.

Definition - The fixed price at which the owner of an option can purchase, in the case of a call in the case of a put, the underlying security or commodity.

   a. Strike price
   b. Moneyness
   c. Naked put
   d. Swaption

4. An _____ is a contract written by a seller that conveys to the buyer the right -- but not the obligation -- to buy (in the case of a call _____) or to sell (in the case of a put _____) a particular asset, such as a piece of property such as, among others, a futures contract. In return for granting the _____, the seller collects a payment (the premium) from the buyer.

For example, buying a call _____ provides the right to buy a specified quantity of a security at a set strike price at some time on or before expiration, while buying a put _____ provides the right to sell.

   a. Option
   b. AT'T Mobility LLC
   c. Annuity
   d. Amortization

Chapter 24. Options

5. An _____ can be defined as a contract which provides an income stream in return for an initial payment.

An immediate _____ is an _____ for which the time between the contract date and the date of the first payment is not longer than the time interval between payments. A common use for an immediate _____ is to provide a pension to a retired person or persons.

   a. Intrinsic value
   c. Amortization
   b. AT'T Inc.
   d. Annuity

6. The _____ is the price the buyer of the options contract pays for the right to buy or sell a security at a specified price in the future.
   a. ABN Amro
   c. AAB
   b. A Random Walk Down Wall Street
   d. Option Premium

7. In banking and finance, _____ denotes all activities from the time a commitment is made for a transaction until it is settled. _____ is necessary because the speed of trades is much faster than the cycle time for completing the underlying transaction.

In its widest sense _____ involves the management of post-trading, pre-settlement credit exposures, to ensure that trades are settled in accordance with market rules, even if a buyer or seller should become insolvent prior to settlement.

   a. Share
   c. Clearing house
   b. Procter ' Gamble
   d. Clearing

8. _____ is a form of corporation equity ownership represented in the securities. It is dangerous in comparison to preferred shares and some other investment options, in that in the event of bankruptcy, _____ investors receive their funds after preferred stockholders, bondholders, creditors, etc. On the other hand, common shares on average perform better than preferred shares or bonds over time.
   a. Common stock
   c. Stop-limit order
   b. Stock market bubble
   d. Stock split

9. The institution most often referenced by the word '_____' is a public or publicly traded _____, the shares of which are traded on a public stock exchange (e.g., the New York Stock Exchange or Nasdaq in the United States) where shares of stock of _____s are bought and sold by and to the general public. Most of the largest businesses in the world are publicly traded _____s. However, the majority of _____s are said to be closely held, privately held or close _____s, meaning that no ready market exists for the trading of shares.
   a. Corporation
   c. Depository Trust Company
   b. Protect
   d. Federal Home Loan Mortgage Corporation

10. _____ are those dividends paid out in form of additional stock shares of the issuing corporation or other corporation They are usually issued in proportion to shares owned (for example for every 100 shares of stock owned, 5% stock dividend will yield 5 extra shares). If this payment involves the issue of new shares, this is very similar to a stock split in that it increases the total number of shares while lowering the price of each share and does not change the market capitalization or the total value of the shares held

a. Time-based currency
c. Database auditing
b. The Hong Kong Securities Institute
d. Stock or scrip dividends

11. A _____ or stock divide increases or decreases the number of shares in a public company. The price is adjusted such that the before and after market capitalization of the company remains the same and dilution does not occur. Options and warrants are included.

a. Stock split
c. Stop order
b. Contract for difference
d. Stop price

12. A _____ is an exchange of promises between two or more parties to do an act which is enforceable in a court of law. It is where an unqualified offer meets a qualified acceptance and the parties reach Consensus ad Idem. The parties must have the necessary capacity to _____ and the _____ must not be either trifling, indeterminate, impossible or illegal.

a. 4-4-5 Calendar
c. Contract
b. 529 plan
d. 7-Eleven

13. A _____ is a payment made by a corporation to its shareholder members. When a corporation earns a profit or surplus, that money can be put to two uses: it can either be re-invested in the business (called retained earnings), or it can be paid to the shareholders as a _____. Many corporations retain a portion of their earnings and pay the remainder as a _____.

a. Dividend yield
c. Dividend puzzle
b. Special dividend
d. Dividend

14. A _____ is a financial contract between two parties, the seller (writer) and the buyer of the option. The put allows its buyer the right but not the obligation to sell a commodity or financial instrument (the underlying instrument) to the writer (seller) of the option at a certain time for a certain price (the strike price.) The writer (seller) has the obligation to purchase the underlying asset at that strike price, if the buyer exercises the option.

a. Bear spread
c. Bear call spread
b. Debit spread
d. Put option

15. In finance, a _____ is a debt security, in which the authorized issuer owes the holders a debt and, depending on the terms of the _____, is obliged to pay interest (the coupon) and/or to repay the principal at a later date, termed maturity.

Thus a _____ is a loan: the issuer is the borrower, the _____ holder is the lender, and the coupon is the interest. _____s provide the borrower with external funds to finance long-term investments, or, in the case of government _____s, to finance current expenditure.

a. Puttable bond
c. Catastrophe bonds
b. Convertible bond
d. Bond

16. _____ is the process of determining the fair price of a bond. As with any security or capital investment, the fair value of a bond is the present value of the stream of cash flows it is expected to generate. Hence, the price or value of a bond is determined by discounting the bond's expected cash flows to the present using the appropriate discount rate.

a. Collateralized debt obligations
b. Catastrophe bonds
c. Bond fund
d. Bond valuation

17. In economic models, the _____ time frame assumes no fixed factors of production. Firms can enter or leave the marketplace, and the cost (and availability) of land, labor, raw materials, and capital goods can be assumed to vary. In contrast, in the short-run time frame, certain factors are assumed to be fixed, because there is not sufficient time for them to change.
   a. 4-4-5 Calendar
   b. 529 plan
   c. Short-run
   d. Long-run

18. In finance, 'participation' is an ownership interest in a mortgage or other loan. In particular, _____ is a cooperation of multiple lenders to issue a loan (known as participation loan) to one borrower. This is usually done in order to reduce individual risks of the lenders.
   a. Doctrine of the Proper Law
   b. Loan participation
   c. Securitization
   d. Short positions

19. A _____ is a fungible, negotiable instrument representing financial value. They are broadly categorized into debt securities (such as banknotes, bonds and debentures), and equity securities; e.g., common stocks. The company or other entity issuing the _____ is called the issuer.
   a. Securities lending
   b. Book entry
   c. Tracking stock
   d. Security

20. In finance, _____ is the process of estimating the potential market value of a financial asset or liability. they can be done on assets (for example, investments in marketable securities such as stocks, options, business enterprises, or intangible assets such as patents and trademarks) or on liabilities (e.g., Bonds issued by a company.) _____s are required in many contexts including investment analysis, capital budgeting, merger and acquisition transactions, financial reporting, taxable events to determine the proper tax liability, and in litigation.
   a. Share
   b. Valuation
   c. Margin
   d. Procter ' Gamble

21. The _____ is an American stock exchange. It is the largest electronic screen-based equity securities trading market in the United States. With approximately 3,200 companies, it has more trading volume per day than any other stock exchange in the world.
   a. 7-Eleven
   b. 529 plan
   c. Nasdaq
   d. 4-4-5 Calendar

22. The _____ is a stock exchange based in New York City, New York. It is the largest stock exchange in the world by dollar value of its listed companies securities. As of October 2008, the combined capitalization of all domestic _____ listed companies was $10.1 trillion.
   a. 529 plan
   b. 7-Eleven
   c. 4-4-5 Calendar
   d. New York Stock Exchange

Chapter 24. Options

23. A _____, securities exchange or (in Europe) bourse is a corporation or mutual organization which provides 'trading' facilities for stock brokers and traders, to trade stocks and other securities. _____s also provide facilities for the issue and redemption of securities as well as other financial instruments and capital events including the payment of income and dividends. The securities traded on a _____ include: shares issued by companies, unit trusts and other pooled investment products and bonds.

   a. 7-Eleven
   b. Stock Exchange
   c. 529 plan
   d. 4-4-5 Calendar

24. _____ is the name of a method of communication between professionals on a stock exchange or futures exchange which involves shouting and the use of hand signals to transfer information primarily about buy and sell orders. The part of the trading floor where this takes place is called a pit.

Examples of markets which use this system in the United States are the New York Mercantile Exchange, the Chicago Mercantile Exchange, the Chicago Board of Trade, and the Chicago Board Options Exchange.

   a. Equity investment
   b. Intellidex
   c. Open outcry
   d. Insider trading

25. In finance, a _____ is collateral that the holder of a position in securities, options, or futures contracts has to deposit to cover the credit risk of his counterparty (most often his broker.) This risk can arise if the holder has done any of the following:

- borrowed cash from the counterparty to buy securities or options,
- sold securities or options short, or
- entered into a futures contract.

The collateral can be in the form of cash or securities, and it is deposited in a _____ account. On U.S. futures exchanges, '_____' was formally called performance bond.

_____ buying is buying securities with cash borrowed from a broker, using other securities as collateral.

   a. Share
   b. Credit
   c. Procter ' Gamble
   d. Margin

26. The collateral can be in the form of cash or securities, and it is deposited in a _____. On U.S. futures exchanges, 'margin' was formally called performance bond.

Margin buying is buying securities with cash borrowed from a broker, using other securities as collateral.

   a. Risk-neutral measure
   b. Forward contract
   c. Dollar roll
   d. Margin account

27. _____, in bookkeeping, refers to assets, liabilities, income, and expenses recorded on individual pages of the so called book of final entry or ledger. Changes in _____ value are made by chronologically posting debit (DR) and credit (CR) entries to its page. Examples of _____s are cash, _____s receivable, mortgages, loans, land and buildings, common stock, sales, services provided, wages, and payroll overhead.

Chapter 24. Options

a. Account
b. Accretion
c. Alpha
d. Option

28. In finance, _____ refers to the value of a security which is intrinsic to or contained in the security itself. It is also frequently called fundamental value. It is ordinarily calculated by summing the future income generated by the asset, and discounting it to the present value.

a. Intrinsic value
b. Alpha
c. Accretion
d. Amortization

29. _____ is the difference between price and the costs of bringing to market whatever it is that is accounted as an enterprise (whether by harvest, extraction, manufacture, or purchase) in terms of the component costs of delivered goods and/or services and any operating or other expenses.

A key difficulty in measuring profit is in defining costs. Pure economic monetary profits can be zero or negative even in competitive equilibrium when accounted monetized costs exceed monetized price.

a. Economic profit
b. A Random Walk Down Wall Street
c. AAB
d. Accounting profit

30. A _____ is a professionally managed type of collective investment scheme that pools money from many investors and invests it in stocks, bonds, short-term money market instruments, and/or other securities. The _____ will have a fund manager that trades the pooled money on a regular basis. Currently, the worldwide value of all _____s totals more than $26 trillion.

Since 1940, there have been three basic types of investment companies in the United States: open-end funds, also known in the US as _____s; unit investment trusts (UITs); and closed-end funds.

a. Net asset value
b. Financial intermediary
c. Trust company
d. Mutual fund

31. A put option is a right to sell a particular stock to the writer of the option at a certain price (the strike price) on or by the expiration date. If the contract writer does not have an offsetting short position in the stock that the contract is written on, the put writer is considered uncovered for the loss incurred if the current price of the stock is below the contract price. If the writer has enough cash in his brokerage account to pay for the stock at the strike price then, although he is still considered to be in a _____ position, he may also refer more specifically to his position as a cash-covered put.

a. Moneyness
b. Debit spread
c. Bear put spread
d. Naked put

32. In finance, a _____ is an investment strategy involving the purchase or sale of particular option derivatives that allows the holder to profit based on how much the price of the underlying security moves, regardless of the direction of price movement. The purchase of particular option derivatives is known as a long _____, while the sale of the option derivatives is known as a short _____.

An option payoff diagram for a long _____ position

A long _____ involves going long, i.e., purchasing, both a call option and a put option on some stock, interest rate, index or other underlying.

    a. Put option
    c. Moneyness
    b. Bear call spread
    d. Straddle

33. A _____ is a transaction in which the seller of call options already owns the corresponding amount of the underlying instrument, such as shares of a stock or other securities. These owned shares provide the 'cover' as they can be handed over to the buyer of the options when he decides to exercise them, instead of having to buy the optioned shares at unfavorable market prices in the case of 'uncovered' or short call. Thus, the _____ limits the (potentially unlimited) loss that results from a short call when the price of the underlying stock moves above the strike price of the option.

    a. 529 plan
    c. 4-4-5 Calendar
    b. 7-Eleven
    d. Covered call

34. In economics and finance, _____ is the practice of taking advantage of a price differential between two or more markets: striking a combination of matching deals that capitalize upon the imbalance, the profit being the difference between the market prices. When used by academics, an _____ is a transaction that involves no negative cash flow at any probabilistic or temporal state and a positive cash flow in at least one state; in simple terms, a risk-free profit.

    a. Issuer
    c. Efficient-market hypothesis
    b. Initial margin
    d. Arbitrage

35. In the valuation of a life insurance company, the actuary considers a series of future uncertain cashflows (including incoming premiums and outgoing claims, for example) and attempts to put a value on these cashflows. There are many ways of calculating such a value , but these approaches are often arbitrary in that the interest rate chosen for discounting is itself rather arbitrarily chosen.

One possible approach, and one that is gaining increasing attention, is the use of _____ or hedge portfolios. The theory is that we can choose a portfolio of assets (fixed interest bonds, zero coupon bonds, index-linked bonds, etc.) whose cashflows are identical to the magnitude and the timing of the cashflows to be valued.

    a. 7-Eleven
    c. 4-4-5 Calendar
    b. 529 plan
    d. Replicating portfolios

36. In finance, _____ or 'shorting' is the practice of selling a financial instrument that the seller does not own at the time of the sale. _____ is done with intent of later purchasing the financial instrument at a lower price. Short-sellers attempt to profit from an expected decline in the price of a financial instrument.

    a. Short ratio
    c. 4-4-5 Calendar
    b. 529 plan
    d. Short selling

37. In finance, a _____ is a position established in one market in an attempt to offset exposure to the price risk of an equal but opposite obligation or position in another market -- usually, but not always, in the context of one's commercial activity. Hedging is a strategy designed to minimize exposure to such business risks as a sharp contraction in demand for one's inventory, while still allowing the business to profit from producing and maintaining that inventory. A typical hedger might be a farmer with 2000 acres of unharvested wheat in the ground, who would rather tend his crop without the distraction of uncertain prices.

Chapter 24. Options

a. Hedge
b. 7-Eleven
c. 4-4-5 Calendar
d. 529 plan

38. In financial mathematics, _____ defines a relationship between the price of a call option and a put option--both with the identical strike price and expiry. To derive the _____ relationship, the assumption is that the options are not exercised before expiration day, which necessarily applies to European options. _____ can be derived in a manner that is largely model independent.
   a. Hull-White model
   b. Rendleman-Bartter model
   c. Put-call parity
   d. Cox-Ingersoll-Ross model

39. _____ most frequently refers to the standard deviation of the continuously compounded returns of a financial instrument with a specific time horizon. It is often used to quantify the risk of the instrument over that time period. _____ is typically expressed in annualized terms, and it may either be an absolute number ($5) or a fraction of the mean (5%).
   a. Volatility
   b. Portfolio insurance
   c. Currency swap
   d. Seasoned equity offering

40. _____, static projection, and static scoring are pejorative terms for statistical analyses for which existing trends are projected into the future simplistically, or beyond what is possible to predict in any manner, producing results often wildly unrealistic.

Its opposite, dynamic analysis or dynamic scoring, is an attempt to take into account how variables may change or interact. One common use of these terms is budget policy in the United States, although it also occurs in many other statistical disputes.

   a. 4-4-5 Calendar
   b. 7-Eleven
   c. Static analysis
   d. 529 plan

41. In financial mathematics, the _____ of an option contract is the volatility implied by the market price of the option based on an option pricing model. In other words, it is the volatility that, given a particular pricing model, yields a theoretical value for the option equal to the current market price. Non-option financial instruments that have embedded optionality, such as an interest rate cap, can also have an _____.
   a. Interest rate future
   b. Interest rate derivative
   c. Equity derivative
   d. Implied volatility

42. In finance, the value of an option consists of two components, its intrinsic value and its _____. Time value is simply the difference between option value and intrinsic value. _____ is also known as theta, extrinsic value, or instrumental value.
   a. Conservatism
   b. Debt buyer
   c. Global Squeeze
   d. Time value

43. _____ is a fee paid on borrowed assets. It is the price paid for the use of borrowed money, or, money earned by deposited funds. Assets that are sometimes lent with _____ include money, shares, consumer goods through hire purchase, major assets such as aircraft, and even entire factories in finance lease arrangements.
   a. Insolvency
   b. A Random Walk Down Wall Street
   c. AAB
   d. Interest

44. An _____ is the price a borrower pays for the use of money they do not own, and the return a lender receives for deferring the use of funds, by lending it to the borrower. _____s are normally expressed as a percentage rate over the period of one year.

_____s targets are also a vital tool of monetary policy and are used to control variables like investment, inflation, and unemployment.

a. A Random Walk Down Wall Street
b. AAB
c. ABN Amro
d. Interest rate

45. _____ means regulating, adapting or settling in a variety of contexts:

In commercial law, _____ means the settlement of a loss incurred on insured goods. The calculation of the amounts of compensation to be paid by or to the several interests is a complicated matter. It involves much detail and arithmetic, and requires a full and accurate knowledge of the principles of the subject.

a. Intelligent investor
b. Asset recovery
c. Equity method
d. Adjustment

46. In finance, a _____ is a standardized contract, to buy or sell a specified commodity of standardized quality at a certain date in the future, at a market determined price (the futures price.)

The price is determined by the instantaneous equilibrium between the forces of supply and demand among competing buy and sell orders on the exchange at the time of the purchase or sale of the contract.

In many cases, the items may be such non-traditional 'commodities' as foreign currencies, commercial or government paper [e.g., bonds], or 'baskets' of corporate equity ['stock indices'] or other financial instruments.

a. Financial future
b. Repurchase agreement
c. Heston model
d. Futures contract

Chapter 25. Futures

1. In finance, a _____ is a standardized contract, to buy or sell a specified commodity of standardized quality at a certain date in the future, at a market determined price (the futures price.)

The price is determined by the instantaneous equilibrium between the forces of supply and demand among competing buy and sell orders on the exchange at the time of the purchase or sale of the contract.

In many cases, the items may be such non-traditional 'commodities' as foreign currencies, commercial or government paper [e.g., bonds], or 'baskets' of corporate equity ['stock indices'] or other financial instruments.

   a. Repurchase agreement
   b. Financial future
   c. Futures contract
   d. Heston model

2. In finance, a _____ is a position established in one market in an attempt to offset exposure to the price risk of an equal but opposite obligation or position in another market -- usually, but not always, in the context of one's commercial activity. Hedging is a strategy designed to minimize exposure to such business risks as a sharp contraction in demand for one's inventory, while still allowing the business to profit from producing and maintaining that inventory. A typical hedger might be a farmer with 2000 acres of unharvested wheat in the ground, who would rather tend his crop without the distraction of uncertain prices.

   a. 7-Eleven
   b. Hedge
   c. 4-4-5 Calendar
   d. 529 plan

3. The _____ or cash market is a commodities or securities market in which goods are sold for cash and delivered immediately. Contracts bought and sold on these markets are immediately effective. _____s can operate wherever the infrastructure exists to conduct the transaction.

   a. Foreign exchange controls
   b. Spot market
   c. Currency swap
   d. Non-deliverable forward

4. The _____ or spot rate of a commodity, a security or a currency is the price that is quoted for immediate (spot) settlement (payment and delivery.) Spot settlement is normally one or two business days from trade date. This is in contrast with the forward price established in a forward contract or futures contract, where contract terms (price) are set now, but delivery and payment will occur at a future date.

   a. Cost of carry
   b. Market price
   c. Spot price
   d. Central Securities Depository

5. An _____ is a contract written by a seller that conveys to the buyer the right -- but not the obligation -- to buy (in the case of a call _____) or to sell (in the case of a put _____) a particular asset, such as a piece of property such as, among others, a futures contract. In return for granting the _____, the seller collects a payment (the premium) from the buyer.

For example, buying a call _____ provides the right to buy a specified quantity of a security at a set strike price at some time on or before expiration, while buying a put _____ provides the right to sell.

   a. Annuity
   b. Amortization
   c. AT'T Mobility LLC
   d. Option

6. _____ denotes the total number of derivative contracts, like futures and options, that are currently active on a specific underlying security, having specific terms.

Namely, the total contracts for a specific strike price and expiration date, that have been traded, but have not yet expired, have not yet been closed through a closing transaction, or have not yet been terminated via early exercise. A closing transaction occurs when a counterparty that longs the contract sells, or, conversely, when a counterparty that shorts the contract buys.

  a. International Swaps and Derivatives Association   b. Equity derivative
  c. Equity swap   d. Open interest

7. _____ is a fee paid on borrowed assets. It is the price paid for the use of borrowed money , or, money earned by deposited funds . Assets that are sometimes lent with _____ include money, shares, consumer goods through hire purchase, major assets such as aircraft, and even entire factories in finance lease arrangements.
  a. AAB   b. Insolvency
  c. Interest   d. A Random Walk Down Wall Street

8. In banking and finance, _____ denotes all activities from the time a commitment is made for a transaction until it is settled. _____ is necessary because the speed of trades is much faster than the cycle time for completing the underlying transaction.

In its widest sense _____ involves the management of post-trading, pre-settlement credit exposures, to ensure that trades are settled in accordance with market rules, even if a buyer or seller should become insolvent prior to settlement.

  a. Procter ' Gamble   b. Share
  c. Clearing   d. Clearing house

9. A _____ is a fungible, negotiable instrument representing financial value. They are broadly categorized into debt securities (such as banknotes, bonds and debentures), and equity securities; e.g., common stocks. The company or other entity issuing the _____ is called the issuer.
  a. Tracking stock   b. Securities lending
  c. Book entry   d. Security

10. The institution most often referenced by the word '_____' is a public or publicly traded _____, the shares of which are traded on a public stock exchange (e.g., the New York Stock Exchange or Nasdaq in the United States) where shares of stock of _____s are bought and sold by and to the general public. Most of the largest businesses in the world are publicly traded _____s. However, the majority of _____s are said to be closely held, privately held or close _____s, meaning that no ready market exists for the trading of shares.
  a. Federal Home Loan Mortgage Corporation   b. Depository Trust Company
  c. Corporation   d. Protect

11. The _____ requirement is the amount required to be collateralized in order to open a position. Thereafter, the amount required to be kept in collateral until the position is closed is the maintenance requirement. The maintenance requirement is the minimum amount to be collateralized in order to keep an open position.
  a. Arbitrage   b. Issuer
  c. Efficient-market hypothesis   d. Initial margin

Chapter 25. Futures

12. The _____ is the amount required to be collateralized in order to open a position. Thereafter, the amount required to be kept in collateral until the position is closed is the maintenance requirement. The maintenance requirement is the minimum amount to be collateralized in order to keep an open position.
   a. AAB
   b. A Random Walk Down Wall Street
   c. Initial margin requirement
   d. ABN Amro

13. In finance, a _____ is collateral that the holder of a position in securities, options, or futures contracts has to deposit to cover the credit risk of his counterparty (most often his broker.) This risk can arise if the holder has done any of the following:

   - borrowed cash from the counterparty to buy securities or options,
   - sold securities or options short, or
   - entered into a futures contract.

   The collateral can be in the form of cash or securities, and it is deposited in a _____ account. On U.S. futures exchanges, '_____' was formally called performance bond.

   _____ buying is buying securities with cash borrowed from a broker, using other securities as collateral.

   a. Share
   b. Credit
   c. Procter ' Gamble
   d. Margin

14. The collateral can be in the form of cash or securities, and it is deposited in a _____. On U.S. futures exchanges, 'margin' was formally called performance bond.

   Margin buying is buying securities with cash borrowed from a broker, using other securities as collateral.

   a. Margin account
   b. Dollar roll
   c. Risk-neutral measure
   d. Forward contract

15. _____, in bookkeeping, refers to assets, liabilities, income, and expenses recorded on individual pages of the so called book of final entry or ledger. Changes in _____ value are made by chronologically posting debit (DR) and credit (CR) entries to its page. Examples of _____s are cash, _____s receivable, mortgages, loans, land and buildings, common stock, sales, services provided, wages, and payroll overhead.
   a. Account
   b. Accretion
   c. Alpha
   d. Option

16. The variation margin or _____ is not collateral, but a daily offsetting of profits and losses. Futures are marked-to-market every day, so the current price is compared to the previous day's price. The profit or loss on the day of a position is then paid to or debited from the holder by the futures exchange.
   a. Total return swap
   b. SPI 200 futures contract
   c. Delivery month
   d. Maintenance margin

17. The _____, sometimes called the maintenance margin requirement, is the ratio set for:

- (Stock Equity - Leveraged Dollars) to Stock Equity

- Stock Equity being the stock price * no. of stocks bought and Leveraged Dollars being the amount borrowed in the margin account.

- E.g. An investor bought 1000 shares of ABC company each priced at $50. If the initial margin requirement were 60%:

- Stock Equity: $50 * 1000 = $50,000

- Leveraged Dollars or amount borrowed: ($50 * 1000)* (1-60%) = $20,000

So the maintenance margin requirement uses the above variables to form a ratio that investors have to abide by in order to keep the account active.

The point is, let's say the maintenance margin requirement is reduced from 60% to 25% - At what price would the investor be getting a margin call? Let P be the price, so 1000P in our case is the Stock Equity.

- (Stock Equity - Leveraged Dollars) divided by Stock Equity = 25%

- (1000P - $20,000)/1000P = 0.25

- (1000P - $20,000) = 250P

- P = $26.67

So if the stock price drops from $50 to $26.67, investors will be called to add additional funds to the account to make up for the loss in stock equity.

Margin requirements are reduced for positions that offset each other.

a. 7-Eleven
c. 529 plan
b. 4-4-5 Calendar
d. Minimum margin requirement

18. A _____ is something for which there is demand, but which is supplied without qualitative differentiation across a market. It is a product that is the same no matter who produces it, such as petroleum, notebook paper, or milk. In other words, copper is copper.

a. 4-4-5 Calendar
c. 529 plan
b. 7-Eleven
d. Commodity

19. In the context of financial futures, _____ can be defined as the spot price minus the futures price. There will be a different basis for each delivery month for each contract. In a normal market, basis will be negative.

Chapter 25. Futures

a. Legal and regulatory risk
b. Controlled foreign corporations
c. Municipal Okrug #7
d. Basis of futures

20. _____ in finance is the risk associated with imperfect hedging using futures. It could arise because of the difference between the asset whose price is to be hedged and the asset underlying the derivative, or because of a mismatch between the expiration date of the futures and the actual selling date of the asset.

Under these conditions, the spot price of the asset, and the futures price, do not converge on the expiration date of the future.

a. Credit risk
b. Currency risk
c. Basis risk
d. Liquidity risk

21. _____ is a risk-adjusted measure of the so-called active return on an investment. It is the return in excess of the compensation for the risk borne, and thus commonly used to assess active managers' performances. Often, the return of a benchmark is subtracted in order to consider relative performance, which yields Jensen's _____.

a. Annuity
b. Option
c. Alpha
d. Amortization

22. In business and accounting, _____s are everything of value that is owned by a person or company. The balance sheet of a firm records the monetary value of the _____s owned by the firm. The two major _____ classes are tangible _____s and intangible _____s.

a. Accounts payable
b. Income
c. EBITDA
d. Asset

23. _____ is a term used to refer to how an investor distributes his or her investments among various classes of investment vehicles (e.g., stocks and bonds.)

A large part of financial planning is finding an _____ that is appropriate for a given person in terms of their appetite for and ability to shoulder risk. This can depend on various factors; see investor profile.

a. Asset allocation
b. Investment performance
c. Investing online
d. Alternative investment

24. _____ is a futures market term. It describes a situation where the amount of money required for future delivery of an item is lower than the amount required for immediate delivery of that item. For example, immediate delivery of gold may cost $1,000 an ounce, whereas delivery in two months only costs $900 an ounce, with that $900 to be paid at time of delivery.

a. Risk-neutral measure
b. STIRT
c. Backwardation
d. Delivery month

25. _____ is a term that refers both to:

- a formal discipline used to help appraise, or assess, the case for a project or proposal, which itself is a process known as project appraisal; and
- an informal approach to making decisions of any kind.

Under both definitions the process involves, whether explicitly or implicitly, weighing the total expected costs against the total expected benefits of one or more actions in order to choose the best or most profitable option.

A hallmark of _____ is that all benefits and all costs are expressed in money terms, and are adjusted for the time value of money, so that all flows of benefits and flows of project costs over time (which tend to occur at different points in time) are expressed on a common basis in terms of their present value.

a. 4-4-5 Calendar
b. 529 plan
c. 7-Eleven
d. Cost-benefit analysis

26. _____ is a term used in the futures market to describe an upward sloping forward curve (as in the normal yield curve.) Such a forward curve is said to be 'in _____' (or sometimes '_____ed'.)

Formally, it is the situation where, and the amount by which, the price of a commodity for future delivery is higher than the spot price, or a far future delivery price higher than a nearer future delivery.

a. Delta One
b. Commodity tick
c. Single-stock futures
d. Contango

27. A _____ is an adjustment to the cost of carry in the non-arbitrage pricing formula for forward prices in markets with trading constraints.

Let $F_{t,T}$ be the forward price of an asset with initial price S_t and maturity T. Suppose that r is the continuously compounded interest rate for one year. Then, the non-arbitrage pricing formula should be

$F_{t,T} = S_t e^{r(T - t)}$.

a. 529 plan
b. 4-4-5 Calendar
c. 7-Eleven
d. Convenience yield

28. In finance, the term _____ describes the amount in cash that returns to the owners of a security. Normally it does not include the price variations, at the difference of the total return. _____ applies to various stated rates of return on stocks (common and preferred, and convertible), fixed income instruments (bonds, notes, bills, strips, zero coupon), and some other investment type insurance products (e.g. annuities.)

a. Macaulay duration
b. Yield to maturity
c. 4-4-5 Calendar
d. Yield

29. The _____ is an American financial and commodity derivative exchange based in Chicago. The _____ was founded in 1898 as the Chicago Butter and Egg Board. Originally, the exchange was a non-profit organization.

a. Chicago Mercantile Exchange
b. Public Company Accounting Oversight Board
c. Financial Crimes Enforcement Network
d. Gamelan Council

Chapter 25. Futures

30. In economics, business, and accounting, a _____ is the value of money that has been used up to produce something, and hence is not available for use anymore. In business, the _____ may be one of acquisition, in which case the amount of money expended to acquire it is counted as _____. In this case, money is the input that is gone in order to acquire the thing.
   a. Marginal cost
   b. Fixed costs
   c. Sliding scale fees
   d. Cost

31. The _____ is the cost of 'carrying' or holding a position. If long, the _____ is the cost of interest paid on a margin account. Conversely, if short, the _____ is the cost of paying dividends, or opportunity cost the cost of purchasing a particular security rather than an alternative.
   a. Cost of carry
   b. Delta hedging
   c. Spot price
   d. Secondary market

32. A _____, also FX future or foreign exchange future, is a futures contract to exchange one currency for another at a specified date in the future at a price (exchange rate) that is fixed on the purchase date. Typically, one of the currencies is the US dollar. The price of a future is then in terms of US dollars per unit of other currency.
   a. Currency future
   b. Currency swap
   c. Foreign exchange controls
   d. Non-deliverable forward

33. _____ refers to an assessment of the viability, stability and profitability of a business, sub-business or project.

It is performed by professionals who prepare reports using ratios that make use of information taken from financial statements and other reports. These reports are usually presented to top management as one of their bases in making business decisions.

   a. Value investing
   b. 4-4-5 Calendar
   c. 529 plan
   d. Financial analysis

34. A _____ is a futures contract on a short term interest rate (STIR.) Contracts vary, but are often defined on an interest rate index such as 3-month sterling or US dollar LIBOR.

They are traded across a wide range of currencies, including the G12 country currencies and many others.

   a. Dual currency deposit
   b. Financial future
   c. Real estate derivatives
   d. Notional amount

35. The _____ , largely the creation of Leo Melamed, is part of the Chicago Mercantile Exchange (CME), the largest futures exchange in the United States and the second largest in the world after Eurex, for the trading of futures contracts and options on futures. The _____ was started on May 16, 1972. Two of the more prevalent contracts traded are currency futures and interest rate futures.
   a. ABN Amro
   b. A Random Walk Down Wall Street
   c. AAB
   d. International Monetary Market

36. The _____ of an asset is the return obtained from holding it (if positive), or the cost of holding it (if negative)

Chapter 25. Futures

For instance, commodities are usually negative _____ assets, as they incur storage costs, but in some circumstances, commodities can be positive _____ assets as the market is willing to pay a premium for availability.

This can also refer to a trade with more than one leg, where you earn the spread between borrowing a low _____ asset and lending a high _____ one.

a. Bankruptcy remote
b. Financial assistance
c. Carry
d. Cramdown

37. In economics and finance, _____ is the practice of taking advantage of a price differential between two or more markets: striking a combination of matching deals that capitalize upon the imbalance, the profit being the difference between the market prices. When used by academics, an _____ is a transaction that involves no negative cash flow at any probabilistic or temporal state and a positive cash flow in at least one state; in simple terms, a risk-free profit.

a. Efficient-market hypothesis
b. Issuer
c. Arbitrage
d. Initial margin

38. A _____ is a payment made by a corporation to its shareholder members. When a corporation earns a profit or surplus, that money can be put to two uses: it can either be re-invested in the business (called retained earnings), or it can be paid to the shareholders as a _____. Many corporations retain a portion of their earnings and pay the remainder as a _____.

a. Dividend
b. Special dividend
c. Dividend puzzle
d. Dividend yield

39. A _____ is a method of measuring a section of the stock market. Many indices are cited by news or financial services firms and are used to benchmark the performance of portfolios such as mutual funds.

a. Stop order
b. Stock market index
c. Trading curb
d. Program trading

40. _____ is the last hour of the stock market trading session (3:00-4:00 P.M., New York Time) on the third Friday of every March, June, September, and December. Those days are the expiration of three kinds of securities:

- Stock index futures.
- Stock market index options.
- Stock options.

The simultaneous expirations generally increases the trading volume of options, futures and the underlying stocks, and occasionally increases volatility of prices of related securities.

With the introduction of

- Single stock futures expiring on the same days, triple witching has become quadruple witching

The term 'triple witching' is conventionally thought to originate from the three witches in Shakespeare's play Macbeth. While the terms 'double witching' and 'quadruple witching' are sometimes used too, it doesn't carry the same foreboding connotation as triple witching. The phrase is intended to connote the extra volatility leading up to the event resulting from the expiration dates of three financing instruments.

a. Quality spread differential
b. Repurchase agreement
c. Triple witching hour
d. STIRT

Chapter 26. International Investing

1. The _____ is the market for securities, where companies and governments can raise longterm funds. The _____ includes the stock market and the bond market. Financial regulators, such as the U.S. Securities and Exchange Commission, oversee the _____s in their designated countries to ensure that investors are protected against fraud.

   a. Delta neutral
   b. Spot rate
   c. Capital market
   d. Forward market

2. A _____ is a portfolio consisting of a weighted sum of every asset in the market, with weights in the proportions that they exist in the market (with the necessary assumption that these assets are infinitely divisible.)

   Neha Tyagi's critique (1977) states that this is only a theoretical concept, as to create a _____ for investment purposes in practice would necessarily include every single possible available asset, including real estate, precious metals, stamp collections, jewelry, and anything with any worth, as the theoretical market being referred to would be the world market. As a result, proxies for the market are used in practice by investors.

   a. Delta neutral
   b. Central Securities Depository
   c. Market price
   d. Market portfolio

3. _____ is a technique to adjust income payments by means of a price index, in order to maintain the purchasing power of the public after inflation.

   Applying a cost-of-living escalation COLA clause to a stream of periodic payments protects the real value of those payments and effectively transfers the risk of inflation from the payee to the payor, who must pay more each year to reflect the increases in prices. Thus, inflation _____ is often applied to pension payments, rents and other situations which are not subject to regular re-pricing in the market.

   a. ABN Amro
   b. A Random Walk Down Wall Street
   c. AAB
   d. Indexation

4. The _____ is one of the measures of national income and input for a given country's economy. _____ is defined as the total cost of all finished goods and services produced within the country in a stipulated period of time (usually a 365-day year.) It is sometimes regarded as the sum of profits added at every level of production (the intermediate stages) of all final goods and services produced within a country in a stipulated timeframe, and it is rarely given a monetary value.

   a. Recession
   b. Behavioral finance
   c. Gross domestic product
   d. Macroeconomics

5. _____ is a type of risk faced by investors, corporations, and governments. It is a risk that can be understood and managed with proper aforethought and investment.

   Broadly, _____ refers to the complications businesses and governments may face as a result of what are commonly referred to as political decisions--or 'any political change that alters the expected outcome and value of a given economic action by changing the probability of achieving business objectives.' .

   a. Political risk
   b. Capital asset
   c. Single-index model
   d. Mid price

Chapter 26. International Investing 171

6. A _____ is a fungible, negotiable instrument representing financial value. They are broadly categorized into debt securities (such as banknotes, bonds and debentures), and equity securities; e.g., common stocks. The company or other entity issuing the _____ is called the issuer.
   a. Book entry
   b. Tracking stock
   c. Securities lending
   d. Security

7. The term _____ is used to describe a nation's social, or business activity in the process of rapid industrialization. _____ are generally less-wealthy than the developed world, and are wealthier (or the wealthiest of) the developing world. According to The Economist many people find the term dated, but a new term has yet to gain much traction.
   a. A Random Walk Down Wall Street
   b. Emerging markets
   c. AAB
   d. ABN Amro

8. The _____ is the weighted-average most likely outcome in gambling, probability theory, economics or finance.

In gambling and probability theory, there is usually a discrete set of possible outcomes. In this case, _____ is a measure of the relative balance of win or loss weighted by their chances of occurring.

   a. ABN Amro
   b. A Random Walk Down Wall Street
   c. AAB
   d. Expected Return

9. _____ refers to a portfolio management strategy where the manager makes specific investments with the goal of outperforming an investment benchmark index. Investors or mutual funds that do not aspire to create a return in excess of a benchmark index will often invest in an index fund that replicates as closely as possible the investment weighting and returns of that index; this is called passive management. _____ is the opposite of passive management, because in passive management the manager does not seek to outperform the benchmark index.
   a. ABN Amro
   b. AAB
   c. A Random Walk Down Wall Street
   d. Active management

10. An _____ is a contract written by a seller that conveys to the buyer the right -- but not the obligation -- to buy (in the case of a call _____) or to sell (in the case of a put _____) a particular asset, such as a piece of property such as, among others, a futures contract. In return for granting the _____, the seller collects a payment (the premium) from the buyer.

For example, buying a call _____ provides the right to buy a specified quantity of a security at a set strike price at some time on or before expiration, while buying a put _____ provides the right to sell.

   a. Option
   b. AT'T Mobility LLC
   c. Amortization
   d. Annuity

11. The _____ or spot rate of a commodity, a security or a currency is the price that is quoted for immediate (spot) settlement (payment and delivery.) Spot settlement is normally one or two business days from trade date. This is in contrast with the forward price established in a forward contract or futures contract, where contract terms (price) are set now, but delivery and payment will occur at a future date.
   a. Market price
   b. Spot price
   c. Cost of carry
   d. Central Securities Depository

12. In finance, the _____ between two currencies specifies how much one currency is worth in terms of the other. For example an _____ of 102 Japanese yen to the United States dollar means that JPY 102 is worth the same as USD 1. The foreign exchange market is one of the largest markets in the world.

   a. AAB
   b. ABN Amro
   c. A Random Walk Down Wall Street
   d. Exchange rate

13. _____ is a form of risk that arises from the change in price of one currency against another. Whenever investors or companies have assets or business operations across national borders, they face _____ if their positions are not hedged.

   - Transaction risk is the risk that exchange rates will change unfavourably over time. It can be hedged against using forward currency contracts;
   - Translation risk is an accounting risk, proportional to the amount of assets held in foreign currencies. Changes in the exchange rate over time will render a report inaccurate, and so assets are usually balanced by borrowings in that currency.

The exchange risk associated with a foreign denominated instrument is a key element in foreign investment. This risk flows from differential monetary policy and growth in real productivity, which results in differential inflation rates.

   a. Tracking error
   b. Credit risk
   c. Market risk
   d. Currency risk

14. The _____ is a daily reference rate based on the interest rates at which banks borrow unsecured funds from banks in the London wholesale money market (or interbank market.) It is roughly comparable to the U.S. Federal funds rate.

During 1984 it became apparent that an increasing number of banks were trading actively in a variety of relatively new market instruments, notably interest rate swaps, foreign currency options and forward rate agreements.

   a. Risk-free interest rate
   b. Shanghai Interbank Offered Rate
   c. London Interbank Offered Rate
   d. Fixed interest

15. In business and finance, a _____ (also referred to as equity _____) of stock means a _____ of ownership in a corporation (company.) In the plural, stocks is often used as a synonym for _____s especially in the United States, but it is less commonly used that way outside of North America.

In the United Kingdom, South Africa, and Australia, stock can also refer to completely different financial instruments such as government bonds or, less commonly, to all kinds of marketable securities.

   a. Bucket shop
   b. Share
   c. Margin
   d. Procter ' Gamble

16. _____ is the standard framework of guidelines for financial accounting used in the United States of America. It includes the standards, conventions, and rules accountants follow in recording and summarizing transactions, and in the preparation of financial statements. _____ are now issued by the Financial Accounting Standards Board (FASB).

Chapter 26. International Investing

a. Revenue
b. Depreciation
c. Net income
d. Generally accepted accounting principles

17. _____ in finance is a risk management technique, related to hedging, that mixes a wide variety of investments within a portfolio. Because the fluctuations of a single security have less impact on a diverse portfolio, _____ minimizes the risk from any one investment.

A simple example of _____ is the following: On a particular island the entire economy consists of two companies: one that sells umbrellas and another that sells sunscreen.

a. 7-Eleven
b. 529 plan
c. 4-4-5 Calendar
d. Diversification

18. In probability theory and statistics, _____ indicates the strength and direction of a linear relationship between two random variables. That is in contrast with the usage of the term in colloquial speech, which denotes any relationship, not necessarily linear. In general statistical usage, _____ or co-relation refers to the departure of two random variables from independence.

a. Variance
b. Geometric mean
c. Probability distribution
d. Correlation

Chapter 1

1. a	2. a	3. d	4. d	5. a	6. b	7. d	8. d	9. b	10. d
11. b	12. a	13. b	14. c	15. b	16. d	17. d	18. d	19. d	20. b
21. d	22. d	23. d	24. d	25. c	26. c	27. b	28. c	29. d	30. d
31. d	32. d	33. d	34. c	35. d					

Chapter 2

1. d	2. d	3. d	4. d	5. a	6. d	7. d	8. c	9. d	10. a
11. d	12. a	13. d	14. d	15. d	16. a	17. a	18. b	19. b	20. b
21. d	22. d	23. c	24. d	25. c	26. c	27. b	28. d	29. d	30. d
31. d	32. c	33. b	34. d	35. a					

Chapter 3

1. c	2. b	3. a	4. a	5. d	6. b	7. d	8. d	9. b	10. b
11. c	12. d	13. b	14. d	15. d	16. d	17. d	18. d	19. d	20. d
21. d	22. d	23. d	24. d	25. d	26. d	27. c	28. a	29. a	30. a
31. b	32. c	33. b	34. d	35. b	36. d	37. d	38. b	39. c	40. d
41. d	42. d	43. d	44. a	45. a	46. d	47. d	48. d	49. a	50. d
51. a	52. b	53. a	54. a	55. b	56. d	57. d	58. c	59. b	60. b
61. b									

Chapter 4

1. b	2. d	3. d	4. a	5. d	6. b	7. b	8. d	9. d	10. c
11. d	12. d	13. d	14. c	15. a	16. c	17. d	18. d	19. c	20. d
21. c	22. c								

Chapter 5

1. c	2. d	3. c	4. a	5. d	6. d	7. a	8. d	9. d	10. b
11. b	12. b	13. b	14. d	15. d	16. c	17. a	18. d	19. a	20. a
21. a	22. b	23. c							

Chapter 6

1. b	2. b	3. a	4. d	5. d	6. d	7. d	8. c	9. c	10. a
11. d	12. a	13. d	14. d	15. a	16. d	17. b	18. b	19. d	20. b
21. d	22. b	23. d	24. b						

Chapter 7

1. d	2. d	3. d	4. d	5. d	6. d	7. a	8. a	9. a	10. d
11. a	12. c	13. d	14. d	15. c	16. c	17. d	18. d	19. d	20. d
21. a	22. d	23. d							

Chapter 8

| 1. b | 2. d | 3. a | 4. d | 5. d | 6. d | 7. d |

ANSWER KEY

Chapter 9
1. d   2. c   3. d   4. d   5. c   6. d   7. c   8. d   9. d   10. d
11. c   12. b   13. b

Chapter 10
1. d   2. c   3. a   4. a   5. a   6. b   7. c   8. b   9. d   10. c
11. c   12. d   13. b   14. a   15. b   16. d   17. d   18. d   19. a   20. b
21. a   22. a

Chapter 11
1. c   2. b   3. d   4. d   5. c   6. a   7. a   8. d   9. d   10. a
11. d   12. d

Chapter 12
1. d   2. d   3. d   4. a   5. d   6. d   7. d   8. b   9. d   10. a

Chapter 13
1. a   2. d   3. b   4. d   5. a   6. d   7. a   8. d   9. b   10. d
11. d   12. c   13. d   14. d   15. d   16. d   17. d   18. d   19. c   20. a
21. d   22. b   23. d   24. d   25. d   26. d   27. c   28. a   29. c   30. c
31. d   32. d   33. d   34. c   35. c   36. d   37. c   38. c   39. d   40. d
41. d   42. a   43. d   44. a   45. c   46. b   47. b   48. c   49. d   50. d
51. c   52. d

Chapter 14
1. a   2. d   3. d   4. d   5. d   6. a   7. d   8. d   9. a   10. d
11. d   12. c   13. d   14. b   15. b   16. d   17. a   18. d   19. c   20. a
21. a   22. c   23. a   24. d   25. d   26. c   27. d   28. c   29. c   30. a
31. a   32. d   33. d   34. a   35. d   36. b   37. d   38. d   39. d   40. d
41. c   42. a   43. a   44. d   45. a   46. c   47. d   48. a   49. c   50. a
51. d   52. b   53. a   54. d   55. d   56. d   57. d   58. d

Chapter 15
1. c   2. d   3. c   4. d   5. b   6. d   7. a   8. b   9. d   10. d
11. a   12. a   13. d   14. c   15. d   16. d   17. a   18. b   19. b   20. a
21. d   22. a   23. c

Chapter 16
1. d   2. c   3. c   4. d   5. c   6. d   7. b   8. d   9. a   10. c
11. c   12. b   13. a   14. c   15. c   16. d   17. b   18. d   19. c   20. a
21. d   22. c   23. d   24. d   25. d

Chapter 17

1. c	2. d	3. c	4. d	5. d	6. c	7. b	8. d	9. d	10. c
11. d	12. d	13. c	14. d	15. a	16. d	17. d	18. b	19. d	20. a
21. a	22. c	23. b	24. d	25. d	26. d	27. c	28. d	29. d	

Chapter 18

1. b	2. b	3. d	4. d	5. b	6. c	7. b	8. d	9. d	10. c
11. c	12. b	13. d	14. a	15. d	16. c	17. d	18. d	19. d	20. d
21. a	22. d	23. a	24. d	25. d	26. b	27. d	28. d	29. d	

Chapter 19

1. d	2. b	3. d	4. c	5. d	6. d	7. d	8. b	9. d	10. d
11. d	12. b	13. d	14. d	15. d	16. d	17. d	18. c	19. d	20. d
21. a	22. a	23. c	24. c	25. b	26. d	27. a	28. d	29. d	30. d
31. a	32. c	33. c	34. c	35. d	36. d	37. c	38. a	39. c	40. d
41. d	42. d	43. b	44. d	45. d	46. d	47. a	48. d	49. d	50. d
51. b	52. d	53. d	54. b	55. a	56. d	57. d	58. d	59. c	60. b
61. b	62. d	63. b	64. d	65. d	66. b	67. a	68. c	69. d	

Chapter 20

1. d	2. d	3. d	4. d	5. d	6. a	7. d	8. d	9. a	10. c
11. d	12. c	13. d	14. b	15. d	16. d	17. b	18. a	19. c	20. d
21. c	22. d	23. d	24. d	25. d	26. d	27. b	28. d	29. c	30. d
31. b	32. d								

Chapter 21

1. d	2. d	3. d	4. a	5. d	6. d	7. a	8. a	9. c	10. a
11. c	12. d	13. d	14. d	15. d	16. c	17. b	18. d	19. d	20. a
21. d	22. d	23. d	24. c	25. a	26. b	27. a	28. b	29. a	30. d
31. c	32. d	33. a	34. b	35. a					

Chapter 22

1. d	2. d	3. d	4. a	5. b	6. d	7. b	8. d	9. d	10. c
11. d	12. b	13. a	14. d	15. d	16. d	17. d	18. a	19. c	20. d
21. a	22. d	23. d	24. d	25. c	26. d	27. d	28. d	29. c	30. d
31. d	32. d	33. c	34. b	35. d	36. c	37. a	38. a	39. a	40. d
41. d									

Chapter 23

1. a	2. d	3. d	4. b	5. d	6. b	7. b	8. c	9. d	10. d
11. d	12. d	13. b	14. a	15. d	16. d	17. d	18. b	19. d	20. d
21. c	22. b	23. d	24. b	25. b	26. d	27. d	28. d	29. c	30. c
31. d	32. d	33. b	34. d	35. c	36. d	37. c			

ANSWER KEY

Chapter 24

1. a	2. d	3. a	4. a	5. d	6. d	7. d	8. a	9. a	10. d
11. a	12. c	13. d	14. d	15. d	16. d	17. d	18. b	19. d	20. b
21. c	22. d	23. b	24. c	25. d	26. d	27. a	28. a	29. d	30. d
31. d	32. d	33. d	34. d	35. d	36. d	37. a	38. c	39. a	40. c
41. d	42. d	43. d	44. d	45. d	46. d				

Chapter 25

1. c	2. b	3. b	4. c	5. d	6. d	7. c	8. c	9. d	10. c
11. d	12. c	13. d	14. a	15. a	16. d	17. d	18. d	19. d	20. c
21. c	22. d	23. a	24. c	25. d	26. d	27. d	28. d	29. a	30. d
31. a	32. a	33. d	34. b	35. d	36. c	37. c	38. a	39. b	40. c

Chapter 26

1. c	2. d	3. d	4. c	5. a	6. d	7. b	8. d	9. d	10. a
11. b	12. d	13. d	14. c	15. b	16. d	17. d	18. d		

www.ingramcontent.com/pod-product-compliance
Lightning Source LLC
Chambersburg PA
CBHW082202230426
43672CB00015B/2872